THE BLACK BODY

Edited by Meri Nana-Ama Danquah

Seven Stories Press
NEW YORK

A Seven Stories Press First Edition

Seven Stories Press
140 Watts Street
New York, NY 10013
www.sevenstories.com

In Canada: Publishers Group Canada, 559 College Street, Suite 402, Toronto, ON M6G 1A9

In the UK: Turnaround Publisher Services Ltd., Unit 3, Olympia Trading Estate, Coburg Road, Wood Green, London N22 6TZ

In Australia: Palgrave Macmillan, 15–19 Claremont Street, South Yarra, VIC 3141

College professors may order examination copies of Seven Stories Press titles for a free six-month trial period. To order, visit www.sevenstories.com/textbook or send a fax on school letterhead to (212) 226-1411.

Book design by Jon Gilbert

Library of Congress Cataloging-in-Publication Data

The black body / edited by Meri Nana-Ama Danquah. -- 1st ed.
p. cm.
Includes bibliographical references.
ISBN 978-1-58322-889-0 (pbk.)
1. African Americans--Race identity. 2. Human body--Social aspects. 3. Body image--Social aspects. 4. Anthropometry--Social aspects. I. Danquah, Meri Nana-Ama.
E185.625.B5545 2009
305.896'073--dc22
2009034061
Printed in the USA

9 8 7 6 5 4 3 2 1

For
Mina and Caillou

may the tide
that is entering even now
the lip of our understanding
carry you out
beyond the face of fear

—Lucille Clifton

CONTENTS

ACKNOWLEDGMENTS

First and foremost, I would like to thank God for the miracles and blessings. I am deeply grateful for all the beauty and love that exist in my life, and for each day that I am able to wake up and experience it once more. Thank you, again and again, to Reverend Dr. Michael Bernard Beckwith, Rickie Byars Beckwith, Akili, Mama Alice, LaTerri and the entire community at the Agape International Spiritual Center for loving me, urging me forward and encouraging me to shine these past two decades.

I was in the middle of working on this book when my life suddenly came undone. I thank my family for welcoming my daughter, Korama, and me back home to Ghana with open arms, hearts and minds, especially Etwie Atta Akyea; Nana Addo Dankwa Akufo-Addo; Kwasi Twum; Hilda Danquah; George Brobby; Eric Fiifi Ofori-Atta; my mother, Josephine Danquah; Iris Asamoah; Dr. Charles Wereko-Brobby; Ken & Angie Ofori-Atta; J.B. Danquah Adu; Reks Brobby; Nana Asante Bediatuo; Frank Adu; Asare "Gabby" Otchere-Darko; Nana Yaw Kuntunkununku Ofori-Atta; the incomparable Nana Yaa Ofori-Atta; and, of course, the late great Ferdinand Ayim.

Many thanks to this book's contributors for their patience and understanding and for writing with such grace, courage and honesty. I feel extremely honored to have been able to work with all of you—particularly Gail Wronsky, who was my ninth grade English teacher and who introduced me to a world of black literature I didn't even know existed.

My heart is filled with so much love for the friends who keep me laughing, talking, dreaming, and writing. Thank you: Annie

Burrows, David Goldsmith, Michael Taylor, Andrew Solomon, CCH Pounder, Agyeman Ossei, Jamal Kadri, Jaime Pressly, Herman Chinery-Hesse, Kimball Stroud, Eric Burns, Ama Dadson, Komla Dumor, Anedra Shockley-Elsesser, Greg Tate, Bee-be Smith, Alhaji Aliu Mahama, Stephanie Covington Armstrong, Michael Blum, Anna Bossman, Sharla Crow, David Hatcher, Jonathan Burrows, Lisa Black-Cohen, George Koomson, Dianna Cohen, Frank Roman, John Dramani Mahama, Jackson Browne, Don Mensah, Hill Harper, Nnamdi Mowetta, my uncle Opoku Akyeampong, and my sister Paula Danquah-Fischer.

I am grateful to Ama Ata Aidoo, one of the African women writers upon whose shoulders I stand, and to the phenomenal poet, Kofi Awoonor, for their friendship and encouragement.

I am also grateful to: my uncle, Duke Danquah, for the many great conversations and Bloody Mary–soaked Sunday brunches at Sarabeths; William Assibey, Richard Druyeh, and Joe Nanor who so generously supplied bailout funds to help me keep the wolf away while I was writing; my father, N. Duke Brobby for his support; Cindy Spiegel for still believing in me; my lawyer Kenneth Burrows; Rick Solomon, for choosing me to mentor when he decided to "give back"; and my agent David Vigliano, for being exactly who he is and exactly what I needed.

In matters concerning publication, I would like to thank Wayne DeSelle for coming through on such short notice with our gorgeous cover design; Steven Malk and Simon Lipskar at Writers House for being so kind and attentive, and for rescuing this project. Likewise, I would like to thank Theresa Noll, Veronica Liu, Anna Lui, Ruth Weiner, Ashley Roberts, Lars Reilly, Jon Gilbert, and everyone at Seven Stories Press for taking such pride in the books that you produce, and for handling me and this project with such care and respect. I would especially like to express my gratitude to Dan Simon for daring, in a time of tremendous corporate greed, to create this independent publishing house and to keep its doors open and lights on month after month and year after year. Dan, I am just awed by your tireless efforts, your love of literature and your commitment to writers such as myself. Seven Stories Press really is like "The Little Engine That Could," and you really are pretty amazing and inspiring. Thank you for giving this project a home.

Last but certainly not least, I would like to say thank you to my daughter, Korama Danquah, hot cocoa maker and rainbow keeper. A statement of fact: I love you more than I ever thought I could love anyone. You bring meaning to the whole journey, the whole experience, even the silliest parts; and you help me see things with new eyes. A question: *Do u glass?*

Yeah, thought so.

One likely reason for the paucity of critical material on this large and compelling subject is that, in matters of race, silence and evasion have historically ruled literary discourse. . . . It is further complicated by the fact that the habit of ignoring race is understood to be a graceful, even generous, liberal gesture. To notice is to recognize an already discredited difference. To enforce its invisibility through silence is to allow the black body a shadowless participation in the dominant cultural body.

—Toni Morrison, *Playing in the Dark: Whiteness and the Literary Imagination*

If this fire determined by the sun, be received on the blackest known bodies, its heat will be long retain'd therein; and hence such bodies are the soonest and the strongest heated by the flame fire[.] . . . Let a piece of cloth be hung in the air, open to the sun, one part of it dyed black, another part of a white colour, others of scarlet, and diverse other colours; the black part will always be found to heat the most, and the quickest of all; and the others will each be found to heat more slowly, by how much they reflect the rays more strongly to the eye; thus the white will warm the slowest of them all, and next to that the red, and so of the rest in proportion, as their colour is brighter or weaker.

—Hermann Boerhaave
A New Method of Chemistry, 2nd edition (1741)

BODY LANGUAGE

The idea that eventually became this book was rooted in my fascination with the black body, which began when, at the age of six, I emigrated with my family from Ghana to America. I don't remember ever being aware of my blackness before then; I guess that was one of the privileges of living in a predominantly black country.

In America, it was the exact opposite. I was always keenly aware of my blackness nearly every second of every day, of how the adjective *black* suddenly seemed to precede every nominative description of me—*black* student; *black* girl; *black* friend. I even got into the habit of counting black bodies—in classrooms, on buses, at parks and beaches, wherever two or more were gathered. I don't know what the point of doing that was, what conclusions I expected to draw; I just know that I felt compelled to do it.

Back then, I hadn't formed any opinions or judgments about the black body. I was a child, a stranger in a strange land. What did I know of the history of the black body? I hadn't yet learned of chattel slavery, of the countless numbers of black bodies—Africans, like me—that had been brought to America. I hadn't yet learned of the chains and shackles, the brandings, the auction blocks, the plantations, the beatings and rapes. When I looked at a black body, what I saw was myself. It was an assurance that I would not disappear, that this sea of whiteness into which I'd been submerged would not somehow swallow me.

As I got older, it became apparent that I wasn't the only one who

13

paid attention to the black body. In fact, people seemed to be obsessed with it.

There were so many jokes about the black body; so many stereotypes that were whispered, passed around and perpetuated.

What do you call a black man in a three-piece suit?

There were so many representations and misrepresentations.

All black men have big penises.

The black body had its own mythology; it had its own language.

Rub a nigger's head for good luck.

The black body, whether whole or broken down to its parts, was "*ized*" in every single way something could be. It was racialized, fetishized, romanticized, demonized, infantilized, criminalized, dehumanized, sexualized, criticized, ostracized, ritualized, and, much more often than we think, it was also prized.

I loved how black people always found a way to celebrate the black body, even as it was being denigrated by what seemed to be a majority of their white counterparts. The white girls I went to school with would sneer or scrunch their noses disapprovingly when they talked about black girls' bodies: the plump lips were not to their liking, the nose was too flat and broad, and forget about the butt—oh, it was way too big. A lot of the black girls pretended they weren't bothered. They promenaded around the hallways switching their bubble butts to the rhythm of Experience Unlimited's go-go classic, "Da Butt."

When you get that notion, put your backfield in motion . . .
That's right! Shake your butt.

If only it was that easy. More often than not the pride that was being celebrated didn't go below the surface. Deep down those of us who couldn't boast a "typical" ballerina's frame or fit easily into the mainstream society's standard of beauty, felt the sting of exclusion. We wondered if there was something wrong with our bodies. We were taught that our butts were supposed to be hidden. We

MERI NANA-AMA DANQUAH

were encouraged to wear clothes that "flattened" our figures. We were made to feel inferior.

Saartjie Baartman had a big butt—which is one reason, the only reason, she became the ultimate icon of racial inferiority. In 1810, when Baartman first met the British Marine Sergeant William Dunlop, she was a twenty-year-old South African slave. Dunlop told her that if she went with him to England, she could earn both of them a fortune. What he failed to tell her was that she would earn that fortune with her body—or, more specifically, her buttocks. How? It would work like this: members of the European elite would pay top dollar for the chance to either glimpse or gape at Baartman's naked posterior which, based on their standards of physical beauty and normality, they considered to be perversely large and uncivilized. It was something of a high society pay-per-view, and it went on for four years, until Baartman was sold and moved to Paris, where she was then exhibited by her new owner, a French animal trainer, as part of his traveling circus.

In addition to the constant public peek-a-booing, Baartman was also subjected to a series of intrusive and degrading examinations by the eminent French scientists of the day. Once the sensation of the "Hottentot Venus," as Baartman had been dubbed, had lost its titillating thrill amongst polite Parisian society, she was abandoned by the animal trainer and forced into prostitution in order to survive. She died in 1815 at the age of twenty-five, an alcoholic, suffering from syphilis and tuberculosis.

The story of Saartjie Baartman's butt doesn't end there. After her body—just her her butt, her brain and other organs, actually—was preserved in formaldehyde, it, along with her skeleton, was handed over to the Musee de l'Homme (Museum of Mankind). There, in the museum, Baartman's skeleton and all her parts were displayed for the next century. Yes, you read that right: her ass was pickled and bottled in a jar and exhibited for public viewing in a museum for 100 years.

Don't be fooled into dismissing this as a tale of how the black body was treated in the past, in the 1800s, when Western society was not as "enlightened." What this story does is confirm that even after two centuries the black body, as evidenced by the treatment of Saartjie Baartman's remains, continued to be an object of much curiosity, of much controversy.

Let me explain:

In 1994 then-South African president Nelson Mandela submitted a formal request to have Saartjie Baartman's remains returned to her native country. By that time, a number of international campaigns attempting the same results had already been mounted. Despite all of those efforts, the Musee de l'Homme asserted its ownership of the remains. They claimed that it was in the interest of "scientific research" for them to keep her remains. In other words, they said they owned her ass and they weren't going to give it back.

Then-French president Francois Mitterand made a personal promise to Nelson Mandela that he would do everything in his power to make sure the matter was resolved. And though Mitterand eventually made good on his promise, it took several years for the necessary legislation, including a special act of parliament, to be passed. Finally, in April 2002, Saartjie Baartman's skeletal remains, along with her butt and the other organs that had been preserved, were repatriated and given a proper burial.

For Christmas in 2001 a white friend, for reasons I still don't understand, presented me with a copy of the book *Ota Benga: The Pygmy in the Zoo*. It is the story of a twenty-three-year-old Congolese pygmy who was brought to America in 1904 to be "displayed" in the St. Louis World's Fair. After he had been "displayed" in the fair for several months, Ota Benga was taken to the Bronx Zoo where he, his hammock, and his bow-and-arrow were placed in the Monkey House with the monkeys, chimpanzees, and gorillas. There he stayed—sharing a cage with an orangutan and a parrot—on exhibit for the zoo's visitors as a way of affirming current racial myths and stereotypes. The director of the zoo insisted that there was no difference "between a wild beast and the little black man." On some days Ota Benga attracted as many as 40,000 visitors. They—children and adults alike—would stare at him, poke him, and chase him around the park.

The public outcry against Ota Benga's situation—or, one might say, incarceration—was immediate. Ota Benga himself also did much to help his own case, securing a knife on one occasion and brandishing it around the park at those who tried to chase him; using his bow-and-arrow on other occasions to retaliate against people who threw things at him and poked him. Within a short period of time, he was removed from the zoo and placed in an orphanage asylum, where attempts were made to formally educate him. He eventually settled into a job at a tobacco factory and became somewhat independent. He also became extremely depressed by the realization that he might never be able to return to his homeland, that he might remain in a country where he was the subject of freakish fascination. He borrowed a pistol and shot himself in the heart.

The book was captivating, but I found the story of Ota Benga incredibly disturbing. It reminded me of Saartjie Baartman and her plight, especially since the return of her remains was making headlines around the same time that I was reading about Ota Benga. I wondered about the people who'd gone to see them—Ota Benga and Saartjie Baartman—when they were on display. What were their fears and prejudices? What emotions had spiraled through them when they'd seen those black bodies? Had they looked at those bodies and deduced that those people were human beings? Or had they reached another conclusion altogether?

A few months later, in the summer of 2002, I stumbled on an article about Merriam Webster's official addition of the words *booty* and *bootylicious* to the dictionary. I was drop-jawed. How bizarre, I thought. On the one hand, it had taken years and an act of parliament for a country to return one black woman's well-preserved ass to her homeland, and on the other hand, here was Destiny's Child, three curvaceous black women shaking, loving, and owning their asses straight into Webster's dictionary. Is that wildly ironic or just plain ignorant?

> *I don't think you ready for this jelly.*
> *'Cause my body's too bootlyicious for ya baby.*

Isn't it remarkable, the black body's nimble curvature of white space? That is, after all, what happens; or haven't you noticed? The black body seems to exist in white space in such a way that it— white space—has to transform itself in order to either receive or reject it. Popular culture, especially music and sports, has always been the best way to see this curvature in action. Then came the phenomenon known simply as hip hop, which took it to a-whole-nother level.

The prism of hip hop reflects the light of pop culture attention onto the black body more intensely than anything before it ever has. That is to say, hip hop has brought to the fore the power of the black body to not simply command the attention of the world but to also create capital. Think about the commercials you now watch on TV, the print ads you now see in magazines. Everywhere you look, the black body is there—even when it's not there, when its presence is merely suggested.

One company that utilized the black body to rock many a boat (and sell a whole bunch of clothes) is Benneton, whose United Colors campaign's print ads, which rarely featured any of the store's products, ventured into the arena of provocative photo journalism. In 1989 the company hired the celebrated photographer Oliviero Toscani to capture the image of a bare-breasted black woman nursing a newborn white infant. In the photograph, the black woman is headless and faceless. She is just torso, cradling arms and dark, engorged nipples.

Essence, a magazine for black women, refused to run that ad, as did a number of other publications in the United States. "The black community in the US," the Benneton company noted on their website, "reacted strongly . . . because, in their opinion, it perpetuated the stereotype of the black nanny, relegated to a subordinate role. The true spirit of the photo—that equality goes beyond the kneejerk reactions and conventional perceptions—was, however, understood internationally. The photo received awards in Austria, Denmark, France and Holland. In Italy, it won the Confindustria prize for the best print campaign in the textile category and the overall Grand Prix for the best photo in print advertising. [It] became the most-awarded image in Benneton's advertising history."

Was the outrage in the US over the photo truly the opposite of the praise that it received elsewhere in the world, or were they simply different expressions of what was actually the same impulse? The impulse that caused those crowds to stare at Saartjie Baartman in Europe and go to visit the caged pygmy, Ota Benga, in the Bronx?

What is it about the black body that draws people in, makes them so fascinated?

Obviously, this isn't a new question. I've read more theory on this topic than I care to admit. But this go-round, I wasn't all that interested in theory; I wasn't searching for an academic angle, some new slant on history and its implications. People don't live inside of textbooks; we live in the world. Thus, I found myself extremely curious about human experiences, human emotions— which are often complex, illogical and sometimes defy reasonable explanation. But that's the way the world works. I guess you could say that what I wanted was story, not theory. And not the same old stories, either. I wanted contemporary anecdotes, ones that would take the black body and transform it from object to subject.

I've always been more reader than writer, publishing to support my expensive and time-consuming habit of reading. So I went in search of a book that would satisfy my curiosity. I wasn't able to find one that was quite right for me. To make matters more difficult, I wanted a text that also included white people in this discussion because after all, what would the black body be in the Western world without white people? Would we have ever been acquainted with the black body of Josephine Baker had she performed her "Danse Sauvage" in Liberia or Cameroon? Or the black body of Jesse Owens, who won four gold medals in the 1936 Olympics in Berlin, had he been running in Kenya? Owens, the son of a sharecropper and the grandson of a slave, became an overnight sensation in Germany—the Germany of Adolf Hitler, the Germany whose exclusion of non-Aryan athletes from their teams sparked an international boycott of the games that, as it were, would be the last Olympic competition for a dozen years.

You see, in my opinion, if you try to have an emotionally honest conversation about the black body without the inclusion of white people, you're not only ignoring the racial dynamics and history of this country, but that of the entire Western civilization. So, when I couldn't find exactly the book that I was looking for, the one I wanted to read, I decided to put it together myself.

I began working on this book, *The Black Body*, in 2003, long before most of the world had heard about Barack Obama, the man who would become the 44th president of the United States of America. President Obama has often called his journey, as the first black man to hold the highest office of the land, an improbable one. In his celebrated speech on race, Mr. Obama said, "[It] is an issue that I believe this nation cannot afford to ignore right now." He called upon Americans to have an open and honest conversation

MERI NANA-AMA DANQUAH

about race. He was certainly not the first to make that declaration. It seems that after every major event or incident that brings to light the county's racial or social inequities, we citizens are suddenly called upon to "talk about race." It happened on the heels of the 1992 Los Angeles riots, then immediately following California's 1994 passage of the anti-immigration Proposition 187, and in the midst of the 1995 O.J. Simpson murder trial. In 1998, President Clinton even launched what was intended to be a series of national "conversations about race."

Despite these various attempts to jumpstart this all-important conversation, we never seem to move past "go." Surely not because there is nothing to be said. Black folks and white folks alike have a whole lot to say about race. We just don't seem to be speaking openly or honestly; we don't seem to be speaking to each other, across the lines that we've been told divide us. The feelings we confide to our friends and family members (of the same race) are not the same feelings that we offer in public forums, where we tend to talk around race, stick with the status quo, regurgitate platitudes or resort to pretense, acting as though it's not a significant issue, one that affects our everyday lives. The topic of race simply does not lend itself to truth-telling. Black people don't want to be perpetually portrayed as angry, and white people don't want to risk being viewed as racist. Editing this collection has given me a glimpse of how deep those fears really are. I'd always felt really privileged to be surrounded by people, of all colors, with whom I could speak candidly about race. I soon discovered that this candor was, disappointingly, quite conditional.

The first prospective white contributor I spoke to was a colleague and friend, a respected and well-known author who was extremely interested in the topic and had an awful lot to say. A gay man, he'd slept with a number of black men and the stories he told offered tremendous insight into race, representation, and desire in that segment of American society and culture. He and I spoke at length about the gay white photographer Robert Mapplethorpe's *Black Book*, published in 1986.

It's a collection of black and white photographs that Mapplethorpe took of black men. A significant number of the photographs in the book picture completely nude black men, their faces covered; they are posed, literally, on pedestal-like objects, or they are wearing loincloths and holding spears. Regardless of what the black male subjects of Mapplethorpe's photographs are standing on, what they are doing, or what they are wearing, one thing they all have in common is their exposed genitalia.

"Would you write an essay about this for the book?" I asked my colleague/friend toward the close of our conversation.

"Oh God, no," he responded, rather emphatically. "Are you kidding? I would never commit anything like that to print." He was afraid his words would somehow be used against him, that he would either come off sounding terribly "PC" or inexcusably insensitive.

I got different variations of this same answer again and again and again from so many of the white writers I approached.

"You want me to write an essay about *what*? The *black* body? Oh."

No matter how many assurances I gave these writers that it was not my intention to "set them up" as racists, they ultimately refused.

"All I need," one writer, a *New York Times* bestselling author laughed, "is for a reviewer to quote something out of context. That could be disastrous, with the Internet, blogs, Facebook; it would spread like wildfire. You just can't undo damage like that. It could wreck someone's career."

The first white writer to say "yes" to the query was my friend, Anne Beatts. Thinking back on it now, it makes perfect sense. As one of the original writers for *Saturday Night Live*, for which she won two Emmy awards, Anne was used to breaking new ground

MERI NANA-AMA DANQUAH

and tackling controversial topics. But that wasn't why I thought to ask her. I decided to ask Anne because of the fearlessness with which she approached the topic of race in our friendship.

Anne and I met nearly two decades ago when we were regular attendees and sometimes-featured artists at a poetry reading series in Los Angeles. She'd once heard me read a poem entitled, "An African American," about being an African immigrant. One of the first gifts she gave me, which was clearly inspired by that poem, was a tiny woven basket from Africa. Inside the basket was a watermelon brooch, along with a note from Anne that read: *In celebration of both of your cultures.* At first, I didn't know whether to laugh or be offended; but, knowing Anne, I figured that she'd intended it as a loving and light-hearted gesture, so I laughed. It was the beginning of what would become one of my most emotionally honest friendships with a white person. Nothing about race is off-limits in our conversations.

I knew that Anne, having worked as the original director of *The Cosby Show* spin-off *A Different World*, had a lot of wonderful stories to share. She'd also recently adopted a young African-American girl who'd been in the foster-care system. I was thrilled when Anne agreed to contribute to *The Black Body*; and Anne's essay about her relationship with her daughter is as brave as it is heartwarming.

Though it continued to be a struggle, in time I was able to convince others to say "yes," which enabled me to meet my goal of including a fair number of white contributors in *The Black Body*.

Steven Kotler sheds some light on black blood, from the one-drop rule to the heredity of hipness. Susan Matus's move to Harlem offers her the opportunity to overcome fear and recognize the not-so-obvious humanity that exists within others, and within herself. Werner Disse's observations about growing up in South Africa under the system of apartheid sum up the concept of race in a new way: "Suddenly, something clicked. This was my opportunity to find relevance. . . . This was my opportunity to explore truth."

Annie Burrows remembers how in the Louisiana of her youth, blacks and whites were united in their love of food and music, but little else. Kimball Stroud recalls how in her hometown of Texarkana partying with the black kids was cool, but kissing them was taboo. This taboo is precisely what Philip Littell explores in his meditation on the black body as a source of inspiration, as an object of desire. When her Jewish father disapproves of her budding relationship with a young black boy, Susan Hayden learns that there is sometimes a price to be paid for that desire, and she discovers that even those who are sensitive to discrimination can fall prey to their own prejudices. Hayden shares how she used soul music to bridge the divide in her family; Kenny White recognizes that had it not been for soul music, he might have missed his calling and found himself on the wrong side of the dial.

David Goldsmith details the push-and-pull of a passionate interracial love affair. "I liked being the white guy," Goldsmith confesses, "who was man enough for the beautiful black woman, because that meant that apparently I had somehow managed to leapfrog over all those available black men. And who's to say who should be at the head of that line?"

Gail Wronsky tells why, as a college student, she chose to work as a nurse's aide in a hospital with a staff and patient roster that were both predominantly black. She writes: "It had something to do with being raised in a middle-class, white, suburban world in which the body was almost systematically denied and ignored." At the hospital, Wronsky learned to see and understand the body, its strength and its fragility, in a way she hadn't even known was possible.

Joel Lipman tackles the world of sports, and explains what it is that makes someone a hero. "Society and race," he writes, "are a fucked-up set of twins, scared of their own shadows. But the athletic public, the crowds, the fans, the rabid—we don't care if your color is black, blue or white—just do that thing you do—and do it for US. Fuck Jim Crow, kick his skinny white ass back in the closet with his kid sister—he hates to hate and hates EVERYTHING, including himself."

Recently, a friend who was unimpressed with the inclusion of white writers in this collection said to me, "White people have been writing about the black body for centuries."

"Yeah," I admitted. "That's true. But they haven't been telling the truth. They haven't implicated themselves in any of the mythology or lies; they haven't shed any light on their own personal relationship to blackness."

Make no mistake: I do not mean to suggest, in any way, that I find the contributions and admissions of the white writers to this collection more courageous, revelatory, or enlightening than those of the black writers. "Until you've walked a mile in my shoes," Whoopi Goldberg wrote in her book, which was aptly titled *Book*, "you can't know how deep the snow really is." To write, no matter how sincerely or respectfully, about the black body; to encounter, experience, or even love a black body, is one thing, but to live in a black body is something else entirely. To write about what it's like to live in a black body is no easy task. Many of us African Americans are just learning to claim ownership of our bodies, to see and appreciate them for what they really are, not what the mainstream (read: white) society would have us believe they are.

In this collection, so many of the essays by black writers are about negating or negotiating the harmful effects of stereotypes and negative imagery. They are about trying to undo the damage that was done by the dishonest documentation of the black body by white writers, the damage that is still being done by the advertising and entertainment industries.

"Imagine a black woman in 1925 who wanted to be a scholar," writes Elizabeth Alexander. ". . . Now imagine that woman wanted to study the black body—that which has so persistently been reduced to perverse stereotype—and who imagined its study could teach black people something important about themselves. What would it mean to scrutinize the disarticulated black body with love, to put it back together, in a sense, and do a new arithmetic that attempts to bring light to the study of who we are?"

With the white writers, my editorial objective was merely to have them address, in a raw and open and deeply personal way, the experience of the black body in their lives. I felt that was more than enough. With the black writers, my editorial objective was to have them "scrutinize the disarticulated black body with love," and in so doing, to "bring light to the study of who we are." Nearly all of the black writers were invited to select a part of the black body to which they felt especially connected and write about it. The rest were invited to write about more specific themes like imagery, health and healing.

Greg Tate waxes poetic on the historical and biological brilliance of the black brain. Brent Jennings writes with grace and aplomb about the vagina and how he learned to view it as much more than a thing to be conquered, enjoyed, and then discarded. Peter J. Harris takes on the myth of the well-hung penis and talks about what it really means to be a sexually empowered black man. S. Pearl Sharp tells the story of how ignorance and racism distorted and animalized the black body in the imaginations of many white people. Meanwhile, Kenji Jasper recounts his childhood fascination with a classmate's butt. "Yet and still," Jasper writes, "I found myself moving my knee toward the back of Tosha's desk until it kissed her soft and cushy prize. I felt the cap of the joint sinking into the warmth of the junk in her trunk. And then I pulled back, having held just long enough for it to be dismissed as a mistake, written off as the unintentional side effect of me reaching down to retrieve a lost pen or pencil."

Nzingha Clarke describes the world she inherited from her parents that exists in her hands, a history written into her palms; Tonita Austin-Hilley traces her lineage through the journey of the feet, proudly claiming the freedom of movement as a right earned for her by her forebears. Meanwhile Lynell George talks about "good hair" and all the ignorance, insults, implications, and innuendos it seems to invite. "My hair is not remarkable," she writes. ". . . My hair, juxtaposed against my skin, however, is just different enough to tally up silent questions, quiet judgment, or merely confusion. I don't have to open my mouth. My hair speaks for me, unbidden.

Back in the day, before the ubiquity of weaves and down-to-the tailbone extensions, my hair said to some:

She stuck up.

She lost.

She self-hating.

She trying to be white.

And now: She white."

Kenneth Carroll and Stephanie Covington Armstrong both explain their relationship to the stomach and the particular hunger that it produced in their lives. "My son knows nothing about the days when my stomach was flat and barely full," Carroll confesses. "He knows nothing of the agitated conversations of parents who fret about job security, evictions and a future clouded by the twin evils of racism and poverty. Back when my stomach was flat, like the world, when my seven siblings and I lived so close to the hungers that poor children are faced with that we could hear them whisper at night. Growing up in the sixties and seventies in DC's rapidly disintegrating public housing, I never knew a really fat kid. They were the oddities, the kids to pick on. Fat kids either had a medical condition or their parents were able to secure extra food by hustling."

"What I wanted," Covington Armstrong recalls, "was to be admired, to be adored and revered. Rarely had I seen that happen to anyone in real life, certainly not the women I knew and certainly not by anybody in my neighborhood. It happened to the waifish women on television and to the butt-less, stick-figured supermodels who graced the covers of fashion magazines. To me they appeared sacred, glamorous, absent of any flaws; it was as if nothing bad could ever happen to them. If I couldn't be like them then I wanted to be ignored, just left alone."

The lack of admiration, adoration and reverence for black women is exactly what Carolyn L. Holbrook condemns in her narrative. Hill Harper envisions a future in which the presence of successful, high-profile African Americans in all fields, not just entertainment and sports, will send a powerful message of possibility for all children and encourage the creation of positive, constructive images of black people. "But what good are those images if black people don't have soul?" asks Yolanda Young as she laments what she believes is the loss of that untouchable, all-powerful part of our anatomy. A. Van Jordan, on the other hand, makes visible what so many refuse to see: the black male heart, its capacity for love.

"I am always captivated," A. Van Jordan insists, "by the squirming of the world under the heartbeat of a black man. The world calls for this level of self awareness, for this level of self assurance, in order to get ahead, but, in the chest of a black man, it carries with it the misinterpretation of a man who is either threatening or crazy. He isn't employable because he isn't easily manipulated; he isn't desirable as a son in-law because you fear for the future of your daughter; he isn't ideal for a son or a father because his expectations are too high—at least, this is all we're seasoned to believe."

My own contribution explores how such limited and limiting expectations factored in my daughter's experiences with overt racism, experiences which ultimately led to her self-abuse. Tajamika Paxton provides insight into the ways in and through which healing can take place, for the mind, the spirit and, yes, the body.

One of the most thought-provoking conversations I'd had about race in the recent past was with a group of white acquaintances. All supporters of Barack Obama, we were applauding his victory, stating all the reasons why we felt his election was a sign of great things to come. "He's the first black president," I beamed.

"But is he?" one of the men in the group asked. He went on to explain that technically President Obama is just as white as he is black, so it wasn't really accurate to call him our first black president. I wasn't having any of that; I did not want to hear it. "He's black," I snapped, folding my arms across my chest and crooking my neck.

"No, he's not," the man snapped back.

"Oh, yes he is," I yelled. He issued the same response, and we went back and forth for a few minutes, each of us growing noticeably angrier and more defensive. Gone were all the feelings of hope and change that had ushered in the discussion; he and I were a few minutes away from coming to blows.

"What makes him black?" the man asked; he was trying, no doubt, to use biology to back me into a corner.

"The people who decided that one drop of black blood makes a person black," I told him. "I think they were white." He wasn't ready with a response, but it didn't matter. I didn't need one to realize that the reason I'd just given to justify my position was the same argument generations of white people have used to justify segregation, discrimination and disenfranchisement. I was truly disgusted with myself. For days afterward, I kept wondering, *what makes a body black? Who gets to create that definition, set the standard?*

Jason Luckett takes us on a guided tour of the many paths he traveled to figure out whether he could or should define his body as white like his mother's, or black like his father's. "The summer I would turn eighteen," he writes, "before my second year at UCLA, I went to get the gap in my teeth fixed. The orthodontist pulled out diagrams of black and white norms and showed I was in between. It calmed me in a peculiar way. Being called the "black guy" always felt so inaccurate. Here I finally had skeletal proof that in fact I was different from my father and whatever the monolith of blackness was supposed to be. But truly this 'evidence' just determined I'm neither fish nor fowl."

Will race ever be irrelevant in our society? Who can honestly say? I would've never guessed even four years ago—especially four years ago—that a man of color named Barack Obama could become president at any point in my lifetime, let alone in the next election cycle.

Be that as it may, race is a relevant issue right now. I hope the essays in *The Black Body* will do what I believe all art should do—inspire dialogue. Some of them, I know, will express opinions you agree with and swear by; others, I suspect, will make you clench your fists and ask how somebody could a) feel that way and b) have the nerve to write about it. Perhaps the inclusion of white writers will encourage black readers to speak about race with their white friends; perhaps white readers will be introduced to new ways of seeing and understanding the black body.

With any luck, we'll start talking to each other about race. The more we talk, the more heated or confrontational or provocative our conversations become, the closer we might get to a time when race really will be an irrelevant issue in this country.

—Meri Nana-Ama Danquah
Los Angeles, California
April 2009

"READING" THE BLACK BODY: OR, CONSIDERING MY GRANDMOTHER'S HAIR

by Elizabeth Alexander

Imagine a black woman in 1925 who wanted to be a scholar. The first black woman received her PhD in 1923; the first crop of black women PhDs—Otelia Cromwell, Eva P. Dykes, Georgina Shepherd, and Anna Julia Cooper (who earned the degree at the age of sixty-seven)—went on to work as teachers in black high schools because discrimination prevented them from teaching at universities. So the black woman who wanted to be a scholar was simultaneously inventing herself and bushwhacking a brand new trail. Now imagine that such a woman wanted to study the black body—that which has so persistently been reduced to perverse stereotype—and that she imagined its study could teach black people something important about themselves. What would it mean to scrutinize the disarticulated black body with love, to put it back together, in a sense, and do a new arithmetic that attempted to bring light to the study of who we are? What would it mean to disentangle this enterprise from concurrent work that saw black bodies as grotesquely emblematic racial markers? What of a black woman in the 1920s who became an anthropologist, one of the first of her color and gender in a field where those of her color are the studied, rather than the studiers? And what of that black woman anthropologist turning the calipers on her own people? What did she think she would discover?[1]

The history of the violent isolation of our body parts is too extensive for us to accede to the notion that parts can tell us anything about the whole, and that the individual whole can tell us anything about the body politic, its putative essence. Think of the macabre American practice of selling souvenir black body parts in the market after lynchings. How much for a finger, an ear, a penis? A basket of fingers, a garland of ears, the severed penis a symbol of feared black masculine power in its most mythical bloom. Chopped-off black hands in the Congo, bits of dissected Khoi genitalia in the Musee de l'Homme in Paris, parts displayed as object lessons, pieces standing for the whole, often in the name of "science." Yet we want to know ourselves better and we long for science and epistemology that will help us think about Us.

Such was the mission of a black woman anthropologist called Caroline Bond Day. In 1932, when she graduated from Harvard, she became the first woman of any color to earn a Masters degree in physical anthropology. At the time, to the best of my knowledge, there were only two other African-American women who had studied or were studying anthropology: Zora Neale Hurston, who studied at Barnard College with Franz Boas and whose work was published in 1933 in *Mules and Men*, and Katherine Dunham, who was studying at Northwestern University in Chicago with Melville Herskovits, and who published her research on Haiti and Jamaica in *Journey to Accompong* and *Island Possessed*. Day's thesis, *A Study of Some Negro White Families in the United States*, was published in 1932 by the Harvard African Series. These three women had no predecessors in their field.[2]

When I was a child I loved looking at the books on my parents' shelves, and *A Study of Some Negro White Families* was one that I returned to time and again. The book chronicled over three hundred families of mixed black and white ancestry using the methodologies of physical anthropology available at the time—the measurement of skull widths, nose breadths, hair texture, and so forth—along with sociological inquiry into subjects' home, work, and social habits. Who were these people sitting on porches with their high white collars and crocheted shawls, their voluminous hair

ELIZABETH ALEXANDER

arranged carefully, people named Archibald and Florida, Nancy and Josephine, Ulysses, Nellie, Sinai, Etnah, Daisy, Augustus, and Inez? Within *A Study*'s pages what most compelled me were the photographs, many taken by Day herself, not only of her subjects, but of their hair. Under each portrait and hair sample was a racial breakdown, fractions of "N" (Negro), "W" (White), and "I" (Indian) in the subject's racial makeup. This information was ascertained through interviews and knowledge of family history. The racial ratios captioned the pictures of the hair samples, so that they became representative of racial types. Hair was described along a spectrum from "frizzled" to "curly" to "deep waves" to "low waves" to "perfectly straight." Day wrote of the extreme mutability of hair textures and emphasized "It is doubtful if two people are ever seen with hair which is exactly alike."

The book amazed me. It was unlike anything I had ever seen, or have seen since. It seemed to both expose the secret lives of black people and conceal further secrets behind its pages. There were notable names among the family trees: W. E. B. DuBois (5/8 N, 3/8 W), Josephine St. Pierre Ruffin (3/8 N, 1/8 I, 4/8 W), artist Laura Wheeler Waring (4/8 N, 1/8 I, 3/8 W), civic leader Walter White (5/32 N, 1/32 I, 26/32 W), opera singer Lillian Evans (nee Evanti) (7/16 N, 9/16 W). Its pages led me to think about myself, about what my own bloodlines "added up to." I liked the structure of proper family trees, the lines and branches that connected. I would ruminate on a stopping point, the ancestor beyond which we could not go, where the information stopped. Often, of course, it stopped where the slave ships let off, on the shores of the United States. Day's charts stopped with "pure" racial types, full blood Africans, Indians, or Caucasians, who were always men. I cut a snippet of my own hair and held it next to the samples. What might I be? Did my hair reflect my "blood"?

We owned this book because Day was my grandmother's older half-sister, my mother's Aunt Carrie, my own Great Aunt. She had died when my mother was a girl, but growing up I heard many stories about her. My grandmother revered "Sister" and found in her a model for a life of intellectual engagement and of service to others—both sisters were social workers for many years. Aunt Carrie also offered a model of independence within the conventions of black middle class society. Her working papers are kept in the Peabody Museum of Harvard University, donated in 1931 by Day's professor, Earnest A. Hooten. They are the only extant working notes of a project taken on by a black woman at that time. The archive contains the cards on which Day kept notes on the measurements and physiognomy of her 2,537 subjects. There are large, careful charts and family trees. Perhaps most fascinating is her correspondence with her subjects. In these letters we see her energy and tenacity—she pursued the project for over a decade, through serious illness, other jobs, and geographical dispersal. They also show the extent of her social network. Day's subjects were often people she knew, so her letters addressed not only the research at hand but also the affairs of the day. She consulted "older people in the community who were not related but whose unofficial business it was, seemingly, to remember the ancestry of everybody else." Her powers of persuasion are also evident in these letters, not least of all when the thorny issue of racial "passing" arose.

Day's subjects seem to have supported her work in its initial stages, perhaps because they were proud to back one of "their" women endorsed by a grant at Harvard University. But when she wrote people asking permission to publish her findings, objections frequently arose. "My brother is strictly w—in Boston," one wrote, "you understand."[3] Other subjects were described as fearful of exposure because they were "passing for white" or had "gone to the other side." Day notes, "Of 346 families, 35 of the families state that there are one or more members who "are 'passing,' either entirely, or only temporarily for purposes of obtaining lucrative employment." She knew of fifty more families with passing members who

ELIZABETH ALEXANDER

were not part of her study and wrote, "practically every family with whom I have talked can give me an additional few names."

Day developed methodological quirks that illustrate the fact that her inquiry could only have been conducted from within the group being studied. With regard to the hair samples, for example, Day noted, "errors due to artificial straightening were partly eliminated by Mrs. Day, who knew most of the subjects and had notes on their true hair form." The work gives a sense of the lived reality of the acute gaze with which people try to read physical racial signs, and the extent to which those markers limited human experience and definition.

In her book, Day is careful to explain her attempts to make a cross section, class-wise, of black communities. She explicitly did not want the achievements of members of her group "to argue for the advantages of race-crossing[;] it is my firm belief that Negroes who are of unmixed blood are just as capable of achievement along all lines as those who are mixed." She seemed to understand the bias and misuse of the work she was doing, and the danger of any "reading of the body."

Day's anthropology would not hold up against what we now know about race and biology. She often mixed what we would call sociology with hard science, imagining certain traits as representative. What did these metaphorical tea leaves of physiognomy suggest to her? In the end, for me, the Caroline Bond Day project is about a tenacious young black woman trying to move beyond preconceived ideas about race, to let a relatively new science tell her things she did not already know. She nudged her social group, many of whom did not want to be pushed or investigated, to tell their stories and reveal secrets that might be helpful to a broader understanding. That she made black people believe that having their bodies calibrated and measured, their very body hair snipped and analyzed and saved, would tell them something they did not know, seems simultaneously discomforting, audacious, and visionary to me, especially as we look at the state of the "art" and "science" involved with the boom in DNA ancestry research today. It is as though Day imagined the disarticulated black body could be put back together again in a new light, draw new conclusions about what she already knew: the full span of Negro endowment and achievement.

Day's work also offers a glimpse "within the veil," as DuBois would have put it, to a world which exists in lore and that has been passed on, refigured as something else, and often, vanished completely, as those old-fashioned names have, too. Sometimes we still "read" racially ambiguous bodies, looking for that telltale frizzle at the hairline, shadow curling around the rim of an ear, a breadth of facial feature that tells what the body's wishes silenced. It's still a mystery, this thinking about "the Logan head," "my mother's hips," "my father's nose," when the body parts in question are thought to be racialized ones.

Now we can send a tissue scraping from inside our cheeks or a strand of hair to various sites that can analyze our DNA and learn the truths Day was aiming for: what percentage this, that, and the other we are, right down to where in Africa our people came from. The wish to go beyond where the family tree stops can be powerful in any of us. Imagination takes us there, and sometimes desire takes us there as well. The urge to know is, I daresay, natural, but what we make of it is tellingly romantic, a way of explaining ourselves. "Send your hair to Howard," says a friend, in a compressed shorthand that also glories in the fact that a historically black school is a place where, through an object as ephemeral as a strand of hair, one could come closer to knowing what has been systematically suppressed and eradicated over hundreds of years. When my mother describes a strand of her family tree, she muses that there were the narrow-headed Logans and the round-headed Logans. She doesn't elaborate on what that means, but it is a way of understanding family visually as part of a lineage, part of a primordial survival fantasy wherein you would "know your people" anywhere you saw them, know where you belonged.

It comes down to Aunt Carrie, to telling her story without trying to draw lessons from it or to crisply lay out what is applicable in the present. Caroline Bond Day believed that the knowledge she collected could help her let the world at large know about a proud community that was invisible. She believed that with this physical data she could disprove myths of Negro inferiority by first showing that Negroes existed in diversity and then writing about who lived in those once-anatomized bodies, their quotidian habits and accomplishments. And I think as a social scientist who quested to get her work done for over ten years, tenaciously, she also believed in the scholar's first tenet: pursue what you do not know. That she herself was by type and in fact one of the subjects only makes the quest to know more, from the inside, ever more poignant and exemplary.

There was one thing left to check on my trip to the Peabody archive: the hair samples. Amazingly, they are there, folded four times into pieces of white paper, hundreds of hair cuttings from people in her study, cuttings she photographed and then placed on pages indicating the racial mixture: 1/4 N, 1/4 I, 1/2 W, hair of differing degrees of length, bend, curl, frizzle, and shine, smudges of hair like smoke, hanks of shiny hair marked 3/4 I, boxes full of nearly hundred-year-old hair.

Properly, the hair shouldn't be kept at the Peabody, the archivist told me. Organic material is supposed to be kept elsewhere. Needless to say, I wasn't allowed to touch the hair or even look at most of it. But Caroline Bond Day had one subject in particular whose hair I had to see: her half-sister, Wenonah Bond, nineteen years old in 1927 when the sample was clipped, my grandmother.

What can I say about sitting in an archive at Harvard University holding a piece of my grandmother's hair? In the thirty-one years we shared, I was her treasure. She brushed and braided my own hair throughout my childhood—she would have said she "disciplined" my hair—working the ends of my pigtails around a spit-moistened index finger and oiling the frizzling edges. In adulthood, she kept her own hair carefully set and arranged. It was blue-grey and lustrous all the years I knew her. When she died at eighty-six, the last thing I did in her presence, in the presence of her body, was stroke her beautiful hair. It felt wavy and soft as it always had and was slightly crisped with hairspray, though she had been dead for an hour. Her spirit was still in the room but was quickly leaving, and we could feel it, and that was that. It was time to go.

Her hair, now before me. Hers was the same color as mine at nineteen: dark brown with a slight reddish undertone, not as curly as mine, a bit mussy, as befits a young woman on the go, as she was then, away from Washington, DC; from the inevitable Teacher's College and early, imminent marriage; from the South, where most of the people she knew came from; and towards learning and Sister and all the possibilities she enacted and represented.

I touched the hair, though I was not supposed to. I am reverent about libraries and archives and their rules, so I justified my transgression with the thought that I was the only person on earth who might ever need to touch this particular hank of hair. Oh, my Nana, there you are. Here is your hair between my fingers. My mind went to an odd place, to a book I'd recently read with my children, about extinct ice-age wooly mammoths. One was discovered in Siberia, frozen for tens of thousands of years in a block of ice. Paleontologists used hair dryers to meticulously defrost small parts of it, so they could snip a bit of fur and see if they could find an unbroken strand of fragile woolly mammoth DNA. As the dryers melted the ice, the book said, the refrigerated research room filled with the musky animal smell of the thousands-of-years-old creature. If they found that unbroken strand, for which they still search, would they try to clone another wooly mammoth and place it in the paleontological park now under development? Why would you, if you could, and why wouldn't you?

I held my grandmother's hair, which felt like the end of her—except, stranger still, it was the before of her, before I knew her, before she even had a child who would be my mother. This was a

ELIZABETH ALEXANDER'

Wenonah Bond I never knew, nor did my mother. No, not Wenonah. Just a hank of her hair at nineteen and her sister's notations, 1/2 Negro, 1/4 Indian, 1/4 White. What did it, what could it possibly, tell me?

Taking care not to disturb its pattern, I put the cutting back onto the paper, folded the packet four times, and returned it back to the archivist, who put it in a glassine envelope in an acid-free box in a basement at the Peabody Museum at Harvard University, where it remains, in the Caroline Bond Day Papers.

NOTES

1. See Marita Bonner's 1925 essay "To Be Young, a Woman, and Colored," for one meditation on these questions. Bonner entered Radcliffe College in 1918 and no doubt knew Caroline Bond Day. Her essay is reprinted in Marita Bonner, *Frye Street and Environs: The Collected Works of Marita Bonner*, ed. Joyce Flynn (Boston: Beacon Press, 1989), 3–8.
2. See Lee D. Baker, *From Savage to Negro: Anthropology and the Construction of Race, 1896–1954* (Berkeley and Los Angeles: University of California Press, 1998), for a discussion of how anthropologists have contributed to the formation of racial categories; and Ira E. Harrison and Faye V. Harrison, eds. *African American Pioneers in Anthropology* (Urbana: University of Illinois Press, 1999), for essays about important African American figures in the field and a genealogy of their participation in and exclusion from the discipline.
3. As quoted in Adele Logan Alexander, *Homelands and Waterways: The American Journey of the Bond Family, 1846–1926* (New York: Pantheon, 1999), 377.

BLOOD AND FIRE

by Steven Kotler

If we have learned anything from our history it is that black blood is a mercurial thing. Black blood, which has meant both so little and so much, simultaneously. It leads one to wonder, how can something that has been spilt with deliberate, wanton glee stain so deeply?

F. James Davis, in his book *Who is Black? One Nation's Definition*, reminds us that the question of who is considered black in America is a historical one. Historically, black meant that someone was of African descent. But black blood also was contagious. So frightened were whites of the intermingling of the races, and, perhaps, so powerless to resist fleshy temptation, that some numb-nuts came up with "the one drop rule." One drop of black blood was enough to contaminate white blood. One drop was enough to stain a body black. We have a whole language that developed to define the intermingling: mulatto, mixed, quadroons, octoroons. An octoroon, who has seven out of eight white grandparents, is still considered black. And yet never, to the best of anyone's recollection, has the inverse been true. A drop of Caucasian blood has never been enough to alter anyone's shade. Which would lead you to logically conclude that black blood is more powerful than white blood. Which leads you back to that earlier question—how can something so obviously powerful be shed so freely?

Science is of little help. What do we find so potent in that one droplet? A random dictionary definition of blood: the fluid (red in vertebrates) that is pumped by the heart; blood carries oxygen and nutrients to the tissues and carries waste products away; the ancients believed that blood was the seat of emotion. The average human has five liters of blood pulsing through his or her veins, 55

41

percent of which is the straw-colored liquid known as plasma, the carrying mechanism for solid cells—both white and red—and clot-inducing platelets, the substance that keeps us from bleeding to death in the face of a paper cut. A single drop of blood contains millions of oxygen-carrying red blood cells. A single drop contains between 7,000 and 25,000 white blood cells—the frontline of the immune system, our first defense against disease. Does any of this bring us any closer to the truth?

Maybe this is a question of scale. Maybe we need to head micro-scopic, where DNA answers many a question. We now know, for instance, that humans share 25 percent of their DNA with lettuce. That is among the information that has flowed towards us from the miracle of the human genome project. For years we thought we shared 98 percent of our DNA with chimpanzees—a startling figure that caused scholar and physiologist Jared Diamond to spend four hundred pages in *The Third Chimpanzee* attempting to deduce what is it in that meager remainder, that two percent, that makes us dis-tinctly, uniquely, sometimes disastrously, human. That number—98 percent—has wavered somewhat as of late, dipping as we have done further research, recently dropping as low as 96 percent. This fact may or may not bring relief to the Creationists on the Christian Right, but it has done little to assuage our curious souls. And it raises even greater questions when we wonder about the mighty staining prowess of black blood.

In the early twentieth century, an Austrian scientist named Karl Landsteiner noticed two distinct chemical molecules present on the surface of the red blood cells. He labeled them, imaginatively, "A" and "B." If the red blood cell had only A molecules on it, that blood was called type A. If the red blood cell had only B molecules on it, that blood was called type B. If the red blood cell had a mix-ture of both molecules, that blood was called type AB. If the red blood cell had neither molecule, that blood was called type O. His quartering of blood earned him a Nobel Prize.

On Landersteiner's back rode the great breakthrough of the blood transfusion. The most intimate of procedures—the donation of blood, the co-mingling of blood, the saving of a life. Transfusions require a precise match, ethnic, genetic, exact. The slightest error leads to rejection. From further research into Landersteiner's work we now know that African Americans have an inordinate amount of rare blood types and that, because of this, the black community faces a deep and growing crisis—a shortage of blood.

It was surgeon, researcher and teacher Dr. Charles R. Drew who discovered the best way to store and ship blood plasma. He is credited with saving thousands of lives during World War II. He is credited with saving those lives during a period of time when the American Red Cross bent to societies' demands and began the racial labeling of blood and blood products. It was a practice that cost thousands of lives—black and white—and one that went on for decades beyond that war. It was a process that quite effectively outlawed cross-racial blood transfusions.

There is a double irony here. Dr. Drew himself was black. For many years following his death, rumors circulated that Drew was allowed to bleed to death in a Southern, all-white hospital. The story goes that there was no black blood on hand, so instead the doctors refused him his need. In 1994, Drew's daughter, first in a letter to the Washington Post and second in an NPR interview, denied these allegations. While Drew did bleed to death in a Southern hospital, she said, the white doctors in attendance did everything they could to save his life. When it comes to black blood, there is irony everywhere.

Currently, owing to the tremendous insight we have gained through genomics, a heated debate is raging on the question of race. The one-drop rule has become the few genes question. On the PBS website were two conflicting, scholarly essays written for the science program *NOVA*. These essays share the same title: "Does Race Exist?" One begins with C. Loring Brace, a man credited with bringing a Darwinian outlook to the field of biologic anthropology, who writes, "There is no such thing as a biological entity that warrants the term 'race.'" The counter argument is made by another learned scholar, Dr. George W. Gill, who says that there *is* a genetic basis for this sort of racial profiling. Dr. Gill, a forensic anthropologist, is among others who feel that this sort of data could lead to more effective law enforcement. While it is true that many experience an innate bristling at the idea of racial profiling—genetic or otherwise—in law enforcement, Dr. Gill is not alone in his feeling. The split in the scientific community over racial genetics is fifty-fifty; fifty percent believe that race is a technical term, fifty percent do not. This is the very best that modern science can offer. Does it bring us any closer to an understanding of black blood?

One of the basic notions of biology is that a gene's function is to copy itself to ensure transmission. If a gene fails at this process, it's no longer around. In recent years, anthropologists and other cultural researchers, looking for a way to make their science as rigorous and defensible as other, harder disciplines, began applying the tools of population biology to their work. Biologist Richard Dawkins came up with the idea of culture as a "population of memes," with memes being copy-me programs just like genes. Memes are cultural units: songs, jokes, stories, notions, values— things that are passed along through a population. Once you hear a meme—say a particularly funny joke—it gets stored in memory and later shapes behavior. In this case the joke gets retold, and this retelling is the copy-me part of the program. Then the whole process repeats itself and on and on.

This idea of memetic transmission becomes interesting when applied to cultures that have emerged from a long history of repression—like American black culture. In his essay "Are Black People Cooler Than White People," Donnell Alexander wrote what most of America was already thinking—that yes, black people are cooler than white people. The way we know this is true is that for most of the twentieth century, from the era of hip-cats to the era of hip hop, when folks of any color wanted to be hip, they most often borrowed their vision from African American culture. Hipness was the most powerful of black memes. And then Alexander goes on to explain why:

> Cool was born when the first plantation nigga figured out how to make animal innards—massa's garbage, hog maws and chitlins—taste good enough to eat. That inclination to make something out of nothing and then to make that something special articulated itself first in the work chants and slave songs in the field and then in the hymns that rose out of their churches. It would later reveal itself in the music made from cast-off Civil War marching band instruments (jazz); physical exercise turned to public spectacle (sports); and street life styling, from pimp's silky handshakes to the corner crack dealer's baggy pants. Cool is all about making a dollar out of fifteen cents.

Alexander's essay appeared almost a decade ago, in the pages of the now defunct *Might Magazine*, but that simple phrase: "cool is all about making a dollar out of fifteen cents" stuck with me. It stuck in my white boy brain. It stuck fast and hard enough that I slit the article from its binding glue and stuck it in a folder for later reference. Donnell Alexander's vision of cool became a meme strong enough to stay with me and now strong enough to be transmitted to you.

Which brings us back to the "one-drop rule" and the question of black blood. One of the more interesting facets of hip hop culture is what everyone knows—sure it's coming out of the ghetto, if we define ghetto as the core culture of cool, but it's selling in the suburbs. Folks on both sides of this phenomena have all sorts of negative criticisms of this process: it's either corrupting our youth—which, these days, seems to mean nothing more or less than causing them to adopt the black lingua franca—or it's commercializing black culture for that dread demon: the dollar. Either way, no one denies its potency.

The other day I was driving and passed two different convertibles, one a new Porsche, the other a Benz. Both were being driven by graybeards, white men pushing sixty, both pumping hip hop from their speakers. Television advertising is littered with hip hop references, and without meaning to offend, I think it's safe to say that they're not merely targeting a new wave of black buying power. The current sneaker trend, one of the longest lasting shopping trends in recent history, has infiltrated all walks of fashion. Designers high and low are pushing athletic shoes and have been doing as such since the early eighties when Run DMC started rapping about their Adidas. Is this about selling fresh soles in Compton or in Beverly Hills? If you were a Puma pusher which would you prefer?

The point is this: if the great white fear has been that one drop of black blood will contaminate, well then, how much of this was phobia and how much prophecy? Because here in the late twentieth century, where cool has become the ultimate commodity, black folks have most certainly cornered the market. One drop of blood: 55 percent plasma, over 1,000,000 red blood cells, roughly 15,000 white blood cells, some DNA tossed into the mix.

One drop of black blood: more than enough to re-color an entire nation.

PLAYING THE VERSES STRAIGHT
by Jason Luckett

They both walked naked around the house. I didn't really look like either of them. My hair was thin and loosely curly. My skin was beige. And my penis was hairless and small. My dad used to tell a story about my childhood castration anxiety. He woke me up early one morning because he knew I'd have a piss hard-on and took me to the bathroom. He pointed to my penis and said, "Look, your penis is big like Daddy's!"

I don't remember this incident, but I heard the story many times. I'm not sure that my flaccid penis has ever been as large as my father's. He'd wash himself in front of us well into our young adult lives. Both my parents were psychotherapists.

I am biracial. My mother is white. My father is black. My relationship with my father is difficult. My father is dead. My mother is alive and just sent me a birthday package. My mother's gifts come at expected intervals. My father's did not. My father gave me my first electric guitar the day before my sister's fifth birthday. My parents divorced when I was twelve. We lived with my mom, in the suburbs, where roads were regularly paved and trees were held up by sticks. When my sister and I had both finished college my mother retired. I drove her across the country where she met a white Englishman thirteen years her junior. She married him. Then they roamed the nation camping or doing outreach with the mentally ill. She's now a minister. That makes her seem interesting.

In my childhood my mother was overshadowed by my father's charisma and antics. She was support. He was praise and damnation. The first body I knew was my mother's. The first skin, the first home, the first nourishment was from her.

Dad often told the story of walking a few paces behind Mom and me with a gun in my diaper bag. This was the summer of 1966. In June of that year James Meredith was shot staging a one-man March Against Fear from Memphis to my father's hometown of Jackson. Meredith integrated Ole Miss in 1962, and family legend has it that Medgar Evers had recruited my father for that role. Dad's family nixed the idea, so he went to the local black college and took what he called "the hate money" for his graduate education in Hawaii. (No public graduate schools in Mississippi at the time would admit blacks.) After James Meredith was shot, Martin Luther King, Jr. and others decided to continue the march in his name. Police arrested Stokely Carmichael during the march and he delivered his first "Black Power" speech upon his release.

To me, Dad was blackness. We lived in Hawaii, Los Angeles, then Irvine, California. By the time we had arrived in Irvine in 1973, Dad had cut off from his Mississippi family. It wasn't until I went back to Jackson on my own at the age of twenty-four that I ever really felt part of a black family. I knew my face gave me access to black culture, but I always felt like a silent imposter when I was assumed to be part of it. The black girls at UCLA flirted with me freely. The LA jazz musicians would engage me as if I were one of the few black youths interested in the music. But I felt as white as Keith Richards seeking out Chuck Berry. So blackness had power, but in my youth, embodied in my father, it was just power over me.

My father was in school working toward his PhD during much of my childhood. Then he was off in extramarital affairs. It's ironic that we visited Mississippi the summer of the March Against Fear; so many of my father's actions were based on fear. He ran away from Mississippi. He initially called off his wedding, fearing the implications of bringing a white woman to the black women who raised him. They told him, "Go back and marry that woman."

He told me he was involved with several women as a young man. He misaddressed love letters to them. The only one who forgave him was my mother. Her forgiveness assuaged his fear of rejection. As I watched him over the years, it seemed every perceived slight in a relationship was healed by adding a new woman to his life. That next woman would validate his sadness, or give him permission to vent, or simply add levity. Three women, sisters, none of whom he understood to be his biological parent, raised him. One was a nurse, one a teacher, and one a domestic.

My fear was that I would somehow be like my father. When my actions contradicted his framework, he would often disown me. My most vivid memory of this was during my sole psychedelic drug experience at age thirteen. I'd dropped acid after a school dance and was playing guitar with a friend in my bedroom. My father came home an hour or so later. He thought I'd call him for a ride home, and when I didn't, he took it as a sign of disrespect.

"Why do you treat me like this? You treat me like a dog. A fucking dog!" he barked. He slapped me. He became a Doberman.

Back in human form he told me he would not have me in his house if I treated him that way. "I'll keep food on the table and make sure you have shelter until you are eighteen. But after that, I'm through with you!"

He drove my friend partially home, left him in the street to walk the rest of the way. Then he dropped me at my mother's place, the condo where Sis, Mom and I lived because he would not let us have, nor sell, the family home. There the above scene was repeated, minus the hit and hallucination. He left.

No, I did not feel very connected to my father. Also, living in a place with few reference points, I felt ambivalent about my "blackness." TV had *Good Times*, *Sanford and Son*, and *The Jeffersons*. I remember thinking black men were supposed to walk with a slight limp and lean, a Freddie "Boom Boom" Washington attitude. While we lived in Los Angeles I wanted to be Michael Jackson. A year in the 'burbs and I wanted to be Paul McCartney. I did not feel black. The posters on my adolescent walls were of The Who, Queen, and Led Zeppelin. Roger Daltrey, Brian May, and Robert Plant had curls that more closely matched mine. Hendrix drummer Mitch Mitchell's perm looked closer to my head than my guitar hero Jimi. I told people I was Indian. And that was one-sixteenth true.

I was fairly glam in a rock 'n' roll way. But the Reagan Era girls turned me down, not yet ready to break a racial barrier. I'd been searching for freedom and/or home through women since I was at least ten or eleven. I wanted to escape youth, Irvine and America. I pursued my babysitters. They let me touch them. I lost my virginity at thirteen. My eighteen-year-old friend, who had driven me to her apartment, walked in on us and watched for a moment. That wasn't the last time he'd spy on me with a groupie. One former sitter practiced fellatio on me when I was a little older, about fourteen or fifteen. An older adult sister of a friend allowed me to kiss her. She and her friends introduced me to areas of sexuality I've rarely been interested in revisiting. I was pretty. Female classmates would dress me as a girl. I enjoyed the attention and the softness of their touches. I'd always try to be first to seduce the new girls in town before the racial weirdness of Irvine kicked in. Soon they'd discover it wasn't alright to be with a "black" guy. One high school girlfriend used to say I had a mouth like Mick Jagger. She also used to ask me to imitate my father's voice for her over the phone.

My first year at UCLA, black girls flirted openly with me. Their freely expressed interest puzzled me. The assumptions of our shared reference points dazed me; I didn't really want to come out and say I wore a "Disco Sucks" t-shirt to school, knew English rock bands inside and out, but had only a vague knowledge of the names Teddy Pendergrass or Luther Vandross. In this new phase in a more diverse setting, my sexual confidence grew. There may have still been those attracted or hindered by some taboo associated with my racial makeup, but I felt that when it was stripped away, I was desirable. I took that newfound confidence and tried to sleep with women from all areas of the globe.

The summer I turned eighteen, before my second year at UCLA, I went to get the gap in my teeth fixed. The orthodontist pulled out diagrams of black and white norms and showed I was in between. It calmed me in a peculiar way. Being called the "black guy" always felt so inaccurate. Here I finally had skeletal proof that in fact I was different from my father and whatever the monolith of blackness was supposed to be. But truly this 'evidence' just determined I'm neither fish nor fowl.

In other matters of measurement, I discovered on my sexual world tour that it's usually the lighter partner who will comment on the "beautiful" contrasts in our skin tones. When our coloring is the same it's an even bet as to who will comment first.

Then there's scent and feel. My arms feel a little like Karen, my first regular black lover in college. My skin is soft with sparse fine hair that seems to curl more as I age. That reminds me of her. She was a few shades browner than I.

Jenny was Chinese. Her skin was soft and firm, less pliable than most of my white lovers. And definitely more so than mine. Naked she smelled of fresh linen with a hint of tonic.

Alisa felt like a black woman. Her taste brought back the scent of women I knew as a young child. Her hands were strong, serpentine. I liked the way I could feel the veins in her arm.

Penelope told me her friend heard me talking in the background while she was on the phone and screamed "White Boy Alert!"

Kat felt like Carrie, who felt like Lyn, with soft white skin that burned in the summer. Molly had skin my color. When I touched her scalp, though, I didn't really understand.

I'm fairly sure I have black lips. I've liked kissing lips with that fullness.

My fatherless father was raised by three women, all blood related to him, while thinking of himself as a doorstep orphan. He idealized family and home. He never kept a formal job for more than a couple years at a time, but I still run into former medical students he counseled at UC Irvine who tell me of his helpful influence. At a housing project in Long Beach, he was memorialized by staff and tenants as a person who always spoke to them on their level, encouraging them to do their best. But his idealism of family and the righteousness of black people was contradicted all the time by his actions. Through tears he'd often state, "I've always been a good father to you. Haven't I?"

I hated that even in his most vulnerable state he'd make a proclamation, rather than truly ask me what I felt. But his idealized images, these images of righteousness and courage, inspired me. The courage of being part of an interracial couple in the early 1960s. The courage of transcending the racist limitations put upon him to get a Master's degree, then a PhD. These images inspired me to write poetry at age six in support of Angela Davis, to write songs encouraging cultural harmony at nine, and to continue exploring topics of social justice and love to this day.

In my early thirties, inspired to carry on my father's legacy of community service, I served as a mentor at a teen camp on diversity. In one of our exercises we separated the campers into racial affinity groups to facilitate the free flow of stereotypes. We then brought a list of these stereotypes back to the whole community for discussion.

"White people smell like dogs," announced one camper. The idea got enough agreement that it made the list we would share later. I'd either heard or could anticipate the other stereotypes that were shared, but was horrified by this. I took aside one of the veteran mentors, who was also biracial, and asked her about it. She said that idea always came up during the exercise. I didn't feel comfortable further exploring this by asking another one of the black leaders if I smelled. The scent of races is not something that's discussed in polite company.

My father arrogantly claimed me. He told me what black people did as opposed to what white people did. He taught me the one-drop theory, the backbone of nastiness in white privilege—while the breast that nourished me was white. He brought unwanted attention from his loud laugh, hard clapping hands, flashy car and extended 35mm camera lens. He shamed me with his poorly concealed infidelities, and by dating my seventh grade teacher—the one black teacher, it seemed, in the entire district—just after his divorce.

For all my cursing, bald anger, and sadness at not feeling considered, I know I'm pretty lucky. I had a man somewhat around to praise me effusively and provide tools and exposure to the things that would feed my dreams. We'd eat warm bread at midnight. We'd talk about slavery and America when I couldn't sleep and he was up late studying.

"Come, ride with me?" he'd ask.

We'd drive in his latest sports car. Jazz mixed with speed as we wove through canyon roads. At stoplights, nearing home, he'd turn to me and pop his hand on my knee. His hands were hard; he did not know his strength. That same strength, in other times, left handprints on my biceps when he squeezed me in anger. Now it was affection that caused me to burn.

Then he'd rub. Three pops, three rubs, then repeat. The rubs pushed the scent of his Polo cologne into my jeans. It would linger in my hamper for days.

The morning he died unexpectedly, the doctor asked if I wanted to see my father. I touched his hands. I touched his face. His mouth had the ventilating tube still in it. I felt the softness of his cheek and stubble of his beard. It was only a body then. My father's body.

I had a closetful of his smell for years after he died. The suits he made me try on—*We could get the pants taken in . . . but your broad shoulders make the jacket work*—were now mine. They smelled like home, not entirely my home, but a home where I know I was wanted and loved.

I used to be angry at the black body epitomized by my father's life. I feared being like him. I fear I will die as he did at sixty. Black men's life expectancy is disgracefully short.

I started this Father's Day with my usual hike in Griffith Park. My Southern DNA makes me greet everyone I encounter. A little ahead of me I saw a man doing the same thing. He had my father's coloring and hair texture. I caught up to him. He was moaning a bit. "My leg is giving me trouble today," he said. "I usually run."

We talked as we walked. He was sixty-nine years old, the same age my father would be, were he alive. This man had been running almost every day since 1983, when he was just a little older than me now. When we got around the bend, he said, "I've got to start running. People see me up here all the time and I can't have 'em see me walking." So I ran with him. He started singing the *Rocky* theme.

Age has lessened my desire to explicitly define myself.

I recently wrote a song called "Stack of 45s" in which my father dances with my imagined wife. The song was inspired by our family's living room dance sessions. We'd march in step to the verses of Paul Simon's "50 Ways to Leave Your Lover," then we'd break into a freestyle for the chorus. The *Rocky* theme was in heavy rotation for a while. Kool and the Gang or the Rolling Stones guaranteed a spontaneous session. None of us really had the proper steps down, but Dad always had an affirmative smile. He'd nod his head on the quarter note. His pointed finger played an imaginary ride cymbal.

> *Tell me what you see*
> *Looking down*
> *As we carry on your medley*
> *What can you tell me?*
> *What can you tell me?*
> *I'm going on . . .*

JASON LUCKETT

HAIR APPARENT

by Lynell George

Two black women walk into a gym.

In the locker room, we un-shoulder gym bags, primp, then make our way out to the training floor. Side-by-side on treadmills: she walks, I run. We hit our separate strides. Twenty minutes in, the walker turns to me. No hello. No preliminary, "By the way . . ." Instead she dives right in. "So which one of your parents is white?" It is important to understand: My skin is the color of turned earth; cocoa at the soft-boil stage. My features—nose, mouth, the cast of my eyes—don't hint; rather, they declare who and what I am. It is a question that I'd never encountered, so consequently there wasn't a spiky retort at the ready.

"Why?" is the best I can muster.

"Your hair."

I don't believe I've seen her before. If I have, she hasn't felt the inclination to speak before now. In any case, she's not a friend or even an acquaintance—just bluntly curious and not concerned about repercussions.

"My hair." I say, not question.

My hair, not at its best at the moment, is pulled up away from my face and neck in gym-rat gal style, best known as the "pineapple." I'm soaked. It's soaked. Two tendrils as wet and black as India ink curl against my neck like commas. But there's not much else to go on. I'm hoping she'll say something else, something illuminating or perhaps outright taunting. I'm angry, but at base I don't know exactly why. Now she's staring at her own image in the mirror. Her hair is pulled back in a quick brown ponytail. Her skin is the color of warm sand. I wonder who asks her who in her family is white based on the mix of tones in her face, her arms, her legs—Latina, Persian, perhaps Italian. Here in Los Angeles, all is possible. People transition in and out all of the time. I consider this as I look, not at her, but at the reflection of her eyes in the mirror. I shrug.

"Neither," I finally answer, conserving my energy. Then I bend into my run once again.

My hair is not remarkable.

It is as black as a new moon. It is neither straight nor uniformly curly. It is thick. But it is fine. If it isn't combed it will curl into itself and "lock." There is a place at the back of my head that women on my mother's side refer to as—"The Ancestors"—that's the first to "go back," that frizzes, naps up, refuses to be silenced.

Currently it's at a length that just grazes my shoulders. It has never been too much longer, but it's been much shorter. My hair juxtaposed with my skin is just different enough to tally up silent questions, quiet judgment, or merely confusion. I don't have to open my mouth. My hair speaks for me, unbidden.

Back in the day, before the ubiquity of weaves and down-to-the-tailbone extensions, my hair said to some:

She stuck up.

She lost.

She self-hating.

She trying to be white.

And now: She white.

Though I don't like to admit it, I struggle with the perceptions or assumptions that people carry. I try to shake them off but, I realize, they linger.

Somehow, I think my skin color makes it more of an issue. The fact that I'm darker-skinned telegraphs a whole other tangled layer as knotty as our "kitchens"—the spot at the nape of the neck

LYNELL GEORGE

known from generation to generation of black women as the most difficult to "clean"—and stowed just as far in the back, and as low. There's a sense I get from some bold enough to go there that I'm dark, yet I was somehow "saved" by my hair. People don't say these things in polite conversation, but they project them.

"Where'd you get that hair?"

But this woman in the gym was expressing less of a question than a judgment. With that kind of comment she's monitoring a door. Telling me I don't quite fit. She's scanning my papers and sending me away on a hunch. It's a small shove of separation no matter how subtly it was dealt. Women, black women in particular, spend so much time, money, effort, and tears worrying over our hair, and the process is a rite of passage, a language all its own. When someone looks at me askance, his or her eyes traveling to, or distracted by, my hairline—is it mine or isn't it—I know they wonder or question if I know the tangled history, the rite of passage; could I ever understand?

Notions

One afternoon my brother I are wandering around a neighborhood five and dime. I'm lost in the notions section; my brother has wandered elsewhere. Since he's younger, he's my responsibility. So I put down the ticking and the pearlized buttons and start toward the toy aisle where, more than likely, he'll be. Suddenly, I feel a hand on one of my braids. A hard yank. Then a voice. A woman's. I turn. "You don't need all that hair. One little girl doesn't need all that hair. I should just cut this one off. Shouldn't I?"

You couldn't help but notice. Even the mightiest, most powerful, most audacious women, scared of nothing . . . no corner-office CEO, no bill collector, no "haint" but would cower come the first sign of a thundercloud. Scatter because of the fog, or camp out in a department store's foyer if the sky opened up for sudden rain.

They were expert at fashioning an umbrella or hood out of a newspaper, some plastic, or a waxy department store bag. Grown, head-of-household women jumping out the way of the sprinkler's mist, or worse, the fog or the South's humidity. For our hair we dodge the elements—and this is evidence of things not seen.

As the late sixties bloomed into the seventies, even at the age of six or seven, I understood the importance of hair, political hair, though I might not have had the language to explain it. It was connected to everything floating around in concert around me—the leather jackets and the picket signs, the stenciled Black Power fist, Billy Paul's "Am I Black Enough for Ya?" declaration.

I had two fat pigtails that looked like they belonged on Sunnybrook Farm. For a while that was OK. It was my playground bargaining chip. Instead of wanting to beat me up (for the infraction of being too quiet) at recess, the bigger girls would argue over who was going to comb my hair. It kept me from having my Turkish Taffy money filched, or sitting alone at recess. My mother would reprimand me when I get home for letting people "mess in my head." But it was worth it. I'd rather get an ass-whuppin' than an ass-kickin'.

But as the world around us continued to change, so did my focus. I wanted to comb my own hair into some sort of "style"— statement—that reflected the moment and all that was happening around me. The separation was palpable. There were the girls who were getting press-and-curls, sporting the burn welts on the tips of their ears or smudged on their necks, brown shiny scars shaped like teardrops at the edge of their foreheads. They were proudly displayed, just as hickeys would be only a few years later.

Then there were the girls who featured their version of the 'fro. Their naturals were beautifully sculpted spheres, like licorice cotton candy, and the step-by-step process taken to achieve this was the feature presentation of much recess-time chatter.

I fell somewhere in the middle: I wasn't allowed to get my hair

LYNELL GEORGE

pressed, but my "natural" didn't correspond with the bushes that bloomed around me. The high-profile standard bearers were Angela Davis, Jim Kelly, the Jacksons and the Sylvers—and we can't forget Teresa Graves' curly interpretation.

The break between the old and new was like a fissure growing after a temblor. Things were perpetually shifting. The message of the moment was muddled. Mixed. It was a transition generation, and we were throwing away old terms—colored, Negro, "good hair," "bad hair"—and feeling the weight and texture of new ones—Afro-American, and Afro, natural. Which one carried more sway? What would ultimately emerge?

I'd watch my brother carefully pick out his middle-of-the-road length 'fro, pat it down, and pick it out again. But at least he had one. He also had a selection of picks: a black one with a fist, one that folded up with one red arm and one green arm that supported the pick. His most impressive was a chrome cake-cutter.

Nothing was going to tease forth anything afro-approximate on my head. I became transfixed by a photo of me as a toddler that showed me in corduroy overalls with a blow-up Rudolph the Red-Nosed Reindeer; my hair somehow seemed to be able to rise heavenward then, but no more. I yearned to figure out how I might attain that head of hair—the right kind of curl—once more. The hairstyle wasn't quite Clarence Williams III, but it was saying something, talking loud. It broadcast the messages swarming around at the time. The mix we had just evolved out of. The bridge we walked over through Civil Rights.

When I thought about it later, my head of hair reflected all of that and then some. My hair was like my mother's, which was like her mother's mother's. Which was also like my grandfather's— we were Louisianans with tangled-up roots. You could map the African's journey through America on our heads. It was all there. Nappy. Straight. Kinky. Wavy. Soft. Course. Confused. Unpredictable. There they all were: black and white, etceteras. But it wasn't just garden-variety white folks, it was Turks, and "the Indians from India," and the "Frenchman" from Acadie, most likely, that my grandfather just referred to as "The Old Man." There were the Prevosts and the McGhee's and the Breaux's and the who knows what all else. In New Orleans my hair looks like my grandfather's springy waves—humidity and sweat win out. No one there ever asks a question. That's why they call it home.

Tender-headed

My mother, of course, has a set of hot-combs. They were stowed in my great-aunt's old maple nightstand. There were two of them, wrapped in a white and spearmint green hand towel marked with old copper colored burn stains. They had old-fashioned silver-tone coil handles, and the combs themselves were brass, brass that had gone dark from sitting in the flame of the stovetop burner. My mother kept them around for touch ups in the case of sudden rain, sudden fog, a party the night before that was sweat out your press hot—that meant dancing to Cha-Cha beats, the rumba. All cares tossed to the night.

At my mother's beauty shop in Southwest LA, none of the women would touch my head. The woman who did my mother's hair, Doris, was as pretty as a movie star. Diana Sands. Diahann Carroll. She always had her hair done up, pressed but with a nimbus of soft curls that dropped down like unscrolled streamers.

"Don't let anyone put a hot comb in your hair," she'd say to me in a "between you and me" voice, moving about the shop in her rolled-up pedal pushers. "Don't let 'em." But I wanted her élan, and those sleepy eyes, made even more mysterious when they were obscured by one of her hot curls. The shop was often loud with talk: work, politics, music or their men. The beauticians would listen and sigh, mumble answers and advice with hairpins jammed in the corner of their mouths as they turned one section and then the next into shiny dark ribbons of hair that smoked.

LYNELL GEORGE

I'd look around the shop at the women on their way home from work, on their way to their second job, arranged on the black cushioned chairs. I sunk into the life of that shop, the smell of cooking hair and grease, of lye and sweet perfume, and the community of women: their tired laughs, their distant stares, their practical shoes. I'd bring a pile of books, but most times I'd find myself just watching the women. Reading their faces. Looking at their mouths work in reaction to their stories.

"Look at all of that hair," Mae, who occupied the station next to Doris', would announce when she passed me by. Then, under her breath, she'd ask me, "Do you throw it around like the white girls? Do you let it blow in the wind?" I didn't know how to answer her. At the time, I didn't know any white girls, except for Debbie Alexander in my second grade class; she was Jewish and her hair was kinkier than mine.

Doris would save me and say, "Let me wash your hair." And she would. Massage my scalp. Let the water run clear. Put me under the bonnet drier and braid it fancy, then attach barrettes like blue agates, pulling the braids up tight against my scalp. She let me feel part of it—part of something.

Hair Food

I started early trying to camouflage it, play it down. I'd worn pigtails way too long—perhaps until I was eleven or twelve. Then I figured out how to braid it into a ponytail. I wore it that way through most of high school. My friend, Jon, a film producer, as blunt in junior high as he is now, told me frankly, "You'd be attractive if you did something to your hair." He articulated what I feared—that my hair was a separate entity of its own.

But I'm as stubborn as he is blunt.

I didn't put a hot comb in my hair until I was fourteen, but then promptly went back to the ponytail that would allow me to play basketball or swim or stand without fear in the rain. Around me things were going the other way. The popular girls had now abandoned their Afros and cornrows for pressed styles. Boys paid more attention. And once swimming became part of our high-school phys-ed rotation, most of the black girls brought notes—sat in the bleachers. Water, you see, might as well have been Kryptonite. The Gatsby, the style of the moment, with its sophisticated nimbus of soft curls on the top that tapered as it moved down the neck, advertised the first bloom of womanhood.

Out of high school into college. I'd periodically get my hair blown out and a light press, but it would revert. I did the same. But by then I was trying to assimilate the other way. I'd wet the front, which I kept short, then pick out the curls and put the rest in a side braid. Or I'd pin it all up in the back in a style my friend Karen referred to as my "I Love Lucy" front. It wasn't quite the look I was going for, but at least it suggested a curl. I'd read somewhere, much later, that somewhere between assimilation and nationalism lies appropriation. I think I'd rather call it self-invention. I look at photos of myself that track this journey. From straight to curled to slicked back and back again. By the time I was living in San Francisco, with rain and fog and just three hours of sun, I kept it pinned up mostly, with that curly front, but braided a couple of pieces in the back and let them hang free; my statement—fed up?

O, My Nappy Hair

After more than a decade in one place, I'm not surprised by the accumulation of books or magazines, LPs and CDs. All of that makes clear sense to me. But when I begin to sort through my bathroom, readying for a move, I'm surprised at what I find: Boxes, bottles, tubes, jars, sticks. Pomades, gels, sprays, sheens, serums, "reconstructors," pure protein, tee tree oil, shea butter, pressing oil, light oil, VO5. Curlers, blow dryer,

LYNELL GEORGE

bonnet dryer, an electric flat iron, a curler. Plastic rollers. Foam rollers. Bobbie pins. Hair pins. Scrunchies. Rubber bands, banana clips, bandanas, sleeping scarves.

The bathroom isn't a bathroom. It's my hair's laboratory. It's a journey of solutions.

I don't think I hide behind my hair. But it has taken me a bit to feel comfortable about not caring about what people think—or what it telegraphs about me—because of my hair.

By the late eighties and into the nineties, black people were ramping up for another revolution. For a moment there was a neo-consciousness movement blooming. It corresponded with conscious rap, Spike Lee and neo-black arts. Again we had something to say and used our bodies to do it. Kente cloth and cowrie shells. 'Locks bloomed, and so did braids and shaved crowns. I tried to get twists. Some people thought they were extensions. Some beauticians looked at me like I was crazy: "Why on earth would you want to do that to that hair?" They'd turn to their neighbor, "You hear? This girl wants twists?"

They were supposed to solve a problem, to let my hair rest. Stress had begun to wreak havoc on my system and my hair started to fall out like the needles on Charlie Brown's Christmas tree. But secretly, beyond it, I was happy to have the question about my hair, for once, silenced. I made some calls. Drove around. Found a shop north of Los Angeles in Altadena. Mia, who had long blond-brown ragamuffin braids, said she could "twist it all up" in two hours. And she did, all the while talking about her wedding plans and the prince charming she hoped would walk into "the club" one night while she was nursing her one white zinfandel—in that order. And one night he did, an actual prince, an African one, or so he told her. It took forever to find a replacement hairdresser. At one busy midtown shop, one man took a look at me and said it would cost me $300. At another shop, one woman informed me: "I ain't trying to stay here late." She handed me over to another operator who was young and new who took five hours to do the work it took Mia two to do. At one moment she sighed, sucking her teeth in exasperation, "Your hair won't do this!? Why don't you just blow it dry?" But that was exactly what I was trying to get away from—the work, the money, the extended explanations. So much for traveling back home.

Two weeks into a new job, one of the administrative assistants, who had exchanged perhaps three words with me, strides up assertively, puts his hand in my scalp and announces, "Oh. It isn't a weave. It is yours." Then turns and is gone.

Not so many months ago, I'm in Oakland on my way to a memorial for a friend and mentor. I've landed and now sit, sunk in sadness, waiting for an airport shuttle. The man who is routing the morning vans strikes up light conversation. He tells me his name is Adom, "Like Adam." He is, he tells me, from Senegal. We talk: about his country and this country, life and death, men and women. Distance and closeness. He asks me if I'm Indian. I feel a familiar clutch in my stomach and simply shake my head no. He pauses for a moment, considering my face. "Then," he asks, "where are you from?"

"Here. California," I say bluntly, not in the mood for twenty questions, or judgments.

"Oh," he says. Then pauses. "Your face. Your hair . . ."

I ready myself for come what may.

"You could be from my country," he announces, an open smile, an open hand. "You'd feel right at home."

EVEN A BRICK HOUSE CAN BLOW DOWN

by Annie Burrows

For a long time, Southern Louisiana seemed to be the perfect example of America's "melting pot" experiment—a veritable "gumbo" blending the best of different races, ethnicities, and cultures to create an atmosphere that was vibrant, decadent, and full of flavor. It was (and still is) a place like no other—with a whole lot of God, but a whole lot of drinking and gambling, too. Life was much more complex than mere coexistence; no matter how different things seemed, everyone and everything still had something in common.

Maybe, as they say, it all started with the roux, and with the sound of the washboard and the fiddle, with the red beans and rice and the Sazerac cocktails—with all the ways Louisianans sustained life and courted death. I'd even go as far as to say that it was in the vernacular: more than white or black, Cajun and Creole were markers of membership, words that seemed to suggest a belonging to the land, with its rice and cane fields, swamps, bayous, and rivers; words that, for better or worse, suggested a belonging to each other. But I know there's more to the story and, after the racial differences and inequities that were exposed by Hurricanes Katrina and Rita, everybody else knows it too.

I was born in New Orleans at a time when the separation of white and black was not only accepted, but also preferred by most. At the very least, this separation was unarticulated and, somehow, expected. I was raised in Lafayette, where I lived with my parents in a typical tract home in a middle-class neighborhood. Lafayette, like most cities back then, was split into two: the north side and the south side. The dividing line was the all-too-predictable railroad tracks. One side, the north side, was where the black people lived and the other side, the south side, was where we, the white people, lived. There were few exceptions back when I was growing up. For sure, no black people lived on the south side and only a few white people lived on the north side.

Even though blacks and whites didn't live side by side back then and they rarely socialized privately, there was always a lot of intermingling in cultural settings and at public events, of which there were plenty. Louisianans in general, and folks in Acadiana (Lafayette and the surrounding area) in particular, like to celebrate. There's a festival or parade for just about everything you can think of: the Crawfish Festival, the Rice Festival, the Boucherie where they kill and roast pigs, and of course, Mardi Gras. At all of these events, black people and white people were cooking and eating, laughing and drinking right there next to each other, as if it was something they did every single day.

But it didn't happen every day—and it still doesn't. Things began to change, though, in the late '70s when I was in high school. My friends and I discovered some black clubs where we were totally welcome to drink, dance, and just hang out. I know during my parents' era, it wasn't something that would have been done, but it was definitely something that we did, and felt extremely comfortable doing. In fact, it was probably my generation that started truly blurring the lines; making it seem as though race was irrelevant because we'd found a way to exist happily in a place of celebration and joy of the shared culture of our Louisiana.

The change began in 1968, when I was in second grade and the schools in Lafayette were integrated. The black kids from across the railroad tracks on the north side were bused to our school. It was a huge deal. A lot of the white parents were angry and horrified. They pulled their kids out and enrolled them in private and parochial schools. My parents didn't turn the situation into some huge drama. They told me that there were going to be some new kids coming to my school. "But you're not going anywhere," they told me. "Everything's going to be just fine." And it was.

Except that we were still very separate. The black kids and the white kids didn't play together. I think, at that stage, it had more to do with fear and a lack of familiarity than with race—though one could argue that all issues of racial separatism have to do with fear and a lack of familiarity. The black kids all knew each other and the white kids all knew each other, so at recess we just played with our same old friends. The busing made it difficult for us to really get to know each other. At the end of the school day, the black kids went right back across the railroad tracks to their homes and we went to our homes and played with the kids in our neighborhood. It would take years before we started to explore the possibilities of friendship.

Sometimes we get our strongest social and behavioral cues not from what the people around us actually say or do but, rather, from what they do not say or do: the ways in which they are silent and, as a result, complicit. My parents weren't racist. While growing up, I never heard them say anything negative about black people—and they especially never used the "n" word, like so many of the white adults and kids I knew. It's true that they didn't treat integration as though it was something terrible and wrong, but it's also true that they didn't treat separation as though it was something terrible and wrong—even when it took place in our own home. I was led to believe that it was just the way things were. And that really bugged the hell out of me because I couldn't understand why things had to be that way.

I couldn't understand why Catherine, our maid, would not sit and eat with us when we were having a meal. It didn't make any sense to me. She would always sit at the counter on a little chair in the tiny alcove by the kitchen where the telephone was, and I would be looking right at her—that's how close she was. Too far to reach out and touch, but close enough to feel the wall that had suddenly come up between us—me and this woman whom I loved like a second mother.

I'm not unaware of all the power dynamics that were at play. Catherine worked for our family. Nevertheless, I suspect that had she been a white woman doing the same job, keeping our home and caring for me, my parents' only child, the very intimacy that's developed in the course of those duties might have granted her some latitude. She probably would have been invited to sit with us at least occasionally. The funny thing is, I also know that if Catherine *had* been asked to sit with us, she would have declined the offer—she would have been uncomfortable sitting at the table with my parents. I also realize that the love I felt for my black care-taker might be easily dismissed by some as childhood dependence. It wasn't. It was, and continued to be, love. Even after I'd reached adulthood and left Louisiana, whenever I returned home, I'd visit Catherine at her home (on the "other side" of the tracks, of course). I considered her a part of my family, and when I got married I made sure she knew it. She sat with us at our wedding and was treated like any other guest.

If hate is what builds walls, then isn't love what burns them down? I know it might sound cliché, but isn't it true? When you love someone, they cease to exist in a category; they become human, in a completely unique and individual way. I think it was my love for Catherine, my ability to see her as something more than just another black person, that automatically made me unable to see every other black person as anything other than a unique individual. That and the fact that I was a product of my time. Those post-civil-rights-movement years were about coming together and recognizing each other's humanity.

The next step in Lafayette's integration happened during eighth grade. For the first time ever, almost all the eighth graders in the entire town had to attend the same school which was on the north side. So instead of having the black kids bused to us, we white kids were now going to be bused to them. It came as no surprise when a number of parents resisted and even petitioned the school board to abandon the idea. Many of them were parents who'd been tolerant and accepting about integration when it was taking place on *their* side of town, but the idea of having their children taken *over there* was just too much for them. But there was no stopping that train and, just as before, my parents told me, "Everything's going to be just fine." And it was even better than that.

By the time eighth grade rolled around, we'd been in school together for so long that we all knew each other. We started talking and hanging out together at school—becoming friends. We were on sports teams together, served in student council together, and attended school events and competitions where we would sit next to each other and work together. The students who were less likely to do that had naturally been weeded out, sent to school elsewhere.

Still, there were one or two incidents that were categorized as "racial." I don't remember a lot of the details, just the tension in the air and the parents' whispers about some impending drama that never quite materialized into anything substantial. I don't know if they were completely race-related or if there were groups of kids getting into fights, groups that just happened to be split along racial lines. Whatever the case, those were isolated occurrences, the kind that made people stop and take notice but were not a regular part of our day-to-day school experience.

Likewise interracial dating, although everyone had a subconscious sense of its inevitability. When you spend time with a community of people, study with them, play with them, dance with them, laugh with them, there's also a chance of falling in love with someone from within that community. I'm not so sure that we, the children who'd been on the front lines of integration in Lafayette, feared that; but our parents did—even the ones who'd been tolerant and accepting of society's changes. And I think we kids—black or white—in turn, feared their disapproval so much that those were waters none of us dared to test. It was an unspoken rule, this "taboo"; a separation that we didn't question or challenge—until college and, for some of us, throughout adulthood.

I'm now married with children, living in Los Angeles, a city that is more divided by class than race, with freeways and area codes instead of railroad tracks. It seems so unreal to think that I once lived in an era when black people and white people could not attend school together, could not buy or rent houses in the same neighborhoods, could not publicly express their love for each other.

Looking back, I realize that I rarely stopped to think about race relations in the era my parents lived through or wonder about what changes they might have seen, what personal experiences they might have had. Recently, before he passed away, my father gave me a glimpse into that aspect of his past.

About ten years ago, my father developed dementia. Toward the end of his life, as the disease progressed, there were significant changes in his personality. He became child-like and combative and a new vocabulary appeared: namely the frequent use of the "n" word. I'd never heard him utter it before and, to my horror, he started using it a lot in certain situations. By then he was in a nursing home and most of the people taking care of him were black. I didn't understand what was going on, but it was clear that his behavior—and his new vocabulary—were somehow linked to his past. Obviously, this language had once come naturally to him and it had been unleashed once again from the deep recesses of his memory. I began asking questions that my father, in his moments of lucidity, would answer. I pieced those answers together with the stories he'd told me before he developed dementia, when I used to ask him to tell me about his youth, and then I started to understand.

My father grew up in Slidell, which is near New Orleans on the

ANNIE BURROWS

other side of Lake Pontchartrain. For a part of his childhood, Daddy and his family lived in a little house with no electricity and no indoor plumbing. His father, my grandfather, ran a plant that made bricks—the sort that people use to build houses. It was a family business and my grandfather had once owned a share of it along with his brothers. My grandfather sold his stake in the business when he decided to go off to the territory of New Mexico to chase his fortune. That fortune never materialized so he returned to Slidell to work once again at the brick plant. This time he worked *for* his brothers, who had attained *their* fortunes.

The vast majority of the employees who worked under my grandfather were black. They called him "Cap'n Johnny"—it was a term of endearment, but a term of subservience as well. My father used to play with their children. As a boy, those little black kids were my father's frequent playmates. They weren't allowed to come into his yard; they'd have to stop at the fence to call for him. When my father wanted to play with them, they all had to go and play in the woods or somewhere else nearby, but not at the house.

On some level, it seems only natural that those would have been his playmates. They were all, in some way, outsiders. Those kids were on the outside because of their race, and my father was on the outside because his father had been "demoted" by the family. Still, it was the 1920s—the Civil War was not so far in the past— and I'm sure that my father was taught to see the differences between him and those black kids, not the similarities.

When they play together, children are so full of trust and joy. They trust their playmates with their safety and look forward to experiencing the joy of discovery with them. How confusing it must have been for my father to then be told that his peers were not in fact his peers—that they were inferior to him. I wonder if it was this part of his background that made my father so resolute in his decision to not pull me out of my school when it was being inte- grated and to not teach me how to undermine what I felt in my heart for my friends and for my caretaker, Catherine, by using that dirty "n" word.

I think when it comes to racism and prejudice, the sign of real change isn't outside of you, it's inside. It's not so much what you think as it is what you *don't* think about anymore. I am firmly planted in the present, in the world my children live in, and many of the injustices I witnessed in the past are a distant memory. But I was reminded when my dad became lost in the fog of aging. My father had traveled so far away from what he'd learned as a child that, when he returned there because of his dementia, he became almost unrecognizable to me.

I was also reminded last year, when my eight-year old son and I were at Toys R Us looking at games. There was a little boy in the same aisle with a woman whom I assumed was his grandmother. The boy was taken with one game in particular. It had a picture of some black kids on the packaging. His grandmother took the game away from him and said, "We're not going to buy that game with the n____s on it." Her tone was so abrasive, almost violent in its anger and palpable hatred. For a moment, I just stood there in shock, my heart pounding. My first thought was to take my son and get out of that aisle as fast as possible, but then I stopped. My son had to know that I would speak up for what I believe in—that I would let her know what I thought of her remark.

"Great! I'm so glad that you're teaching your grandson to be a racist just like you," I barked sarcastically at the woman. I didn't wait for a reaction or a response. But as we walked off, I saw her mouth drop open out of the corner of my eye and I heard her grandson ask her what my words meant.

Back in the car, my son had his own questions about words and their meanings. This was his first encounter with blatant racism, but he knew enough to not repeat that word. Before answering his questions, I thought of my father and how he'd returned to a place and a time in his childhood when it was okay to use that word and

I wished for a time and a place when it would no longer be in existence. But, I also thought how cool it was that my son had made it through until that point in his life without even knowing that such a word existed. It seemed outrageous to me that we could have had such an encounter in Los Angeles in 2008, that we could have heard that word being spoken in public, in a children's toy store of all places. But that lady had better accept that she is a dinosaur, now. I thought of her when, later that year, Zane and I traveled to Nevada to campaign for Barack Obama, who would become the first black president of the United States of America!

When I saw first-hand what Hurricanes Katrina and Rita had done to my home state, I mourned and cried. Like anyone with a television, I saw the outrageous injustices visited upon New Orleans and other parts of South Louisiana and I was stunned. And, given the pathetically slow response of our government, I wondered if things would ever go back to how they were. But now I worry that they will. Neighborhoods are being rebuilt painstakingly, brick by brick. The culture will be what it always was—defined by colorful beads and second line dancing at Mardi Gras, etouffée, café-au-lait, beignets, and boudin. What I hope won't find its way back are the divisions that existed and were thrown into stark relief for all to see when the hurricanes hit. All the lines—real or imagined—that separated people, who in every other way but skin color were, basically, the same. Now that would be something to celebrate!

NOT AS FAST AS JOE

by Joel Lipman

I've always been accused of being lucky and in one way I know that's true: while I was growing up in Chicago, my Uncle Phil owned the player's parking lot at Wrigley Field. When I was a kid comin' up in the early sixties, the Bears as well as the Cubs played at Wrigley. It was Chicago's sports Mecca—the epicenter of a sports town in a sports crazy nation.

My Uncle Phil also owned a junkyard, Lakewood Scrap & Iron, under the El tracks nearby off Belmont Avenue. Lakewood had the paper and scrap collection after every home game—every game. That's eighty-one Cub games and six Bear games!

After every game, once the stands had emptied and the cheering stopped, and the echoes came, Lakewood's big green dump trucks would pull into the stadium under the left field bleachers and his guys would sweep the aisles, making mountains out of all those hot dogs wrappers, Cracker Jack boxes and Pabst Blue Ribbon beer cups. Then they'd load it all in the trucks and drive it over to the yard to be compressed into huge blocks and sold as scrap.

You see, this is where my luck ran good. These two pieces of my Uncle Phil's Russian immigrant empire, the player's parking lot and the junkyard, when cobbled together, were the key to my child-hood wonderland and the formative building blocks of who, at my deepest core, I am. A Chicagoan. A Bear Fan. A Cub Fan.

Every couple of weeks Uncle Phil would give me what every kid dreams of (shit, I'm nearly ancient now and I still dream of it). He'd hand me a little note pad sized stack of paper. A simple, innocuous looking little green pad, glued at the top with green glue. On it were the words that still make my mouth water and my legs itch with anticipation, excitement, and the lucky Jew-bastard knowledge that *nobody* else had these:

Field Pass

Admit One

Gate K only

That's right, a get-in-free pass to Wrigley Field, any game, any day, any time! Wait, it gets better: "Field Pass" means *on the field*. No assigned seat, free roam of the entire ballpark. For Cub games that was tricky 'cause you couldn't be "on the field"—I'd have to find an empty seat (of which there were plenty in the 1960s and 70s)—but for Bear games? I'm on the sideline, Jack! I'm on the grass! Nine, ten years old and I'm free-wheelin', peeking around the players and coaches, the photographers, the umpires and sideline markers.

One of my earliest memories is trying not to get bowled over and killed by Roosevelt Taylor. Rosie Taylor, number 26, Bears corner-back. All of a sudden, like a vicious wind, the world was rushing right at me: run left and Rosie has the corner. I don't remember what team the Bears were playing, or who Rosie had slammed to the turf right in front of me. What I do remember was the shudder of the grass beneath my feet as the force of players steamed in my direction. People scattered like bowling pins in front of me and then like a giant dropped from the sky, Roosevelt Taylor's mile-wide shoulder pads crashed to the chalk line with a spray of dust and grass and dirt right at my feet—his helmet bounced off the turf like thunder and he rolled twice before popping to his cleated feet, inches from my face. I tilted my head up to see him looking down at me. Sweat beads like glass on his black skin. Steam snorting from his nostrils. His coal-black eyes were wild and piercing. He put his hands on my shoulders to stop himself, and I could feel his heart pounding through his hands, his power, this human athletic machine, and he stared right into me—he smiled, the whitest white teeth. The coolest cool. The pinpoint grace. And then like black water at the ebb tide, fluid smooth, he pulled away and ran back to the huddle.

Holy fucking Christ! Right now my skin is tingling. Right this very moment as I type. The hair on my neck shoots sparks, warm with electricity. The red sea opened and Black Moses touched me deep inside—a chiseled myth came to life right in front of me and I saw the flame of him flickering in his eyes. The white 26 blocked on his blue-black jerseyed chest, shading me from the sun and the wicked winter chill. I've still never felt so tiny and so huge at the same instant.

In 1965 Gale Sayers arrived from Kansas. He parked his "rookie car" in Uncle Phil's lot alongside the other player's cars. Man, I couldn't tell you what anybody else drove (except for the Cubbie's Billy Williams' black over blue Buick Wildcat, which was fine); those other rides were beaters, flivers and bolt-buckets compared to Gale's gleaming red Corvette Sting Ray fastback with the license plate "GS 40." That was the chariot, baby—that was the sweetest ride on the lot. That Corvette stood out like Diana Ross at a fat girl parade. I used to wave Gale into his parking space, walk him to the locker room and then ogle his car until game time (hoping one of my friends and his dad would come by, tickets in hand, so I could show off Gale's 'vette).

. . . I Saw The Kansas Comet Streak Across The Earth . . .
I pulled on my sister's
green leotard tights
and quickly stepped into corduroy pants
to hide them
"It's gonna be cold as hell out there"
my father had said
and I wasn't taking any chances

The way the lake-wind ripped through
Wrigley Field was like
razors slashing at your skin

and today with the rain
and yesterday's melting snow
the field would be gooey mush

Now pressed into the stands
hands in gloves
thrust in pockets
stomping feet
Sayers gets the ball
his number, 40
already glopped in mud
he glides off tackle
skids, cuts
and breaks into the open

"Go baby, go baby, go baby, go!!!"
a man behind me screams
coffee sloshing from his thermos cup
and Gale is gone
sleek black ash
hydro-planing into the end zone

Rookie, quick kid, slasher
The Kansas Comet
and next time he touches
the ball
he's off again
leaving broken burly boys burned
face down at the 20
he's making the cold go away
now my father joins the cheer
"Go baby, go baby, go baby, go!!!"
he's in

JOEL LIPMAN

all the way feet like gryption paws
to the 'Niners Keystone Kops

This time they dump him a pass
over the middle
stops on a dime
spins, shakes Matt Hazeltine
like a rag doll
power shifts to gear
mud spinning from his wheels
the mutherfucker's gone again
raking yardage like a surveyor
"Go baby, go baby, go baby, go!!!"
our whole section picks it up
pushes him, goes with him

Gale Sayers is God today
the mud and clots of sod
dance behind him
he's black butter
gliding across a skillet

Rain begins to fall
but nobody makes a move to go
we're in the presence of God
our brother in his athletic robes
our symbol on his headgear
caked and dripping

He's sweating for us
he's killing for us
he's slaying Forty Niners
he's feeding us history

with a broken wooden spoon
he's making us cry with joy
he's stomping his name
in the oozing field of play
today there is no Jim Brown
there is no Hugh McHellany
no Galloping Ghost
no Crazy Legs Hirsch

Now late in the game
he's scored five touchdowns already
Halas sits him down
but we won't have it
we spit at the rain
bare our skin to the cold
"Gale . . . Gale . . . Gale!!!!"
this is not a request
it's a soul scream
from every voice in Wrigley Field
every usher, every hot dog vendor
even the announcers
are leaning out of the booth

And Papa Bear Halas
behind his fogged glasses
under his blocked tweed hat
surveys the stands
hears the steam of one big voice
and motions to the bench

And Gale, soaked to the bone
pushes himself from the pine
and straps on his helmet once more

JOEL LIPMAN

long way from Kansas, baby
long way to this circle of earth
this is the nipple
right here, right now.

He stands at the goal line
waiting to receive the kick
that booms into the grey sky
and like a magnet, finds him at the five
back-step, juke, stutter-step
again Hazeltine bites only mud
Jimmy Johnson beaches at the 30
slow motion, electra-glide, slip 'n' slide
he squirts out from the tangled flesh
"Yes!!! Yes!!!"
now the peasants, we humbled
all of one voice
"Go baby, go baby, go baby, go!!!"
and he does
black lightning, dark thunder
creasing the goal line
for the sixth time today
forever.

Sports is color blind—OK, forget about the color line—put an asterisk on every record before 1947 in baseball. Try and figure out how to straighten out the record books in football, basketball . . . I'm not talking about society now, I'm talking about heroes, I'm talking about kids (and adults) who pray to the feats of athletes, wear their jerseys, sport their numbers—love them, defend them, cry and covet them. Society and race are a fucked-up set of twins, scared of their own shadows. But the athletic public, the crowds, the fans, the rabid—we don't care if your color is black, blue or white—just do that thing you do—and do it for *us*. Fuck Jim Crow, kick his skinny white ass back in the closet with his kid sister—he hates to hate and hates *everything*, including himself. But put some spook in an Alabama jersey and bust off 115 yards on Oklahoma next Sunday and you'll see the unholy Crows dancing in their corn-fields. Hey, Willie Mays would kick the livin' shit out of Babe Ruth all day, every day—to this day, in his day (if they'd let him play).

Why do we (they) love Joe Louis and it took them years to love Ali? Easy, the Nazis are *always* the bad guys. Ali was pointing a finger at *us*! We're the bad guys? Yes, that's the point—especially if you happen to be black. Whose side are you on? Are you with us or a'gin us? Is Ali more a hero if he goes to Viet Nam and gets his ass shot off in a war he was right to disapprove of? Some folks answer a resounding "yes" to that (they happen to be the ones in the closet with their kid sisters). The rest of us marvel in Ali's skill in the ring and ability to look the "white man" in the eye and say "they ain't done nothin' to me." Who hits harder, Joe Frazier or Johnny Law? I gotta say Johnny Law, 'cause he's gonna hit you in every orifice all at the same time, and brother if you can stand up after that, you *are* the Greatest!

Sport has given the underdog a platform to shove it right back up "their" ass—whoever "they" are at any given moment. Step across the color line and look at it from that side. Here is a Man—and he's as good (and hopefully better) than your Man—now bring it. He is going to stand up for Us. He's gonna fight, play, wrestle, run, pass, or throw for Us. For one simple reason: he's a Man and so are you—and that's what's *fair*. Like it or not, bust your lip to prove it, if that's what you need. Knock your ass down if that's what you need. Beat you to the finish line if that's what you need. All day, day after day, if that's what you need. Because that's exactly what you need—you need to share the field, share the locker room, share the winning and the losing. Share the tears and the tears of joy and the tears of Brotherhood.

. . . And Crash and Burn At The 35 . . .
Cool, crisp winter day
wind off the lake
football weather
they call it in Chicago
and the 'Niners came to play

In football you never forget
Never.
The Redskins still want to scalp
the Bears
for kicking their asses
73 to nothing
back in the forties
so yeah
the 'Niners came to play

Late sixties the Bears were a two man team
Butkus was the defense
he'd bring the earth up to meet you
and smash it in your face
spit on your pain and leave you there
and Sayers was the offense
you didn't beat the Bears
you didn't let Sayers beat you
The rest of 'em were street gangers
meat packers
west side Polacks
tee shirt Wops
south side Shines
O'Bradivitch, Buffone, Bukich
MacRea, Petibone, Ditka
the Taylors, Roosevelt and Joe

Ronnie Bull, Brian Piccalo
they didn't win many games
but they bruised your bruises
cracked your ribs
chipped your teeth
made your wife cry out in pain.
Hell was a hundred yards between
Addison Street and Waveland Avenue
but the 'Niners came to play
they had payback
memories of getting singed
by The Kansas Comet

That day in '65 wasn't a fluke
The Comet had torched some grass
since then
he'd left cleat marks, deep
in every face in the league

Now on Sunday he is Wyatt Earp
to every chop block Jesse James
comin' up
his 40 like a target
pinned front and back
waiting to get tagged
there's no secret here, baby
you know who's gettin' the ball
who's gonna shiver slip you
quick spin trick you
and pass between your bones
you know who's gettin' the ball

JOEL LIPMAN

All day like Joe Louis
in your face
pounding you hard
slipping your jab
making you miss
and miss bad
And these man-child chunks
of tissue and flesh
skimmed from the cream
of sand lot
Tar Heels, Sooners, Huskies
Fighting Irish
banded together by
jersey and city
chewed their way to the top
through gristle and bone
swallowing their own teeth
pieces of their bodies
left on playing fields
along the way

Off the field they respect you
marvel at the way you glide
but today their paychecks
are on the line
their oozing egos bubbling
under pads and skin
and it's bigger than the game
years from now
in bars
they want to say they stopped you
and wrestled you down
for a loss of two

these inches are a lifetime
after this
life is just of series of days
until they die

Now the play is called
all eyes fixed
on you, three point stance
jets humming, tensed
the runway laid before you
stripes of chalk

Bukick barks it out
"Red. Red. 45. 19. Hut. Hut. Hut!!"
Pyle slaps him the ball
three step drop
pump fake
play action
guards pull
sweep left
hand off Sayers
red dog
safety blitz
The Comet overruns his block
plants a cleat to cut
but Kermit Alexander
has him in his cross-hairs
plain as day
a Christmas gift
just what mommy promised
he lowers his helmet
mid-air slingshot, a super nova
and they tumble in a tangled mess

JOEL LIPMAN

Alexander springs to his feet
he's Brutus
he's Hercules
but something's wrong at the 35
The Comet lays like a broken toy
Silence, thick as curdled cream
Silence that twists our faces
in the stands
Silence so loud
it becomes a new sound

Men in suits
from the sidelines run
to gather around
the smoldering spark

Then Butkus and Buffone
peel him from the 35
drape his lifeless arms
over their shoulders
and bare him
the crucified Christ
to the sideline
triage
his feet, once flames
wicked with wings
drag, toes down in the grass

My father leans down
and whispers in my ear
words that grab my heart
like an icy hand
"You saw his best game

and now you might have seen his last."

Long way from Kansas, baby
long way to this circle of earth.

I still wear number 40 on my softball jersey; it's the only number I've ever worn when asked to place my uniform order for the new season. I wear it to honor Gale Sayers, to remember him—and if I'm lucky, to embrace and embody a part of him. I hope it calls to The Gods of Sport and announces me as a devotee. I hope it pushes the wind in my direction, anoints my bat, kisses my glove and delivers me one tiny iota of speed, grace, fearlessness and magic.

Isn't competition how we gauge ourselves—or how we are gauged in life? Good is always good, but good is always compared to better and the best. Test scores, profit, architecture—like it or not, everything is measured against something else. Racism is such a big, unwieldy umbrella of a word. So complex and hard to unravel. For me, I see it as simple fear—fear of many things—but fear of being bested by someone that doesn't look like you. Would Babe Ruth have been "Babe Ruth" if Josh Gibson were allowed to play at the same time? Would Jack Dempsey have been "Jack Dempsey" if he would have faced black fighters? You can't deny that these are great athletes, many of whom just played or fought in a time when the color line was thick and bloody red. But you can't be the best until you've beaten the best, or at least faced them and given it your best shot.

Who am I? I don't know, you tell me. But, once, many years ago, I was asked by a publication to "name my greatest achievement." I thought about it long and hard and I remembered the moment when I felt my greatest glory. In junior high school at a track meet I was asked to take the place of one of my teammates who was hurt and race in the 440. I'd never run the 440—I was just the skinny white boy who was a half-assed high jumper. I'd be racing against my

JOEL LIPMAN

friend since grade school, the star of our team: Joe Stewart. Tall, black, muscular—a serious athlete. Joe was All-State champion in the 100, 220, 440. He had real track spikes that the school had bought for him. Joe would later get a full ride football scholarship to Missouri, get drafted by the Oakland Raiders and play pro football.

As we lined up for the race, Joe looked at me and smiled and nodded his head. Bang! The gun went off—and so did Joe. Everybody knew it was his race to win, so I just chased his ass, I ran faster than I've ever run. I'm chasing Joe Fucking Stewart! At the first turn a guy elbows me in the ribs and I look over like "What the hell?" He sneers at me. "So this is how it works," I think to myself, and I elbow him in the stomach. I kick whatever gear I have to try and catch up to Joe, who is now fifteen yards ahead of me. But there's nobody between us—just track and the dust flying off his spikes. I finished second in that race, and with my points we won the meet.

That same publication asked me to "choose five words that best describe you." And you know I didn't have to think long to say, "Not as fast as Joe."

HANDS

by Nzingha Clarke

My brother, mother, and I were not allowed to see my father as he was dying. In the six months after his kidneys failed we were left to wonder how long he'd hold on and how long the siege—a second wife who prevented access to him as she looted his priceless library and his bank accounts—that kept him from us would last. It lasted until he died, and when I went to view his body, I barely recognized the man in the casket. Illness had made him smaller than my father. He was no one I knew without the tilt of his head or the way his brow almost furrowed when he was making a point of paying attention. I looked to my mother, comfortingly familiar as I failed to comprehend the man before me: my father, the other half of the very first things I ever learned about this world. And then I looked down and began to cry. On this man, who I did not recognize, were my father's hands. Chocolate brown shot through with just enough red to make the color rich. The wrinkles couldn't disguise the elegance of his long fingers. His nails, which were always jaggedly cut with a fraction of the attention he would have needed to do the job right, were neatly trimmed for their final viewing. I'd know those hands anywhere, they belonged to my Dad.

The familiar is an anchor when you've dropped through the chute and landed in the surreal. At a wake, surrounded by a few hundred people I hoped I'd never see again, I stared at my father's hands until the world made sense. My last memory of my father was surely one of my first: knuckles and nails, deep lines on dark skin. A palm extending from the wrist. His hands.

Hands are the books of our lives. A close look at a pair of hands could tell you everything you want to know about a person. Our hands are made by the way we use them. For my family, the story and history of our time in America can be collapsed into a conversation about our hands.

My father was born on a sharecropping farm, and he would be the first to say that farm labor was what drove him from the South. He wasn't built for it. That, and he wanted to be a writer. The family my father left on the farm has working hands. Their hands have done hard labor, whether the labor was farming, cleaning houses—or in this generation, working at McDonald's and any number of other dead-end jobs. Everything they have has been hard-won with wages by the hour in jobs that don't use their brains as much as they wear down their bodies, making them old before their time.

So this is the story: I am here because once upon a time, a few hundred years ago, the ancestors who would become my family, who eventually would become me, were brought here, to America, for our labor. For our strong backs, but mostly for our hands. We've had farming hands, craftsman's hands, factory hands and caretaking hands that have raised part of every generation that has grown on American soil.

By leaving the fields of rural Georgia for New York City, my father changed the fate of his hands. He came to New York to learn to write, but before he was known as a writer, he spent decades doing whatever work he could find—working as a short order cook, cleaning floors, anything that a willing set of hands could do. He worked hard and long for too little money, right until the moment someone first paid him for the thoughts in his head. By moving north, my father jumped the queue and folded our family's ascent from poverty to the middle class into one lifetime. Rags to riches. The leap from the hands' labor to the mind's is the Horatio Alger myth that fuels every poor person and every immigrant. It's the story that keeps this country moving forward.

NZINGHA CLARKE

My father was born in 1915 to a family that intimately recalled slavery. Between 1900 and 1960, almost 5 million African Americans migrated from the southern states to the north. In 1929, the year my father left Columbus, Georgia, the Ku Klux Klan was on the rise and the Great Depression had just begun. In the South there were few models of African-American thinkers (rather than laborers), and if his life had to be lived at the limits of his hands, it wasn't difficult for my father to imagine that big city life and a factory job would be an improvement over farming. From slavery to sharecropping to New York City, the history of the Northern Migration is in my father's hands.

My mother's parents came to America able to build a world. Moving from the Bahamas to Miami, Florida, my grandparents and their generation brought, not just the talents and the capacities to make a life for themselves, but an aesthetic for living. They were 'handy'—in possession of a palette of skills that quickly located them at the heart of their new community. My grandfather was an artisan cobbler and a folk painter. He opened his workshop at a time when black people were not allowed into white stores. Miami's black professionals beat a path to his door to buy the one-of-a-kind shoes and bags and belts he made. His sister made a tidy second income with her made-to-order cakes for all occasions. My grandmother worked as a teacher, but there was nothing she couldn't make. She taught me to crochet, to bead, and to weave, and she had plenty more skills on top of those. My mother's family came to America with very little, but you would never have known it. Their genius for taking the ordinary into their hands and transforming it into something special was all they needed to push themselves upward. The history of the rise of the immigrant middle class is in my family's hands.

The early 1900s to the 1940s saw the influx of black immigrants from all over the Diaspora. By 1930, more than 73 percent of foreign-born blacks in America had emigrated from the British West

Indies. They had studied in English colonial schools and arrived empowered from living in countries where they were the majority. They were better educated than their African-American counterparts, but nothing prepared them for the racism they encountered when they got here.

My mother and her sisters are first generation Americans and their story dovetails with the end of segregation, the Black Power movement, and the Women's Liberation movement. The story of their opportunities is in their hands.

My mother is of a generation of black women who fastidiously apply lotion. Their hands are soft by design, against all odds. In the world, they work with their minds. They are teachers and civil servants; lawyers and doctors if they were lucky enough. Impeccably groomed, lotion is their hands' disguise. They want you to know that their hands have been pushed to the margin—they are appreciated, but not necessary. Through hard work they have educated themselves, earned the promotions and become the professionals that few black women before them ever had the chance to become. They have gotten where they are through furious dedication and effort behind the scenes, and admirable equipoise in plain sight. The fiction of their ease is in their hands. Their soft hands and carefully done nails wear the mask. Lotion, baby oil, even sleeping with cotton or satin gloves hides all the hard work those hands really do. These are women who will not abide a dirty house and they would hardly trust anyone to be as thorough as they can be. They scrub and they scour. Hands graze surfaces, searching out dirt wherever it hides. These hands cook and they iron. The exactitude that has pushed these women forward and served them well is in the way their hands 'know' and navigate their worlds.

In the sixties we recovered our agency, took back our hands and declared that we would no longer do anyone's bidding but our own. The Black Panthers took up arms, and the Fruit of Islam studied martial arts and made it clear they didn't need weapons—their hands were all they needed to protect themselves and their community. In the sixties our hands cut hair into afros, sewed dashikis and gave the Black Power salute. The liberation of our hearts and minds was the liberation of our hands.

My culture, African-American culture, is essentially synthetic. No one can make something out of nothing better or faster than we can. It's a state of mind, it's a worldview, but it's also borne of knowing exactly what we've got in our hands. Our hands are, themselves, pure possibility. While my mother is very conscious of her hands, I don't care a whit about mine. This is the luxury my parents bought and gave to me through their labors—my brain is my instrument to such a degree that my hands are superfluous unless I *choose* to give them value. I have computer hands. Hands that do what they want, rather than what they have to, need to, do. My self-sufficiency depends on my ability to manipulate the ultimate intangible: information. But information is a fiction and before I'm lost to the imaginary worlds and the false truths of data, my hands conspire to bring me back to the here and now.

I rescue meaning for my able appendages by climbing rocks. In a way, rock climbing marks the achievement of everything my parents wanted for their kids. Smarts enough, access enough, accomplishment enough that the hardest labor I put my hands to is no more than larking around. That I put my life in my own hands is perhaps the ultimate expression of the choices I've been given. Climbing, my hands work hard, and often they're scratched and nicked. They are strong and the way they look belies their formidable dexterity.

In a roundabout way, my hands tell the story of my privilege. All that my parents gave me for the sake of sparing me a life of manual labor is akin to the way new immigrants fail to teach their children what should be their first language. They want their kids to be American, and speaking only English feels to them like a gift they've given their kids. As they grow, most of these children hunger to speak the language that would tie them to their grandparents. I'm like that with my hands. I cook, and I'm a better carpenter and electrician than almost every man I know. I want to locate my hands in the world. This is irony: my hands look like they work for a living.

My generation is the first to have grown up with the assumption of equal opportunity. We were not the first to integrate historically white environments. In the Northeast where I was raised, integration was an occasional reality decades before I was born, but my cohort was the first to experience the effects of the raft of civil rights legislation aimed at making sure our educations and life paths would, for the very first time, mirror those of our white classmates and colleagues. And in turn, the white kids I grew up with were the first to experience people of color in positions of authority and the certain knowledge that we were their equals. We are the "diversity" generation.

I want this to be a success story, and maybe if I stop right here it would be—with me aloft on the laurels of my family's hard work, America's cultural evolution and the feeling that my hands speak of a life in which everything is possible. But unfortunately, the story takes a turn when I, a habitual expatriate, move back to America.

When I returned to live in Los Angeles, I was appalled to observe that in stores, I walk with my hands behind my back as I shop. It is no longer conscious, and it's a habit I mean to break, but it's a behavior as old as my adolescence, when my friends and I ("good girls" all) couldn't flash our dark skins in boutiques or department stores without being followed. My mistaken, youthful choice was to neutralize my suspect hands, as if that would make any difference.

Recently, an African American friend called, cursing and crying, with a story of being followed as she shopped in a major department store by a clerk who seemed to assume she might steal something and had to be watched. My friend was angry and humiliated to have been treated so poorly. I've had similar experiences, and as if it would comfort her, I confessed my awful habit of hiding my hands.

Ultimately, my friend and I were telling the same story. It's the story of strangers inhabiting a world and a consciousness that is much smaller than the lives my friend and I lead. It's the story of race limiting the ways in which we are allowed to experience our bodies, our intentions, our labor; the way white and ignorant still holds more power in this world than all expressions of blackness, but nothing in our assumptions or in the power we wield in our daily lives ever prepares us for the shock of running headlong into these experiences. We are innocent, but our hands are never above suspicion. And maybe that—wrestling the meaning of our hands from the opinions or limitations of our countrymen—maybe that's the feel-good story for the next generation.

MY ACE IN THE HOLE
by Susan E. Matus

I can't claim to be the first white woman to have ever walked the streets of Harlem, NY. But in the summer of 1997 I could claim to be the first white woman to have moved into a building located at 136 West 111th at St. Nicholas. And for Ace, a black man who was raised on 110th at St. Nicholas, and now claimed the corner bodega at 111th as his personal territory to drink cheap forty-ounce bottles of beer and smoke crack cocaine, that was enough to make me infamous.

My boyfriend, now husband, and I have just fallen in love, and like two whirlwind romantics, are ready to start our life together after dating for only six months. He has a place on the Upper East side, where much of the population consists of old uptight white people, whose faces are oftentimes tighter than their attitudes and whose fear often finds them clinging to their belongings whenever he walks by. Even a trip to the local deli to buy cigarettes or milk is cause for alarm, as the store owner, with a watchful eye, follows him from aisle to aisle to make sure he isn't trying to steal anything. We often joke around, feeding into the paranoid delusions of the local residents by pretending that we are in a fight. He plays the "abusive" boyfriend to my "poor, low self-esteemed" white girl and we watch their righteous reactions pickle up their faces. Then we laugh our way home imitating the stupidity of racism. It is something I had never really experienced before meeting him, and even now my personal experience is secondhand. So it isn't a surprise when he suggests Harlem as a possible place to relocate. Being from a mix of Mexican American and African American heritage, he feels like he can finally plant his roots in the diversity of the community. And I, having lived in cities all my life, feel comfortable in any community. Because unlike him, I look white (even though I, too, am of mixed race), and that means I am welcome anywhere. Well, almost anywhere.

We stumble upon our flat, after being stood up by another landlord in the same neighborhood who had concerns about "someone like *me*" living in his building. Annoyed but not discouraged, we walk into a real estate office that we had spotted earlier across the street. The sign outside reads Alvarado Realty. Inside is a large vacant-looking office space with a couple of desks and a single computer. It is here that we first met Nelson, an ambitious Dominican P-Diddy lookalike, whose father owns three of the largest apartment buildings in the neighborhood. He is sly but friendly, and as luck would have it, he has a vacancy he is willing to show us in one of their buildings. We follow Mr. P-Diddy out the door of his office and around the corner to 111th St. He has a leisurely walk, as though the day is going to come and go no matter what he does or doesn't do. We stop in the middle of the block in front of a large, run-down, brownish-beige building with light teal green fire escapes. I figure they must have had a special sale on that paint, there is no other reason. He pushes open the entrance, a large broken wooden door with bullet-proof glass, and leads us into a corridor with a lingering aroma of cat piss and frying grease. We then follow him up three flights of stairs to an old steel door with 3RW carelessly spelled out in adhesive gold stickers. I figure out that this stood for third floor, rear apartment, west side. Pulling out a large metal ring with an infinite number of mismatched keys, P-Diddy fumbles with the locks as we stand silently, passing secretive glances and wondering what we are getting ourselves into. After several failed attempts he finally manages to unlock the three deadbolts. Heaving open the vault-like door, he leads us into the darkness. He reaches for the light switch and turns on the dangling fluorescent tubes that hang precariously over our heads, revealing a long hallway to an enormous three bedroom flat. Our eyes are wide with disbelief, and when he tells us how little the rent is, it takes everything we have to contain our enthusiasm. Not realizing rent control is on our side, we try to play it cool, pretending not to show our upper hand, until after we sign the lease.

The hum from the switched-on lights gives warning to the thousands of tiny cockroaches who scatter across the floor as we enter each room. The twelve-foot-high ceilings give way to overburdened walls covered in layers of semi-gloss paint that is beginning to peel, and the floors are covered in dingy grey linoleum that reveals the disheveled layout of previous tenants' furniture through the layers of unswept dirt. Basically, it is a dump. But it is a large dump, and in Manhattan during the Clinton era and the stock market boom, being able to afford a closet is a challenge.

A week later we are schlepping our belongings up from the Upper East side to our new three bedroom "estate" in Harlem USA. Tired and hungry, we decide to walk our dog and grab something to eat. The closest venue for food is a place called Mama's Fried Chicken, a mock KFC, down the block near the 1/9 subway station. We walk in and immediately are taken aback by the counter, which is encased in a thick layer of Plexiglas, giving the appearance of giant fish tank. We would later come to realize this was customary decor for all the local merchants, who all had a story to tell about being robbed at gunpoint. We order a bucket of chicken, then stand there trying to decipher the broken English of the Indian man on the other side of the glass, who is attempting to explain how to place our money in a box that spins around like a lazy Susan. In the corner a young Puerto Rican couple, who had been yelling at each other over "who didn't call who," stop to evaluate the situation and to size us up. "There's no dogs in here," the young Puerto Rican man says flatly. I smile, trying to cut through the tension and avoid a stare-down, while my boyfriend, *feeling his roots*, tries to play it cool: "Yeah boss, I got you. We're just getting some chicken to go." No response. No nothing but a cold hard stare. Getting the point, and not wanting to get in a fight our first night in our new neighbor-hood, we decide to head over to the corner bodega to get some beers and toilet paper while our order is being made.

The bodega is in full effect. The outside window is full of people trying to place bets on their "numbers" before closing. A daily occurrence which, I later find out from David, the owner of the bodega, is like an underground lotto. With his shining gold teeth and charismatic smile, he explains to me that with this lotto game "the money is filtered directly back into the hands of the 'commu-nity' rather than being ripped off by our government leaders." A boombox cranks out Marvin Gaye at its optimum decibel, while a local woman with big boobs, missing teeth and matted hair argues with her imaginary friend, spilling her Steel Reserve beer. My boyfriend opens the door and walks in while I hesitate with my dog, not sure if I should wait outside or follow. A young woman with her two young children in tow glares at me, then shoulders me out of her way, making my decision for me. In less than an hour in our new neighborhood, I am beginning to understand all that "someone like *me*" entails. I walk into the bodega and stand up front near the counter by the door, just in case the dog is a problem again, and wait anxiously for my boyfriend.

I feel awkward, unbalanced and vulnerable. Aware of every moment passing, every eye assessing. Some people check me out slowly with no discerning curiosity, like giant fish that stare as they swim by in the aquarium tank, their expression vacant. Others prowl by, like large cats with predatory hunger: heads hung low, eyes focused, moving slow and steady before the kill. A slight man of about fifty wearing a red, oversized sweat jacket with the large hood slung over his head like the Grim Reaper, approaches me. "What type a dog is dat?" he asks, matter of fact. "She's a mutt," I answer, not really ready to engage in conversation, not really sure if he's a curious fish or a predatory cat. He reaches down to pet her, and without warning, she snarls.

I pull her back, thinking it is probably best for me to leave, but before I can turn around, Mr. Hoodie pulls out a knife that he has concealed behind his back and lunges toward her. "Oh yeah, muthafucka, you wan' some dis! I'll fuckin' cut you open, you bite me." I pull her even closer to me, and with the calm grace of Mother Teresa, look him in the eye and say, "She won't bite you." He retracts the knife and laughs wildly.

Thinking at this point it would be best to wait outside, I begin to walk backwards, pushing the door open behind me. Unaware of a presence in the doorway, I stumble into a man whose energy absorbs me like a black hole. I freeze like a deer mesmerized by headlights. He is at least six feet tall and as dark as night. His hair is matted and his eyes are large and bulging with a stare that is both menacing and caustic. Immediately I see images of hellfire, and violent screams filter through my mind as we stand there fixated on each other. The enormity of his energy shakes my core; the moment becomes an eternity as he evaluates my presence: friend or foe? Friend or foe. My heart is racing and my breath is stopped. I'm waiting, waiting. Then a voice rings from the counter like a match bell: "Ace! Leave her alone!" And it's over, the spell broken. He slowly steps to the side, holds the door open, and follows me with his eyes as I step outside. No words exchanged, just the acknowledgment of our existence. I leave knowing this will not be the last time we meet.

Like so many struggling artists in New York City I make ends meet as well as I can by being a waitress. I work nights at a small Italian restaurant in the Upper West side called Romano's, a neighborhood joint owned by an Israeli man named Jerry. Jerry is the Leona in our *Mystic Pizza*. A warm, gentle, honest man who just wants the best for everyone. His staff is made up of six eclectic girls, "his girls," who find themselves spending a moment of time together before becoming who they think they want to be. I love working at Romano's because every night is a fun-filled family experience. Like sisters we sit around telling tales of our latest love or heartbreak, then jump into action during the dinner rush, laughing and squabbling over tables. Our evening isn't complete if we don't find ourselves gathered in force for defense against the cooks in the kitchen. Each side yells at the other over a returned plate or a misplaced or messed up order. Afterwards we all sit around sharing a bottle of wine like performers after a well-done show. Romano's is a sanctuary, a place we can forget about the hassles of New York life and just be, with no worries of where our futures are headed.

I am fortunate that Romano's is only three short stops away on the 1/9 train, with the nearest station only a half a block away from our building. The entrance is down a short flight of stairs just to the left of the corner bodega. In the afternoon I leave for work around three o'clock, when many of the neighborhood night-walkers are still sleeping off binges of cheap beer and crack cocaine. It isn't until my shift ends around 11:30 and I head down into the station to return home that I start to get a sinking feeling: my sanctuary is behind me. I know that once I descend the stairs I will have to come out on the other side and ascend them and at the top, waiting, will be Ace. Most of the time I find him leaning against the wall of the bodega, talking to himself, lost in another dimension. A dimension between pleasure and pain that only the mixture of crack cocaine and alcohol can lead to. If I am lucky he will be too high to notice my presence, and will continue his conversation between himself and his god while I walk quietly home. If not, which is most of the time, he will attempt to stand up, teetering against his inebriated equilibrium, and walk towards me, purposely penetrating me with his demonic eyes. Not wanting to show any fear, I walk as calmly as I can past him. The walk getting to the station by day feels like falling out of bed, but at night, with Ace at my heels, it feels more like a walkabout in the deepest parts of the jungle.

"Think you special?" he hisses from behind. "Think you better than us? Think you gonna come here and change things. What? . . . you too good to talk to me, whitey?" He taunts me, pacing himself behind me with long strides. All I can do is keep walking. I have heard it all before; night after night, he asks the same questions. Night after night I keep walking, partly out of fear, but mainly out of uncertainty. Is he right? Is he telling me a truth that I have never had to ask, let alone answer? I want to be able stop and say, "No. Of course I'm not better. *Of course* I'm not special, *of course* I'm not too good to see that you are a human being, just like me." But I can't. The free thinking bi-racial liberal whose opinion is open and accepting of the world simply becomes a cliché. And one night I realize that this man is calling me out and questioning my Truth. He is expanding my awareness to something far greater than myself. I realize that, through no fault of my own, I have been led to believe that I am "special" and more "deserving." That by the nature of society in general, I am conditioned through generations of prejudice to not truly see him as another human being. Another human be-*ing*.

I go home and cry. I cry for him. I cry for me. I cry for us as people caught in a history of devaluation, a racket of judgment and jury where we lose sight of our own imperfections, our own humanity. I have to stop and see that Ace is not only a black man, not only a drug addict or an alcoholic. Ace is a man, with a beginning, a middle, and someday, an end. Just like me, just like us all.

Not long after that night, Ace and I start to share a dialogue. It happens in small ways at first, a simple "Hey, what's up?" from me or a "Hey, you gotta dollar" from him. On occasion I buy him a beer and he thanks me and goes on his way. He stops following me at night unless he needs some change, which I feel, not knowing his situation, is not for me to judge. Eventually we exchange names; I am no longer "whitey," he no longer a neighborhood nightwalker, and in our own off-kilter way, we become familiar to one another, we become friends.

One evening on my way home, I see Ace, leaning against the wall, a little more strung out than usual. I walk by expecting a comment or request, but he is lost. I turn back and say "Hi, Ace," and there is no response. Not sure of what to make of it, and not certain of what to do, I continue home. Pushing open the still-broken front entrance and walking into the now familiar smell of piss and grease, I head up to the third floor, rear apartment on the west side. I unlock the steel door and step inside, exhausted from a busy evening at Romano's. I kick off my shoes and head for the bedroom, where I am sure my boyfriend is dead asleep. A pounding on the door stops me in my tracks. I know it is Ace. Not certain of his condition, I open the door slowly to find him standing there, looking at me.

"You know why they call me Ace?" he asks.

"No," I muster.

"Because I was the smartest kid on the block. I got all A's in school. I'm real smart, like you. You think you're the only one who's smart around here? I was smart too. Got a scholarship to Howard University. I was the only one on my block who wuz gonna go to college."

"What happened?" I asked.

"Nam. Viet-fuckin'-Nam. I was drafted. When I got home, man, I was fucked up and everything was gone." He stands there lost in thought. I watch this scary man become nothing more than a lost child.

"I'm sorry Ace," I tell him, not sure what else to say.

"You and me. We're the same," he says, looking for my acknowledgment.

"Yes, we are."

We look at each other for a moment, then he turns and walks away.

It's been almost eleven years since Ace and I first met. I now live in Southern California with my husband and my six-year-old son, and new pups have replaced my dog, who passed on of old age. But

SUSAN E. MATUS

to this day, Ace remains in my heart. I think of him often and wonder where he is or if he's still even alive. On a recent visit to New York I was reminded of his fear of change, and what that change meant for him, when I saw that condos have replaced the corner bodega we both once called our own. All traces of Ace and the other forgotten vets have disappeared. I now embrace our tumultuous beginning which blossomed into a friendship that began that summer and lasted five years on the streets of Harlem. I think of him as my hidden advantage, a person who showed his face at the right time in my life to open up my heart. Even now he guides me when I think that life is unfair; he gives me the inspiration and strength to keep fighting the societal ignorance that shuts people into boxes of judgment and preconceived ideas, keeping us away from our humanity. And for this I am grateful. For this, he will always be my Ace in the Hole.

INITIATION OF A DESIRE
by Brent Jennings

It was in a Little Rock classroom, a long time ago. I was in the third grade. My teacher, Mrs. Hollingsworth, was a tall coffee-with-cream colored woman with an easy smile. She was neither young nor old. But she was the first teacher I can remember having a crush on. My first imaginary girlfriend.

Third grade was a year of firsts. I must have been about eight or nine. Young, curious, eager to explore the world and its myriad possibilities. There was an annual fall carnival held at our elementary school called "The Follies." It was modeled after those old vaudeville chorus-line types of shows. The girls danced and kicked like miniature Rockettes. There were four boys called the "End Men," two on each end of the chorus line. Their job was to sing songs, their prepubescent falsettos emulating the early Motown sound of the sixties. They also told jokes and funny stories between the girls' dance numbers. That year, I made my showbiz debut as one of the "End Men." I'll never forget feeling that initial fear as I moved my way through the silence onto center stage, that rush of adrenaline as the words I spoke came to life, that swell of pride and love, pure love, as the audience's laughter and applause filled the room. It was the birth of a consciousness, the initiation of a desire.

That year also marked another birth, that of my youngest brother, Curtis. I can still remember running across the school yard of Capitol Hill Elementary, tearing through the front gate, racing all the way through the white neighborhood, then across the train tracks (the border that separated black from white) and down the long, steep hill that was Jones Street, to my house. How could I ever forget that sense of urgency, the excitement that propelled me home so that I could bear witness to the arrival of my mother with my brand new baby brother?

This was around 1960, an era charged with change. The desegregation of Little Rock Central High School (by the now-famous Little Rock Nine), the landmark civil rights event that had brought Federal "peacekeeping" troops to our streets, took place just three years earlier. It was a volatile and explosive time, filled with so many extremes: hatred and love, fear and courage, violence and peace. It was a time when the changes occurring within our society forced us all, black and white, to take notice of each other, not only as we were, but as we desired to be.

In my small still-segregated classroom, one of Mrs. Hollingsworth's main desires for her third grade students was that we become perfect gentlemen and respectable ladies. She felt that in order to accomplish this, we had to become "comfortable with each other," so she made the boys and the girls sit side by side, adjacent to one another. We were seatmates. Our school desks were the old-fashioned kind that can now usually be found only on the sets of period movies and at museums. Books were stored underneath the desktop rather than underneath the seat. Our classroom was reconfigured into rows of twos. Every day we sat, two by two, male beside female.

My seatmate was a skinny, chocolate brown girl who was slightly bow-legged, always well-dressed and well-pressed. She wore patent leather flats and white turned-down ankle socks and bright, sun-drenched dresses over puffy lace petticoats, the kind worn by Little Red Riding Hood and Dorothy in *The Wizard of Oz*. Her hair was always neat, with decorative barrettes in dizzying colors that held every hot-combed pigtail in its place. Her nose was a little too broad for her face. But when she was smiling, which she always seemed to be doing, her light brown eyes twinkled ever so slightly, daring you to look into them and discover whatever secrets she held deep within her. Her name was Annette Reed. And our seating arrangement allowed us to become very comfortable with each other. In fact, it was that physical closeness which allowed Annette to take it upon herself to school me in the one subject my imaginary girlfriend, Mrs. Hollingsworth definitely could not: the birds and the bees.

One day, as Mrs. Hollingsworth was standing at the blackboard guiding us through our multiplication tables, Annette inched closer to me and whispered, "I bet you don't know where babies come from."

"Yes, I do," I quickly replied, accepting the bait. "They come from my mama's stomach. She just had one taken out last week."

"But how did it get in her stomach? I bet you don't know that." She was right. I didn't. I paused, searching for the right answer.

"God," I said.

"Noooooo. You want to know? Huh? Wanna know?" She picked up her thick black No. 2 pencil and resumed copying her multiplication tables, but as she did, she turned to me, eyes twinkling. "Meet me at recess, and I'll tell you."

Capitol Hill Elementary School was a big three-story Victorian-style brick building. An old, weathered chain link fence ran along the perimeter of the grounds. Behind the red brick building was a wooden structure that housed two first grade classrooms. Adjacent to these classrooms was the cafeteria. The three buildings were connected by a covered walkway. Capitol Hill had a rocky playground. There wasn't a patch of grass anywhere on it. Just rocks. Boys and girls weren't permitted to play together at recess. There was a boys' playground and a girls' playground. Strict separation of the sexes. This was the ultra-conservative south of the late fifties and early sixties. Maybe Mrs. Hollingsworth, in her own way, was rebelling against these puritanical values by forcing boys and girls to sit together in her classroom. After all, doesn't it make more sense to separate kids in high school rather than in elementary? How dangerous can prepubescent children be? There was, however, one corner behind the cafeteria that was secret, safe, neutral. I met Annette there for her lecture.

Knowing that if we got caught together, we'd be in trouble, Annette didn't waste any time. "It's like this," she began. "You have a penis . . . that's what you use to pee with. And I have a vagina . . . and I'll kiss you and you kiss me and stuff and your penis grows and gets hard and . . . it feels good . . . so some stuff comes out of your penis . . . and stays inside of me and a baby grows. That's why your mama's stomach gets big, and it comes out later . . . that's it."

Then she was gone.

I was stunned. I had no idea what this information really meant, or how to use it. But I never doubted is veracity. Annette spoke with authority, the Dr. Ruth of our third grade.

After recess it was quiet time in the classroom. Mrs. Hollingsworth worked at her desk grading papers. Every now and then, she'd look up and reprimand one of us for not being quiet. The classroom would eventually settle down and Mrs. Hollingsworth would, again, give her full attention to the work on her desk. Our assignment during this "quiet time" was to sit at our desks reading our weekly readers. But Annette Reed had decided that it was the perfect opportunity to take my education into the area of field study. She had apparently decided that I needed to know for myself, firsthand, exactly where this magical, mysterious, exotic place was located, the place where pleasure and people could be created. That little girl, innocent as a character from a fairytale, had decided that I needed to know the vagina, her vagina. The touch of it, and the scent of it.

I felt her inch closer. When placed side by side, as Mrs. Hollingsworth had us arrange them, our desks offered some degree of privacy—at least for certain parts of the anatomy, since they protruded out and over our laps. Annette took my hand, placed it under her dress and eased it upward, across her thigh. I immediately panicked and looked around the room to see if anyone had noticed what she was doing. Meanwhile, she slipped my hand under her panties and guided my index finger into her vagina and told me to keep it there. I was shocked, thrilled and confused. I knew that I was participating in an activity that was supposed to be enjoyable, in an adult way.

Once, on a Saturday afternoon as my father was driving my brothers and me home from Woods Barbershop after completing our Saturday grooming ritual in preparation for Sunday church and dinner, I repeated a joke I'd heard Josephus Ingram tell at school. My only objective was to entertain. It was a joke about a traveling salesman who stumbled upon a farmer's daughter. Now, when Josephus, a sixth grader, told this joke to a group of us huddled together in a corner on the boys' side of the playground, everyone laughed, so it must've been funny. But when I told it, my father didn't think so. Although after so many years I can't remember either the set-up or the punch line, but I do remember my father admonishing me in no uncertain terms not to ever repeat that joke in public again. This is how I knew, sitting in Mrs. Hollingsworth's class with my finger touching Annette's vagina, that I was having fun. I didn't know how I was supposed to enjoy it necessarily, but I knew it was a forbidden pleasure. I knew I could never tell my father what had happened at school that day. After some time, I slowly eased my hand away as Annette looked at me with those big, deep brown eyes. Eyes that always twinkled and smiled, eyes that knew things I didn't know and couldn't wait to teach me, eyes that bore no shame.

We repeated this activity, this game, intermittently and clandestinely, throughout the remainder of our year in the third grade, which also happened to be my last year at Capitol Hill Elementary School. My parents bought a home in another part of town and I transferred to a new school. From time to time, as I grew up, I'd run into Annette and we'd talk. Always briefly and cordially, never awkwardly or flirtatiously, but the memory of our third grade year was forever present. I have often wondered how she knew so much at such a young age. Experience and maturity have taught me to question now what I probably couldn't and wouldn't have then. Did Annette read it in a book? Was it possible that her mother and father had schooled her in this carnal knowledge? Broken it down so graphically and specifically?

I have come to suspect, though I will never know for sure, that Annette was most likely the victim of incest or sexual abuse. It's possible. I would even go so far as to say it's probable. We now know that things we once thought of as taboo, things we used to claim were the domain of white folks and could never happen in the black community, were and continue to be commonplace occurrences. The black vagina has always been under attack, by everyone from slaveholders who invaded the wombs of the mothers, sisters and daughters of our ancestors, to itinerant lovers who have seduced our own mothers, sisters and daughters by showering promises of love, family and fidelity upon their longing ears and hearts, only to then disappear, fade away into the night, after taking what they had come for. I have been guilty of this type of deception.

The irony is that my experience with Annette is what initially exposed me to my own predatory potential. My introduction to that part of the female anatomy greatly influenced my future perception of, and relationship with, the female gender. Suddenly they were no longer people, friends and playmates with thoughts and feelings. They were, first and foremost, a vagina. Objects of a desire that Annette had aroused within me. And this desire would, both subtly and overtly, dominate and direct my interactions with members of the opposite sex. There was a time when I didn't ever wonder what the vagina really was, or care who it belonged to. I didn't connect it to a heart, a brain, a mind, a soul, a people, a race. It existed only for me, to please and gratify me. Like so many of my

BRENT JENNINGS

peers, to me the vagina was nothing more than a pawn in a game of numbers. The more I could have, the better I felt about myself. Typical.

Having also discovered what would be my life's work that year in third grade when I performed as one of the "End Men" in "The Follies" production, I left home and Little Rock to attend Emerson College in Boston, Massachusetts to study theater. That was in 1969. It was an era of free love, mind expansion, a time when the norm was to challenge the social and sexual mores and values of society. The Civil Rights movement, Anti-War movement, and the Feminist movement all reached their apex during this period. This atmosphere of change and exploration made it easy for me to finally succumb to my lusts and passions.

As I moved through college, enjoying the comforts and caresses of as many vaginas as possible, I started to also notice a startling and disappointing reality of the black experience. Many of the people I met during those years, men and women, were from homes that were either broken or fatherless. Most of them were like beautiful, elaborate puzzles, meticulously assembled; but there always seemed to be a piece missing. A piece that was vital to the completion and comprehension of the larger picture. In the midst of the struggle for access to the American dream, it became obvious to me that our most immediate struggle and need, as black people, was for the restoration of the black family unit. And this was a feat that could not be accomplished through legislation or by singing or marching, only by our commitment to each other. This destruction of the black family unit was a reality I never wanted to be a part of. I wanted desperately not to contribute to this social malady that, in my view, was weakening my entire race. It seemed to me the most revolutionary thing a black man could do was dedicate himself to his offspring. I vowed to myself I would never leave my seed behind. In the end after it was all said and done, dedication to family would be my political statement.

After graduation, I moved to New York to establish my theatrical career. It was a great time to be in the city. My relationship to the vagina had not essentially changed, but I was by now a responsible Lothario, making sure to protect my vow by always using protection. I was not particularly monogamous, though there were some vaginas that I visited more than others, and there was even the guise of monogamy with several. But strict monogamy was never an option, even when it appeared to be. I needed the notches on my belt, the trophies on my wall. I was on one big, long safari. Hunting vaginas.

But it wasn't just me. It was the same with many of the black men I knew. The subject of the vagina, how to get it and what to do with it, dominated our conversations in locker rooms, on playing fields and courts, on golf courses, on airplanes as we flew through the clouds, even in churches, before and after we prayed for the forgiveness of our sins.

Once, Mr. Bishop, the doorman of my upper-west side apartment, and I had a discussion on the ways and means of persuading a vagina to give itself to you willingly and with full commitment. He offered this: "A woman will have sex to hear I love you. A man will say I love you to have sex." This bit of wisdom, from an old sage, provided me with all the ammunition I needed. It drew for me a psychological profile of the prey, which I then used to my advantage, whenever necessary. I became a master of deceit. If a vagina needed to feel the promise of a deep and personal attachment, I could play that part. For the one that wanted freedom and fun, no problem; I could play that part, too. I used the vagina for emotional comfort and for physical enjoyment. Maybe in some ways I used it to validate my manhood and enhance my self-image, I don't know. For the heterosexual male, the vagina is the conduit to love and affection. Don't we all, the secure and the insecure, need that?

And then one day my steady girlfriend (I'll just call her "Madame X") told me she was pregnant, and wanted to have the child. She was quite adamant; it was not something that was up for

BRENT JENNINGS

discussion. I instantly remembered the vow I had made, to myself and to my race. So, reluctantly and resentfully, I consented. I was trapped by my ideology. Cornered by my lifestyle of deceit and lust. It all seemed so unreal. I couldn't believe this was happening to me. One moment I was a bachelor, a young carefree actor in the Big Apple, just having fun. Then before I knew it, Madame X and I were attending birthing classes to learn how to breathe and count spaces between contractions. It was clear that my life had changed, and that it would never go back to the way it was.

It was a humid summer night when I was initiated into the real world. Madame X went into labor. In what seemed like a flash, we found ourselves in a Manhattan skyscraper hospital. I was given a surgical mask, scrubs and rubber gloves to wear so that I could participate in the birth. Admittedly, I was not much help. It was as though I had suddenly forgotten how to count. As my girlfriend, this woman whom I had gotten pregnant, screamed and pushed, all the while begging God for mercy, my mind began to wander. The operating room had floor-to-ceiling windows that wrapped completely around it. Seventy-five percent of the wall space was glass. I couldn't help but notice how high up we were. It was as though we were floating through the night. It was one of those rare occasions in New York when the sky was so clear that the heavenly bodies were visible. It was a little past midnight. The moon was extremely bright, cutting into the blackness with its silver promises. Everything had vanished, and we were all that was: the woman who would become eventually my wife, our soon-to-be-born child, and me. This was all that mattered, we were all that mattered, all that was real and true.

All of a sudden I heard a voice say, "Here he comes."

I turned and saw this vagina opening wider than I could've ever believed possible. There was a head, a tiny human head, moving through and out of it. Then came the shoulders, turning, sliding, guiding his body towards its entrance. My son's strong black body. I was stunned, dumbfounded. I was in shock, in absolute awe.

I was the first to hold our child. And when I looked into the face of my firstborn son I saw the face of the brother who, twenty-four years earlier, I had run home to greet. I saw my father, my grandfathers. I saw myself.

Shortly after the delivery, the hospital staff prepared my girlfriend, my son's mother, to be moved into a recovery room. She looked like someone who had just fought a tremendous battle—and won. The hospital garment she was wearing was soaking wet; her body was as limp as a dishrag; those luminous eyes into which I had melted as we'd made love were glazed over as if they were peering into a galaxy far, far, away. After all we'd been through, how could I have not understood that there was more to this woman than her vagina? How could I have not understood that there is more to every woman than that?

It is an opening for life, the powerful link between our past and our future. It is what connects us to our history, what perpetuates our existence, creates the limitless possibilities of all we ever were and all we can ever hope to be.

OUR KIND OF PEOPLE
by Kimball Stroud

Prejudice is all about conditioning, seeing the world in the starkness of black and white instead of the fluidity of color, where everything touches, carries a part of the other. Growing up in a small Southern town it can be easy to get used to the presence of boundaries.

Texarkana, where I grew up, gets its name from three different states: Texas, Arkansas, and Louisiana. The town is about a forty-five minute drive from the Louisiana border, only a hop, skip, and a jump.

Technically, there are two Texarkanas: Texarkana, Texas and Texarkana, Arkansas. But those of us who lived there really considered it one town. The main street there is called State Line Avenue. It's a huge, six lane road which splits the town almost perfectly in half. But there's a post office that sits right on the actual state line, so State Line Avenue has to curve around the building.

It's poetic—isn't it?—that the building which reminds the community that it is one, the building in which every member of the community is welcome, is a facility that promotes communication. The minute you step inside that post office, all boundaries cease to exist. Unfortunately, that wasn't always the case outside of it.

Texarkana was idyllic, the perfect place to grow up. It was like something out of a movie. Families vacationed together. People left their front doors unlocked. There were spacious homes with equally spacious front and back yards, residential roads that ended in a cul-de-sac. The neighborhoods were always filled with kids playing, walking, or riding their bikes. Our lives were insulated, but they were also isolated. We were sheltered, and in a lot of ways, that was a very good thing; that was what made our lives feel so protected, so carefree. But being sheltered also kept us apart from everyone who wasn't in our neighborhood or our group of friends.

I grew up on the Arkansas side of Texarkana; my friend, Sally, grew up on the Texas side. When we were younger, we were always friendly, and we knew lots of people in common. Still, we didn't really become close until adulthood, when we'd each made a new home and a life for ourselves in DC.

A year or so ago, Sally and I were talking and our conversation took me back to my youth, and back to all those boundaries, particularly the social ones, the prejudices that we'd been conditioned to at least acknowledge, if not abide by or altogether accept.

Sally is in a committed relationship with Petiri, a black man from Zimbabwe. They were living together, but she hadn't yet told her family—for fear of their reaction. The question of when, and how, to tell her parents about the relationship was causing Sally a whole lot of stress and trauma. During our conversation, she admitted that in her opinion, it would have probably been a whole lot easier to tell her parents that she was a lesbian than to tell them that she was in love with Petiri. After she said that, both of us giggled. Here we were, in 2008; Barack Obama had just become the Democratic presumptive presidential nominee, and my dear friend was losing sleep trying to find the words to tell her parents she was sharing her bed with a black man.

Still, I understood. We'd been conditioned with the idea that it was incredibly taboo for a white woman to date a black man. I can't speak for Sally, but in my case it came from the society in which I found myself, not from my parents. I can't remember anybody actually telling me, "Kimball, black men are off limits." It was just something that was known, imbedded in our brains, much like all the other prejudices that people pick up by osmosis, the ones which purport to define the sort of individuals who are "our kind of people."

As it turns out, a number of the black people I knew *were* "my kind." It took me a while to figure that out, though, because our society was so segregated. I attended junior high and high school in the late seventies and early eighties, so the schools were legally integrated but outside of the classroom the black and white communities didn't mix. It was rumored that there were one or two interracial "couples" at our school, white girls who had secretly hooked up with black guys. Nothing like that ever took place out in the open. It was frowned upon by the communities on both sides of the dividing line, the black people and the white people. Those white girls (for some reason it was always white girls and black guys, never black girls and white guys) were called *nigger-lovers*.

The "N" word was definitely something that we heard a lot back then in Texarkana. To my ears, the word had a very specific sound to it, no matter who said it. It was a sound filled with hostility, fear, hatred, and insecurity masked as superiority. That wasn't something I could have articulated back then; I only knew the sound of the word made me cringe.

For most of the time that I lived in Texarkana, my friends were white. I suppose that was to be expected: I lived in an all-white upper middle class neighborhood; my family belonged—and still belongs—to an all-white country club—except it's been integrated now. I think they had to go out and recruit to get a black member. Back then, the only black people you'd find at that club were the ones who were employed there. That's just the way things were.

The divide between black and white was so wide that in junior high, they had to begin a quota system, almost like an affirmative action program, to ensure that the entire population was being represented in sports and other extracurricular activities. There were eight girls on our cheerleading squad. Five of them were always white and three of them were always black. It had to be like that, no matter what, because of the system that was instituted. This is what usually happened: thirty white girls would try out for five allotted spots and eight black girls would try out for three allotted spots. It didn't make sense, and it never really seemed to balance out. Instead of bridging the divide, that quota system actually caused a lot of resentment and bitterness.

I chose to use the cheerleading squad as an example because to be a cheerleader was the honor of all honors. This was "The South" after all. Try-outs were held in front of the whole school, and the entire student body would vote for those highly coveted spots. It was incredibly competitive.

I'm sure by now you've figured out that I was a cheerleader. And that's the other reason why I chose to use the activity as an example of the problems, as well as the possibilities, that existed in the childhood that I knew. For some people the controversy over the allocation of spots on our cheerleading squad seemed to make their minds all the more narrow. For me, it opened up my world. It allowed me to naturally interact with girls I would never, in any other circumstance, have come into serious contact with. That's how I started becoming friends and socializing with black people. That's how I came to know that some of them were definitely "my kind."

Even as I write this and try to explain how monumental some of those experiences in my childhood were, what huge barriers my siblings and I broke, barriers that our parents allowed us to break, it all seems so nonsensical, as though it's not worthy of the time that I'm spending to shape these words, to tell this story. But I know, I know, it's important that we discuss the issue of race now, just as it was important back then for my family to live without regard to any of the possible consequences of not toeing the party line.

Once, in junior high, I had the cheerleading squad spend the night at my house. If you can believe it, there were people who were shocked that I included the three black cheerleaders, and that my parents allowed me to. But why wouldn't they? To my parents, having them in our house wasn't any more of an issue than having any of the other cheerleaders; they were all my squad-mates, all my friends. Besides, my parents would have done the same; in fact, they did do the same.

During my freshman year of high school, my father was appointed to the Arkansas Supreme Court. Two other justices were appointed that same year, one of whom was African American. My father invited them to spend the weekend with our family at our lake house. I'd never seen any black people at Lake Greeson before but I had seen confederate flags proudly displayed on jet boats. I thought it was just the coolest thing to have my father's colleague and his family there, at the lake, with our family. It's also pretty cool to look back and see how my parents taught and led by example.

By high school, my social life had become much more integrated; and because of sports, so had my older brother's. He and I threw a lot of parties together and, in addition to our white friends, we also always invited our black friends. It was pretty rare, unless it was at a school dance or the prom or something like that, for the black and white students to socialize together outside of school hours. Having our black friends over to our home to dance, listen to music and have drinks was, in essence, us making a statement.

And what a statement it was. Those were the days. We had so much fun. That's how I learned to groove, how I learned to love funk music: going to public high school, being on the cheerleading squad, dancing with my black girlfriends, and partying with our new, makeshift, racially-mixed crew. We listened to George Clinton and Parliament, Rufus, The Go-Gos, Heart, Aerosmith, Michael Jackson, and old-school seventies soul. Maybe it's just the nostalgia of youth, but there was a sense of perfection to those days, and to those interactions. It was as if I knew that this was right, that this was how life was supposed to be, that you didn't have to stand in the post office on State Line Avenue to feel at one with people who lived on the other side, and to connect with the rest of the world.

After graduating from the University of Arkansas, I moved to Washington, DC to work in national politics. I got a job as a receptionist at the Democratic Congressional Campaign Committee (DCCC). My co-receptionist, Tamela, a black girl who was about the same age as me, became my best friend. The office hadn't become non-smoking yet, so we used to sit at our desk, smoking and talking up a storm, she with her Kool Menthols and me with my Benson and Hedges Deluxe Ultra Lights.

Tamela and I hung out after work, too—when she wasn't doing hair, which was her little side gig. We spent time together at each other's places, and we went to a lot of concerts together. She'd bring one of her friends, either Kalima or LaTerri, and I would bring one of my friends, usually Melissa or Jill. We'd pile into Tamela's car, a little red Datsun with roses painted on the window. Her name was also painted on the window, in slanted curlicue letters. We saw Anita Baker, Luther Vandross, Prince, and a bunch of other performers. Tamela welcomed me to DC in style.

In the early nineties, when the governor of my home state decided to run for president, I decided to work for him. Being involved with the Clinton Campaign further opened my world. I'd already grown accustomed to working and socializing with African Americans, but prior to living in DC, I'd never worked with any other group of people, except white people—not even Jewish people. Suddenly my days were filled with constant interactions with Hispanics, Asian Americans, Native Americans, people with all different kinds of ethnic ancestry, immigrants from countries I'd only ever read about. That experience taught me a lot about what it is to be a part of that proverbial American melting pot.

During that time, I met and became good friends with a brilliant young African American man named Nathan, who also worked in Democratic politics. For years, our professional paths crisscrossed. It was inevitable that our personal lives would also eventually become intertwined.

Nathan, whom I still count as a dear friend, is extremely handsome. He was striking and distinguished, incredibly well dressed and educated, with an air of confidence. Even my mother made mention of his looks when she met him at one of the many political events on which he and I worked. "He is so good looking," she told me. "Like a young Harry Belafonte."

I remember hearing her say those words. I remember, too, how that moment became something of a dividing line separating the me who, despite all that I'd learned and experienced in my life, was still that white girl from Texarkana who couldn't break that ultimate taboo or cross that final social barrier, and the me who had suddenly realized that there was no reason not to. Even though I'd never had any reason to believe that my parents would disapprove of my being with a black man, there was something liberating about my mother's words. It allowed me to give myself the permission I'd unwittingly been withholding.

That moment was all I could think about when Sally and I had our conversation about how she would tell her parents of her love for Petiri. I tried to put myself in her position. I wondered what I would do if I met a man whom I believed was "the one," but wasn't sure my parents would accept or celebrate our love because of his race. Do you walk away from love? Or do you walk away from family? Until the choice is really yours to make, I think it's hard to know what you would really do. Thankfully, I've never been in that position and I probably never will be.

Sally did end up breaking the news to her family. They were reasonable in their response; they told her that she was an adult and was free to love whomever she pleased. You could say that they accepted her decision, but I honestly don't think Sally's going to be taking Petiri home to Texarkana for the holidays.

Nathan and I eventually shared a kiss. Okay, maybe it was more like several kisses. It happened, as these things often do, after a night of good food and good drink. The get-together that evening just so happened to be at my apartment. Nathan stayed after everyone else left and things started getting cozy. I was surprised at how nervous I was. Every first kiss is exciting with the usual butterflies in the stomach, but this time seemed different. This was going to be "it." My first kiss by a black man. And then it happened. Nathan and I embraced and we made out like teenagers. I remember pulling away from him at one point and looking at his face and thinking, What is the big deal?

I was struck by how familiar it felt to be in Nathan's arms. Kissing him was, for lack of a better explanation, like kissing a white man. But then, I wonder: what other explanation could there be? So many of us were brought up to believe that there is this huge difference between black people and white people; there isn't. Being with Nathan that night made me realize a body is a body. It made me realize that the black body is my body, just as the white body is his body.

I'm aware that history would have us believe otherwise. And I'm not sure why some people choose to hold on to all that is wrong and bad about that history, why they are so afraid of recognizing themselves in other people. What I do know is that it's difficult to build on a foundation that is flawed. When it comes to race, the truth of our past is extremely complicated—there's nothing we can do to change that. But our future is already changing; and the more it changes, the easier it is to see how simple that truth can be.

Regardless of the color of its skin, every single body is blood and muscle and bone. If we let skin be the most defining factor of a body, then we're going to miss out on everything else that body has to offer us—from its brain, to its heart, to its soul. We'll miss out on the privilege of knowing and loving some pretty amazing people, people we might come to discover are "our kind of people" after all.

A CINEMATIC MONTAGE OF THE BLACK MALE HEART

by A. Van Jordan

Fade In:
EXTERIOR. Inside the Beltway. 1993—NIGHT

Under the moonlight. I am driving along the Beltway, 495 west, just outside Washington, DC, en route home from a movie, *Nothing But A Man*, which was re-released and shown in Georgetown at the Biograph Theater. It's that time of night, the same hour everywhere, when The Quiet Storm comes on the radio. If you aren't in DC, the equivalent is happening wherever you are: Lenny Williams, inevitably, sings "'Cause I Love You"; you, inevitably, shake your head in empathy. This will happen if you are grown; that is, it will happen if you have lived through love and the loss of a relationship—you will shake your head because your heart will say, "Now, ain't that the truth." So when a brother shakes his head to Lenny's voice, it's the equivalent to nodding, "Yes."

There can be the narrow focus of the eyes on the double-yellow lines of the road, the defensive driving of a man who'd rather put his ride on cruise control, or there is the conscious presence of your heart, your internal bass drum, that both is in rhythm with Lenny Williams's voice, which you'll never hear as honestly on wax again, and his inflection, now as the images play out on the screen of your mind, of Ivan Dixon and Abbey Lincoln's hard-won, on-screen love, which you'll never see as poignantly rendered in film again.

Diastole:
INTERIOR. My Heart. 2006—DAY

If it's true that before the words of "'Cause I Love You" can sink in you must have experience, then isn't it also true that without experience you may not *get it*? And if you don't get it, then you suffer the consequences of not knowing what it means to reveal yourself in your most unvarnished form.

Williams' singing is striking, but it's what happens at the center of the song that makes it such a classic. The lyrics are not that which poetry is made of; there are moments you might even describe as cliché, but, after all, it's popular music in the category of soul music, which was still a category in 1978 when the song was first released, so we accept it. What makes it a classic played nightly all over America, however, is the moment when Williams breaks out *of* song—not breaks out *in* song—to speak to a friend about some problems he was having with his lover:

> *And my friend told me, he said, "Lenny,*
> *You just oughta forget about her."*
> *But I told my friend, I said, "You know*
> *Maybe you've never been in love like I've been in love . . .*
> *You know, sometimes you get lonely . . ."*

No single soul or R&B love ballad reveals the vulnerability of a man in love more than "'Cause I Love You." Yes, songs have been written to reveal the hearts of men, but the degree of this nakedness, its willingness to expose itself, is, initially, hard to fathom. In 1978, I was in eighth grade. For me at that time, this song was little more than an excuse to slow grind with a girl under a black light at a house party. Now I hear this song at least twice a week, every week, and every time I hear it, it resonates deeper and deeper. Between 1978 and 2006, I've lost my virginity; fallen in love, a mature adult love; seen hundreds of films; read hundreds of books; published two books; lost family members; gone to college; learned to say "I'm sorry" or "I was wrong"; won awards; seen art exhibits; found religion in many forms, and then found spirituality. Through this lifetime of listening, I've had regrets, I've had epiphanies, I've watched my nephew grow and learned from it, and I've lost friends, gained friends and learned from it. This was all necessary.

The heart has to fill with experience before it can pump. Experiential knowledge is needed in order for your understanding of a work of art to evolve. There's a double strand of artifice at play in any art form, a DNA strand that makes up its genetic code: 1) there is the artifice of its craft, which can be appreciated for its solid design. That is to say, a work of art can be appraised by how well it matches up or progresses its respective field. And 2) there is the delight in the experience of it, which is predicated on what the audience brings to the listening to or the viewing of or the reading of the work.

And if art is used to communicate in a way that we don't practice in our daily lives, shouldn't it also challenge the way in which we live? To some, Lenny Williams may be too naked in this song, too real with his feelings. This may cause discomfort to a closed listener, but also the listener with an open heart. It will simply stir these two souls differently. That it calls for an art that is more vulnerable than we're allowed to show downtown or in the gym or in the boardroom or in bed is evident if we're to call it music.

And this is truly soul music. Most people won't know this song by its title. Whenever I ask someone if they've heard it, they always ask, "Is that that ooh, ooh song?" There comes a moment when words reach their limit to express emotion and you must scream or cry or laugh from your belly. Williams understands this as he sings, for what seems like a whole chorus, "Oh, oh, oh, oh, oh, oh,"—eighty-two times total, interspersed between short phrases, as a preface to simply saying "I love you." What man can remember the phrase *I love you* in this song, even in the title, after having heard Williams evoke sounds of how brothers feel when we're trying to "look like men" and not cry? This is what it would sound like if we let it out and Lenny Williams set it to music. Maybe you've been in love like I've been, and one night you'll call in on the dedication line.

Systole:
INTERIOR. Biograph Theater. Washington, DC. 1993—NIGHT

Ivan Dixon's square jaw and tamed afro. Abbey Lincoln's full, wide, and lonely eyes. They are framed in the windshield of a convertible automobile driven by Dixon's character, Duff, who is taking Lincoln's character, Josie, out on their first date. The couple is now parked. Two white boys walk into the scene with flashlights. They shine the lights in the car and, specifically, over Josie's body. "Just checking her out," other characters in this film would say, but not Duff. He's tired of white men who "can reach right inside you with their white hands and turn you on and off." Duff and Josie are excited for each other, or they are scared for each other. Eventually, their excitement overpowers their fears.

I am watching this film alone in the dark in a Georgetown theater. It's 1993 but the film was first released in 1964, and I can't believe this love story still feels ahead of its time. There are stories that seem to adorn themselves with reality much in the way a privileged, suburban youth affects the look of a common thug or grunge kid, redolent of a lack of authenticity. Then there is *Nothing But A Man*, which can only be described as a look at hyper-reality. That is to say, it's so real, you can hardly look without turning your head. It shows us what we barely have the courage to face in our lives, the beauty and the decay.

130

A. VAN JORDAN

The film is directed by Michael Roemer and co-written by Roemer and Robert Young, both of whom are white, which in no way impinges upon their ability to remain loyal to the cultural nuances of this story. It's in the tradition of neorealism; it reveals a life of poverty with the hope to transcend if given a chance. This style takes on a new twist when African-American culture, especially in 1964, is used as the vehicle through which the story is told. In America, too often, audiences must be reminded that stories like *Nothing But A Man* are universal in the lessons they convey about life. I say *reminded*, because once the principle characters are black, audiences—and, unfortunately, sometimes even black audiences—must be reminded that African Americans can represent the plight of the human spirit. Once we witness this level of perseverance through crises, we usually refer to it as having heart.

The story centers on Duff (Ivan Dixon), a section hand on a railroad in Alabama. He lives in a railroad car parked at the work site with his coworkers, and their lives are hard. There is little respite from the drudgery of their jobs except for drinking, jokes, and card playing. Duff attends a church social one day and meets Josie (Abbey Lincoln), who is a school teacher and the pastor's daughter. He asks her out, and they soon fall in love.

INTERIOR. My Mind. My Heart. 2006—DAY

Here's the problem: the preacher doesn't want his daughter hitched to a railroad hand. Duff lives in a time and place in which docility is expected of blacks in order to get ahead, or even to get along, which makes it hard for a man who won't respond when his boss calls him "boy." Duff has a son from whom he is already estranged, and a strained relationship with his own father. Can this man love a woman in this environment and mend his relationship with his son, too? What's central here is the need for our hero to expose his heart, its strengths and its weaknesses—a timeless struggle for men.

My parents divorced when I was eight years old. I don't have a clear record of the exact date, but I clearly remember seeing my father pack, for good. I say *for good* because I'd seen him pack for the night, but this was different. There was a sense of finality to his leaving that had to extend beyond my scope at that age because, to a large degree, it's beyond my scope now. It's especially difficult for me to make sense of the divorce today; my parents remarried each other twenty-three years later—and they eloped. What I remember more distinctly as a child was the need to vie for his attention. At the time, to put it plainly, I wondered if my father loved me. This question comes up in your mind whenever someone—a mother, a girlfriend, whatever—sets a precedent for what love looks like in your mind. For me, my mother had done that. So I expected certain actions to come from my father that, in my mind, I equated with love: talking about school, showing up to games, disciplining me—in the ways parents did, back then—and, later, comforting me with tough love.

My father died October 22, 2006. I saw my parents dance together for the first time in my life six years ago at one of my cousin's birthday parties. Part of watching my father take my mother's hand on the dance floor felt like a change of lighting on a stage. There's that moment when you realize the lighting is changing, but you're not sure what mood will be set by its beam, not until the spot is fully aglow. I realized then that my father was a subtle lover. It wasn't his showing love for my mother while they danced that I looked for; it was his taking her hand *to* dance that was his act of love, his growth that I witnessed over the years. There were actions that my father was now comfortable with expressing that were emblematic of the complexities of his life—the strained relationship with his father *and* his mother; the lack of a childhood due to a life of labor that started with a lie about his age so he could work, at sixteen, in a Goodyear plant; and the poor examples of love that prefaced his marriage.

The contrast of Duff with his world embodies a black male in touch with the complexities of his heart, too—a man who's comfortable with it. This makes the world squirm. I am always captivated by the squirming of the world under the heartbeat of a black man. The world calls for this level of self awareness, for this level of self assurance, in order to get ahead, but in the chest of a black man, it carries with it the misinterpretation of a man who is either threatening or crazy. He isn't employable because he isn't easily manipulated; he isn't desirable as a son-in-law because you fear for the future of your daughter; he isn't ideal for a son or a father because his expectations are too high—at least, this is all we're seasoned to believe. This story offers a glimpse at what a man with heart can endure and what a man with heart will inevitably face.

EXTERIOR. Inside the Beltway. 1993—NIGHT

It has started to rain. The windshield wipers try to compete with Lenny Williams's voice. They try. I turn the volume up and the rain becomes a silent movie. Through my windshield I see Duff and Josie on their first date. They are about to embark upon a relationship that will become the pebble that disturbs a still lake. They will fight each other when they want to fight others, and they will love each other once they figure this out. No one will encourage their love. They will love anyway, much in the way Lenny Williams wouldn't take the advice of his friend who didn't know love like he did. Under me is the road whirring beneath the weight of my tires; I know this but I don't hear it. I know the moon is still watching over the rain. The watery eye of the night is welling up as the world

that is real, the world that can't face that reality—the hearts that
have stopped and those that keep on keepin' on—tires, loves, and
stays alive.

Fade Out.

THE MEANING OF ASHY
by David Goldsmith

When I first lay eyes on her, she is completely nude.

I am in an experimental theatre, in a progressive town. An *enfant terrible* of a local writer/director is staging yet another of his sometimes-annual political agitprop pageants, a staple of this particular theatre company, and if one subscribes to its eclectic season of plays, one is obliged to attend these occasional assaults on the senses for the good of one's own social awareness (this play is about a Japanese fishing village that had been blighted by thalidomide in the water). It's rather like choking down a mouthful of broccoli on a Thanksgiving plate in order to justify all the stuffing and gravy.

But tonight, there is dessert.

At some random point in the proceedings, a young, vibrant, athletic black woman with an avid smile and a game attitude bounds down the aisle of the theatre and leaps up the stairs leading onto the stage. Like an Olympic gymnast, she catapults herself into the last available spot in a line of actors flanked across the apron of the proscenium, expertly sticking the landing.

She alone among her multiracial colleagues wears not a single stitch of clothing. I still have no idea why.

As this moment continues on, I am stunned that it is happening at all, let alone for as long and lingering. Certain this vision will soon be wrested from my view, I begin to commit this woman to memory, assiduously cataloguing the details of her extraordinary physique and then scaling back my perspective to get the overall image burned into my brain for my own personal use later.

First, I will admit, are the breasts. They are small, but perfect, with dark, proportioned nipples, delicate and feminine. Then there is the long, lean torso and tight belly that leads to a meticulously trimmed, triangular tuft of black, coiled hair, framed by toned thighs that taper at last into a smooth, shapely pair of legs.

While I do register that this aggressively naked, beautiful woman with the shining smile is black, this fact is neither here nor there in what it is about her I find compelling.

That is, until about ten years later, when I start dating her.

We meet at a party of a mutual friend, a Caucasian man; we all work in the same tight-knit theatrical sphere so this sort of thing is bound to happen. Among the mostly white actors, directors, and assorted other artist types, she is impossible to miss. This gazelle-like African-American stranger, so comfortable with herself and her own body.

We are introduced. She smiles at me. It is in this moment, at this party, upon seeing that smile; that I remember.

"I've seen you naked," I hear myself saying.

Though right away I wish I could, I am unable to stuff the words back into my mouth. I attempt to play this off as some sort of edgy new brand of flirtation. Somehow, I am sure having more to do with her graciousness than my skill, I am successful.

There is an instant chemistry between us that catches us both by surprise. An ease she has with me, and with my then six-year-old daughter, who has returned from the buffet table to stand at my side (I am a single father). There is quick, comfortable banter, and common interests rise to the surface. There is also perhaps—just perhaps—that mutual whiff of danger in the prospect of an encounter with the "Other." Add to that the alluring perception of post-racial enlightenment.

She and I bond quickly. Within a week, we are dating exclusively. Within two weeks, we are in love.

I don't know much about her at this point. There's a brother, or is it a sister . . . her parents are still alive, or are they . . . San Francisco, San Diego . . . some story about being left in a steamer trunk . . . and a dog named . . . no wait, a cat . . .

She is amazing in bed. She is easy to be around. She is crazy about me.

And though I'm unwilling to acknowledge it, there is: she's black. How cool is that? Or more to the point, how cool am I?

We are at another party, our first together as a couple. A friend of mine, an African-American woman, has rented a dance hall for her birthday. Chic, multi-culti guests are playing conga drums in several adjoining rooms. Others dance sensuously to the piped-in music. Still more specimens of fabulousness mill around the full bar in the middle of the main room. I enter hand in hand with my Princess.

The reaction is not quite that movie cliché, the sound of a needle scraping off the edge of vinyl, accompanied by a room of slack-jawed stares . . . but that's how it feels. As if all assembled have stopped their merry-making to take stock of the svelte, statuesque black woman with the short Jewish man—think Naomi Campbell on the improbable arm of Jon Stewart—and then have just as quickly gone back to their drinks and their conversation and their dancing.

And as we circulate ourselves into the bloodstream of this party, I can't deny the power I am feeling. It is intoxicating, and I do not need a drink. I shake hands with friends of friends, am introduced to those I have not met before as though I am a visiting dignitary. And a thought flashes through my mind: everyone at this party must think I have a big dick.

Even as I recognize this thought as intellectually absurd, I cannot resist the feeling of empowerment that washes over me. Thank God my new girlfriend is graciously wearing flats so that I don't look ridiculous. I whisper into her ear:

"Everyone at this party thinks I have the biggest dick in the room."

"That's cuz you do, Daddy," she responds without missing a beat.

I'm ready to marry this girl. We've been dating a month.

There are a few race-related moments in our courtship that I find fascinating: the night she tells me she's dated so many white men that her mother finally said to her, "When you bringin' home a black man?"; the morning I watch her slather herself with cocoa butter and discover what "ashy" means. Then there's the day I'm standing in a bathrobe in the kitchen and she begins to seduce me. When the inevitable moment arises for her to be, well, kneeling in front of me, she takes me by the hand and leads me upstairs instead. "I'm not getting down on my knees in front of any white man," she says.

Wow, I think, makes sense. Never thought about that before. Even though we are generations away from certain wrongs of history, there are still those acts, innocent though they may seem, that resonate as anything but.

And yet those are not the reasons why we inevitably crash and burn. The cold, craven reach of history has nothing to do with why we are simply not meant to be.

I keep asking myself, "What do I really know about her?" And the more I know, the more I discover that beneath the surface, at this time in her life, there is too much that is unknowable, even to her.

Our senses of humor don't connect. What passed as glittering banter at a party has not translated into anything deeper in conversation. On The Great Subject—race—we are strangely apolitical with each other. We are, in fact, the embodiment of its irrelevance as a topic. I am useless at sharing my feelings, for fear of creating conflict, and end up lashing out at inappropriate times in unfair ways. We both do. I come to the conclusion that we are two people who just don't belong together in a relationship.

DAVID GOLDSMITH

We break up. We get back together. More than once.

It's hard for her to let go; it's hard for me to let go. But what am I reluctant to forego? The same old things, I guess . . . I don't want to be alone. I want the sexual intimacy that comes with a relationship. I don't want to be "out there" anymore.

But in retrospect, there was more to it for me than that. I was having trouble letting go because, if I'm honest, I really liked that feeling of being looked upon by all who saw me as having the biggest dick in the room. I liked being the white guy that was man enough for the beautiful black woman because that meant that apparently I had somehow managed to leapfrog over all those available black men. And who's to say who should be at the head of that line?

But what could I have represented to her? Was there some reverse fantasy about the black woman with the white man that fed into her willingness to fall for me, stick with me, take me back? And back, and forth?

For my part, one thing was clear. I liked how the shiny surfaces of her blackness reflected off the dull palette of my whiteness. Is that so wrong?

We break up again, this time for good. Our time together hasn't been about a deep connection, intellectual, emotional, spiritual, or otherwise. Ultimately, there are just not enough nutrients in this relationship to keep us going, and all the cocoa butter I watch her elegant hands smooth into her graceful thighs every morning isn't going to change that.

So now I ask myself, Did I love her then, really? Or was I just in love with the fact of her blackness? Did I fall in love with a woman who happened to be black, or did I fall in love with the idea of being with a black woman? By which I mean, of course, did I never really fall in love at all?

Years go by, and somehow she and I never completely lose touch. I follow her career; she follows mine. More years go by. We meet for lunch.

Things have changed between us. I'm not chasing her. I'm not pushing her away. She's not the naked woman; she's not the black woman; she's not my girlfriend. She just is.

And yet as I sit in the restaurant she has chosen, in a neighborhood I would never feel safe going into on my own, I feel the eyes of the black men and women sitting at their nearby tables boring into us. They are probably wondering who that short white man is with the stunning black woman, what he's doing with her, and what he has that draws her to him.

And I find I still sort of like it, that feeling. Of mystery. Of power. Of possibility.

Which finally does, I guess, make me the biggest dick in the room.

1,000 O'CLOCK: JOHNSON TIME

by Peter J. Harris

Since I awkwardly slid my penis into my first lover in the summer of 1971, three months after my sixteenth birthday, I have trusted women's bodies more than I've trusted my own for confirmation and validation of sexual and sensual pleasure. Elevated pussy to first position over my penis. Trusted my lovers' hard nipples, never doubted the silkiness between their open legs, swooned to the music of their sexual scatting as excitement built, and sweetened their involuntary quaking with my own *got to give it up.*

I'm now in my early fifties, *and hallelujah!* Johnson still works just fine, thanks to a dope-free, vegetarian adulthood, and the healthy resolution of most soap operas in my life. My discernment and discrimination have resulted in me having less sex (at least according to the barometer monitored by my *inner knucklehead,* whose annoying ass I've nicknamed *IK),* but sex that's way more satisfying. Now I am aware that I shudder with, like, a *completeness,* only when I trust and absolutely heed the field of attraction generated by my own penis, my own body. Of course, from a strictly biological breakdown, because of the nerve endings, Johnson will always feel good if somebody's stroking him, or if he's tucked up within somebody's *catch and release.* But that's my *IK* talking. Speaking as a grown man, without even a New Jack interlocutor, I know that simply getting a nut is no longer enough. Never really has been.

Which is saying something for an ex-student of the Round the Way Sexual Academy, with its curriculum emphasizing volume over quality, silence over ethical emotional testimony, and other self-defeating behaviors perpetuating the legacy of America's actual and metaphorical assault on the bodies and psyches of Black men.

But it is *1,000 o'clock* and after much independent study I am intoxicated by a peaceful, adult recognition. *I'm on a move to where a grown man gets down.*

For the rest of my life I am on a quest for epic sex. Guided only by the most powerful sex I've ever had—sex that led to dream states, orgasms like geysers, serenity before sinking into sleep; Sunday morning power-sex, followed by the mutual *coma* of renewal, then a brunch of waffles and omelets; or those one or two *first times* that clicked like the harmonies of Ashford and Simpson. Or even that *one* night, when—my right hand raised y'all—I actually stayed hard all night and sis fell asleep beside me, and I was so full of energy I sat up beside her stroking myself gently. And no little pill involved.

Until my libido gives up the ghost, I am on a mission to define for myself what epic sex is. What role Johnson plays. What role partnership plays. What role the quest for pleasure plays. This will be an odyssey and it has not been easy getting to this point, because I still get chills appraising and appreciating an attractive woman's body. But I'm dead-set on choosing beyond surfaces and distilling the most distinctive satisfactions from my perpetual arousal.

When I look back over my sex life, whenever I failed to practice this 'rhythm method,' didn't *do it fluid*, the sex was fulfilling only because—simply put—I *had* sex, nobody got sick, and she didn't get pregnant. Too rushed. Too little time. Wrong day. Too tentative. Always incomplete. Like I could have been doing something better with my time. Not that I had to fall in love or lay the keystone for partnership with every sexual hook up. But even thumbing the dictionary for, uh, the *Satisfaction 101* definition, *arhythmic* sexing left me off-kilter, and clear from the moment I came that I was gone. As I came, my desire dissipated, and instantly it was inconceivable that we should spend any more time together than necessary.

PETER J. HARRIS

There was no way we'd lie around and talk or curl into a sweet sweaty arc or get up to make a meal.

Within this season of expanded awareness, with my kids grown and handling their business, two divorces behind me, and the memories of special, powerful lovers as guides and touchstones, my current search is for consistent joy and seamlessness, which results in less time between peaks and more time between valleys. I have pledged my allegiance to a sensation that has consistently been palpable when I've had the right hook ups: my body's *knowing* vibration blended with this unforced, *luminescent* intimacy that saturates the ebb and flow between me and the woman who makes me hear echoes of Smokey singing *Baby Come Close*. An intimacy that seems preordained.

These days, if I can't sense that throbbing autobiography, then I am saying no, thank you, I don't want *your* sex, I don't want sex with *you, I don't want to spend even one sexual second with you.* I try to say that as respectfully as the situation demands. I'm not trying to devalue, or be harsh, or contribute to any kind of Rejection Field that leaches into her future. Just relying first and foremost on my megahertz, my pulse, so that when I hook up, *I want to hook up*, not just release tension. I want to connect, whether we partner up ultimately, or whether we learn that we're heading for a blues song. I want to cherish the *potential* of each *cum*, hoard it even.

And before I'm tagged as callous or blasé, let the record show that I've been told *no* way more than I've been told yes. So I know that it stings. Swipes a molecule of self-esteem from my reflection in the mirror. But it's not like rejection corrupts my DNA, you know. I get over it. I smack down my inner knucklehead, who wants me to holler bitch this and bitch that. And in my worst sexual droughts, I would still rather know she ain't feeling me, than go through rounds of flirtation only to get trumped by somebody else.

Call it the "Slow Roll Movement," this more deliberate, incremental, resonant relationship with my body, my Johnson. Relying on all my physical and metaphysical senses. Savoring first meeting. Inhaling scent. Absorbing hug. Analyzing the signals my body generates. Swooning to its intelligence. Recalibrating my deepest sensuality.

This goes beyond me being a wiser, mid-level elder (of course I'm wiser and got my IK under control). I'll certainly cop to being mature. But this is a mindful practice. Johnson has become a divining rod, a wick of incandescence, rather than a tool of submission or ownership that gets off dousing for Drama.

I feel like I'm building a foundation for a true happiness and cultivating my sense of whole living. I am asking and trying to answer the questions: What is a happy Black man? How does a happy Black man act? How does a hard dick contribute to a happy Black man's life?

My IK tells me that happiness *is* a hard dick. That happiness means getting pussy and there *ain't* no bad pussy, as long as you don't get sick and die. My IK shouts (echoing every calcified lesson from our male realms of immaturity) that a hard dick ain't got no conscience, and it's a crime when Johnson gets hard and don't get to dip into a woman's wet labyrinth. Man, even beyond obvious and ethical worries about getting or transmitting AIDS or STDs, as critical as that is, what a boring, one-note approach to sex.

I swear I feel I'm being called to fall in love with my mysterious and mystical penis, versus, say, Johnson as a symbol of my power over somebody. This Johnson is symbol of my Maleness without the wolf tickets. My sensualist's baton through which I orchestrate an epic range of celebration. I feel like the only serious use of my introspection is to cultivate—beyond the inspiration of trying to get some pussy—a virtuoso understanding of what takes me to the sexual, emotional and spiritual bridge.

My meditations say make this quest more profound by finding *everything* more joyful: the anticipation, the uncertainties, the awkwardness, the frustrations, the ebb and flow, the wonder in the telephone's ring, the ping announcing an email. *Volunteer*, my inner voices encourage me. Eliminate desperation, embrace this rite of passage, respect my yes and no, handle the consequences without placing blame, regardless of the outcome of testimony, conversation, or an exchange of numbers. If someone I want refuses me, honor the disappointment. Don't beg, don't bogard, and do not expect her to change her mind. Like the Isley Brothers said, *it's your thing . . .*

Spend more time loving self than analyzing why we didn't hit it off. Concentrate on claiming inalienable erotic rights. Rededicate myself to ensuring that I never ever again have bad sex. Never ever again settle for *hit it and quit it* (*my* contribution to bad sex!). Never again fuck just to release my tension. Say no. Choose whose touch I want. Choose which mouth I want to kiss. Whose hands I want cradling my Johnson.

And if I choose someone who chooses me, and we choose to become an item, whether or not it leads to partnership, then definitely do the work, too. The nuts and bolts: Creating the mutual vocabulary of one-on-one. Executing the respect, faithfulness, loyalty, long-distance plans and processes for handling disputes and money. All that and more.

Sounds obvious for a dude my age, I know, but I'm trying to capture the exhilaration I'm stalking, the ecstasy feeding the percussion of this season. When I'm drawn to a woman now, I'm listening for the drumming between us. *Johnson Time!* I'm nodding to the cunning beats surging within me and swooping me to the *suspension* bridge, pants pulled up around my waist, neon pledges radiating off my skin and illuminating the air around me:

> *I bogard no pussy with my Johnson*
> *I enter no body unless I am invited*
> *I dangle before no child with my Johnson*
> *I spread no disease with my Johnson*
> *I issue no false promises with my Johnson*

It is 1,000 o'clock and I want to splash in wet seconds of eternity with somebody, birth on our valuable breath, pleasure our midwife. Her palm—*I am imprinted by her lifeline*—flattens my stomach and I undulate like an appointment with immortality. I want her touch to make me forget I'm always a breath away from needing an undertaker's business card. I want her to hold me like a sculptor cradling stone. I want to walk point at the tip of rejuvenation and end up in the place *spring* go for R&R. I want more than just renewal. I want to *undam* myself.

It is 1,000 o'clock, and I want my skin haunted inside-out by her taste. I want to be sanded by her brilliance, until I couldn't be clever if I tried. I want to stagger mute in her stare. I want her excitement in my ear to *indent* me. I want to moan into the electrons that, yes, I am a hard man to love right now but only because I'm loving myself so hard. I want to shimmer into the man I want to be, shifting dimensions until I can stay dry strolling through falling rain. I am trying to weave words into *do* recalled by my *third cousin's* children. I am standing up, wobbling under weight of my failings in this world of war and inequity, standing for myself, bleeding, but breathing to dislodge the splinters of citizenship and finally feel the acupuncture of a balanced life.

I want a lover who can read all this from the look on my face as the fabled midnight hour melts into 1,000 o'clock, when I no longer know myself without her, and she becomes *inevitable* to me, and I become susceptible to her shake rattle and roll as surely as I am to Earth's orbit rotate and wobble. I want her to speak my name and retune oscillation of my cells. I want her to turn in her sleep next to me and align my spine against new morning's intimidations. I want her to counsel me in crisis, listen to my vulnerable voice, crave my sweat tears and *cum*, and resuscitate amazement in every breath I receive.

It is 1,000 o'clock and I want to make a home in a house built on a foundation bolted to our grandparents' chaingang demands,

PETER J. HARRIS

where the floors creak with *closeted* lovers' Northstar resolve, and the walls, rooms, doors, and roof align with my mother's bedtime prayers. I want to live a barefoot holiday with somebody, measure time by celebration, wilt *he said/she said* with riveting telepathy of two humans face-to-face gossiping with kiss from mouths steady evolving beyond the need for speech.

I want a grown woman in my bed, to inch every skin of her with reverence on my face, her touch calibrated by weightless laughter. We will shake wrong out the sheets, grip with athletic inflammation, eyes open, and root beer, mouths full of carbonation, sarsaparilla easing our conversion from lust to lovers to loved ones. Rising every morning, skin radiant with elation, with nothing, with everything.

I am neutralizing taboos: *Size don't mean shit!* I'm stepping out of the police line-up. Cutting myself down from the lynching tree. I want back in the human race. I see myself through my own eyes. Refuse to be society's family secret any more. Its fetish. Boogeyman. What you *think* you know! I will face my fears and embrace my hard dick *with* a conscience. I will turn my *whole body* into a Johnson, amazing, sacred, confirmed, validated.

> *Psst . . . listen up partner: what had happened was . . .*
> *I have graduated from the Round the Way Sexual Academy.*
> *Schooled my inner knucklehead, glimpsed the joyful path,*
> *and found that no question is taboo.*
> *How big was Jesus? Muhammad? Buddha?*
> *All the OG's we quote during the earthquakes in our lives?*
> *Is it the size of the ship?*
> *Or the motion of the ocean?*
> *Is it 1,000 o'clock?*
> *Who's got the time?*

THE UNBORROWABLE BLACKNESS OF BEING

by Philip Littell

Oh, God, let me be the buffoon in these proceedings. It will all come out.

This can be said, it cannot be printed.

I don't like going to bed with black men.

Sometimes I *do* like going to bed with black men.

I rarely go to bed with black men.

I have had hot sex with black men.

I have had terrible sex with black men.

I have been terrible sex with black men, and good.

The use of the plural (black *men*) is disturbing.

Maybe it's better to write this way:

The black body. More apart than other bodies. I flinch. I summon up representations first. On film mostly. And in photographs. Crucially in paintings. Moving closer, the black body *live* on stage, across the footlights. The Harlem drive-by: no weapon carried but the hungry child's-eye. Then (in my history) the historic contact. Touch. But we have just touched on that.

Ideas influence every encounter, to the point when one properly wonders whether I have ever encountered or considered or experienced the black body directly. Is the experience always mediated? More than others are?

This has been the week of that *New Yorker* cover showing the Obamas at home. We pass over it in silence. It is now already nothing but a wrecked armored vehicle, or a dead horse with its belly swelling. The flies buzz. We are still far from the front.

The aging, damaged Yves St. Laurent is speaking in a documentary on his life. He is asked about his championing of black models. The tremors and the shakes seem to vanish. *What* the black female body *did* to him in his work, *for* his clothes, the *frame*, the *carriage* . . . he is absolutely unafraid of any charges that could be leveled against him of exoticism, of sexual tourism, of objectification, of sentimentalization, exploitation, in fact he is so open to the charges, absolutely heedless, because he is still *so excited*, still inspired. There were consequences, good and bad, to his life, his passions, he is obviously absolutely shot and soon to die, but nowhere else in the course of this interview does he come so alive. Other consequences are known to follow the careers of his models. In the year of his death one of his models is found drowned in the Seine. Was she cursed with beauty or blackness or the great commonality of aging?

Oh, God, let me be as honest.

I have been ashamed of my sexual responses to black men.

I have been proud of my sexual responses to black men.

I have a bunch of rhetorical questions to ask about this.

I won't ask them here.

I will not present my bona fides of black friendships and acquaintances in this matter.

I seek no exculpation of my record of responses on this matter.

In the matter of sexual attraction which is sometimes linked and sometimes not to romantic attraction I recognize forces beyond my control.

My attraction to younger men, to addicts, to great beauties, to neurotics, to famous people, is so strong.

My enjoyment of plural partners, adultery, group sex and exhibition is part of my history. I love to be cheated *with*. I enjoy being cheated *on*.

My preferences as to what kind of sexual activity I like are highly specific, somewhat malleable and always sharpened by curiosity and tempered by capacity.

I recognize some affinities, but more divergences, between my actual practice, my taste in pornography, and my wildest, deepest fantasies.

I am not troubled by these.

I am troubled by the effect reading this will have on a black man.

YouTube has unearthed a treasure for me: the very young Josephine Baker dancing, silent, in the earliest footage of her. A stage show, the whole stage picture recorded without cuts or inserts or a single close-up. My past half-hearted enthusiasm for her based on her leaden talkies and diligent time-defying fabulousness and really tiresome perpetual PR information-loops turns to love. This girl has made her body the instrument of her destiny; her greatest coup is adding insouciance to total nudity (what a breathtakingly hilarious con the African thing is!), but the talent is there to back it up and it runs on what looks like joy and can be read as anything you need it to be. Let's call it energy. She conquered Paris. She conquers me. She is not then nor ever was supported by talented collaborators. The songs, the shows, the settings and scenarios . . . well, stars are too often defined by what they rise above. She is the bomb.

My mother was Mediterranean. French. To my child's eye no star resembled her *but* Lena Horne. It was the skin I knew best. The rest is a sorry snapshot of the times. Black artists are on so many of the record covers in our living room but they do not frequent our home. Apartheid masquerades as mutual respect and respect may have played a real part in the wary social dance of the progressives. Another virtue cited: patience.

But the child I was is lost to desire. Every summer we leave the city, every fall return, and each time the car I'm in is driven through

Harlem. And I want to look and look and look. I want to be a lamppost there, not because I'm afraid, but because I know it's rude to stare. And that's all I want to do. So Beautiful! Allow the child that thought.

Once. Black bodies on the tennis courts of the Bar Harbor Club. Nigerian Olympians. Such alertness within the herd. Nothing terrible happened. Lots of self-pats on the back.

Once. A young black man is taken up by my family and their circle. He is a painter and his father is a famous statesman, a great representative of his race, and this young man who shares his famous name is kind enough to teach me how to draw from life the red rust rocky seaweed smelly beach in Maine, and every day a man's black body sits comfortable and easy, close to me, and guides my hand, and even before my parents' divorce I am starved of a man's attention and for a time the corner of my eye is filled as I draw. So an attempt was being made among the adults. But the weight of it . . . he didn't stay the summer. And how short a summer is to me now, anyway. Had he made a pass at someone? I think so. So many passes were being made. That pass was disallowed.

My father covered Africa for CBS in the sixties. Tired of being married, he prevented our moving to Nairobi with him, the better to cover his affairs. Maybe only one. And, reader, he married her. (An English girl.)

Ball of wax avoided, eh? We would certainly have had "houseboys." There would have been prevailing attitudes. A certain duty to fit in. "Social" is an interesting word.

But the romance of the possibility of Africa endured for us. Our disappointment did not abate. My sister is at home there now with Medecins Sans Fontieres. At home with the reality.

I know we dreamed of having black friends.

I do not tally or otherwise mark my rejection of white, Latino, Arab, Jewish men.

Every rejection of an interested black or Asian man weighs on me.

Every time I refuse or *decline* to get fucked by any man, that weighs on me too.

Quite heavily.

To the point where I tend to deflect anal intercourse in favor of other expressions of sex.

Each rejection of a black man is certainly registered, but it does not deflect me from my pursuit of, or availability to, younger white, Latino, Arab, Jewish men.

I reject men who are overweight usually. Some overweight men have the balls to override my usual response.

Sometimes I am objectified as a white man. I have also been objectified for my looks, youth, age, and even parts of my body.

I do not know what it is to inhabit a black body, black skin or walk in a black man's shoes.

I have always been curious about those things and have rejoiced at every opportunity to experience it imaginatively in art, or conversation, or by observation.

I do not like going to straight parties.

Eleanor Powell. One of the Broadway Melodies. Set on a luxury ocean liner. Plot decrees that everyone show up at a costume ball dressed as their favorite stars. Wonderful tracking shots of a confetti and streamer festooned mass pandemonium, duplicate sets of Marx Brothers and triple Laurels and Hardys, you get the picture. Eleanor is to perform, and she appears as Bojangles to enact his famous step dance on a little set of stairs. This is already a direct *hommage*, but here's the thing: Eleanor Powell was an unsurpassed tap dancer, close to demonic in her virtuosity, and pretty enough, but she had always relied on a fixed smile of astonishing vapidity meant to convey vivacity and joy. A mask, in other words. To get her through. The blackface she has put on enables an astonishing transformation in her: a revelation actually.

As she mounts and descends those tiny stairs, her feet a blur, the camera goes on a fishing expedition for something else to pick out and comes in close on her face. Too close. Her actual face becomes readable under the blacking. It is completely relaxed, rapt with concentration, dead serious and absolutely beautiful. She receives a gift from what is, after all, a travesty: her real self. She is unmasked by a mask, and the care and respect with which she has approached this tribute repaid a thousand fold. And we are rewarded too.

But this was a one-off, I think. Fred Astaire did an equally skilled and respectful Bojangles, and while not shame-making it is merely a very good dance number. And postmodern distancing and ironized blackface remains a lame idea. Not that a lot of us haven't all had it. It never flies.

I can think of no more revealing response to the body than the sexual.

I can understand that my response to the black body is not intentional.

I suspect that my response to the black body is conditioned.

I am still on the hook.

I am on the hook because no matter how many parallels I am able to draw with my response to other bodies, *including the female* . . . my response to the black body *is* different. My defensiveness about it is of another order.

I could say this is where we are.

I must say, rather, this is where I am.

Representation *is* American culture. After all we also *elect representatives*. This is as sly and accurate a political idea as "the *pursuit* of happiness" (ha ha, the laugh's on *you*. You gotta work for it and you *still* won't get it).

But I weary of paradox. And of myself. I want to end with an enigma. Here is what has puzzled me the most.

It is no secret to anybody now that the Civil War screwed everything up, and probably for good.

And the representation of the Negro in American genre painting illustrates this clearly.

After the Civil War, the Negro is either presented in vicious caricature or impossibly ennobled. Both modes repel, are literally sickening.

But before the war the paintings in which the Negro appears show themselves to be concerned with one subject: the Negro's physical relationship to the white figures in the picture. Proximity and distance, the level of social interaction, of mutual awareness. The Negro body and face is painted without inflection, observed truthfully, even curiously. How a person stands or sits in relation to another is such a giveaway that it is usually perceived unconsciously. But not in these antebellum paintings.

For the enigma, I want to cite a group of works by William Sidney Mount. This group is one of the greatest Variations on a Theme I have ever encountered. I have never completely penetrated or understood it.

In every piece there is a small barn one might call a large shed, with a door big enough that it can be opened to reveal the whole interior. In one, a white musician plays a fiddle. A black man outside listens. Or a black man inside is playing an instrument and a white man is outside listening. Or the black man is playing outside and the white man is inside listening. Sometimes the barn is empty. In some of the pictures children are added, white and black. Some portray groups of musicians playing, a pair, or more.

In all, the door is open or closed to varying degrees. And, in a very few, black and white musicians are playing together.

I don't like the word "race." It seems a dumb idea.

I do recognize the continuing validity of the word "racist."

A TAIL TALE
by S. Pearl Sharp

Each night the scrawny little blonde girl ran from Carla's dorm room and disappeared for half an hour or more. It seemed to happen right around the time everyone started getting into their jammies to either hit the bunk or the books. Now, one month into the semester, her nightly exit was more panicked, fleeing from the room like a possessed cat.

In 1960, Ohio's Bowling Green State University officially integrated their dormitories. There had been a few random instances of mixed housing, but now they intentionally placed one "Negro" per floor in each quad of the large pink building that housed some 300 freshman co-eds. I was part of the test pattern. I don't know what the university's strategy was, but we were each suffering from the "The First Negro" syndrome.

Frequently, all eight of us crammed into a cubicle somewhere for self-guided group therapy. Carla, my home girl, was having a unique problem and one night she revealed how the situation was escalating. The next night, when little missy made her regular nocturnal exit, she ran smack into The Colored Wall—seven sistuhs with attitudes! Our position was uncompromising as she cowered before us, shaking, crying, unable to explain herself, but clearly overwhelmed with fear. She crumpled into a tiny mound on the floor.

We wore our newfound Blackness like an honor badge, but we could still recognize someone else's pain. One by one we knelt beside the girl, gently but intensely coaxing her to give it up, whatever it was. Finally worn out, she pointed her skinny, shaking arm toward Carla and whimpered, "Her t-t-t—ta—t—*tail*!" Then, crumpled there on the floor, the girl buried her head in her knees and wept.

"Her *tail*!?" And our anger became strangely quiet.

But we could feel each other thinking. Ain't this deep! We are so amazing that even our *imaginary* body parts are legendary!

If I had known about those advertising "trade cards" distributed in the late 1800s and early 1900s, then I might have been less shocked at the girl's revelation. The postcards, which used Black images to sell products, sometimes showed Blacks with tails going about the business of selling thread and gadgets. You can see a tail sticking out of Negroes in drawings on some of the early popular sheet music.

If I had been informed enough to connect this 1960s moment to our soldiers fighting both Nazism and racism in Europe during World War II, I might have seen Carla's situation coming. Negro soldiers had tails back then—at least that was the word put out by white soldiers in hopes that it would preclude European women's natural attraction to the brothers. Didn't work. The veterans have revealed that some women would put soft pillows on the chairs so that the Black soldier's tail would be comfortable.

If I had known then about Saartjie (or Sarah) Bartman, I would have known what to say to this young white girl, and more important, how to embrace my friend Carla's humiliation. Saartjie was from the Khoikhoi tribe of South Africa, whose women were known for their oversized buttocks and genitalia. In 1810, while still a teenager, she was taken to Europe and put on display in traveling exhibitions as "a living ethnographic specimen," aka: a freak.

Carla was the Khoikhoi of the campus, her huge butt the object of titters and rude stares at this center for higher learning. In one of those ironies that only God can explain, she was put in a room with this wimpy, small town white girl whose parents had taught her that a Black girl's behind is so big because she has a tail, and what strange things could happen to any pure white girl who laid eyes on it.

That experience never left me, and tales of tails keep finding me.

Apparently, the tail has been dangling in tribal mythology for centuries. In *Myths and Legends of the Bantu,* European author Alice Werner documents "tailed heaven-folk": immortals with tails who descend to earth from the sky, bringing creation or destruction, and who are often required by the earth people to cut off their tails if they plan to stay in the community. Well, yeah . . . This mythology, attributed to the African continent, may explain why the tail has the qualities of an apparition—sometimes there, sometimes not.

But contemporary Black folks are not innocent here; we've become believers of our own bad press. When the beloved Nigerian drummer, Babatunde Olatunji, enrolled at Atlanta's Morehouse College in the 1960s, he was asked many questions by African-American students, including "Is it true that Africans have tails?"

"They were not playing," Olatunji recalled. "They were very sincere. They wanted to know. To understand this you have to consider Hollywood's unholy war on Africa."

Which is to say that our tail did not need to be visible, as long as our onscreen behavior showed that it was stuck between our legs.

An interesting aspect of the tail is that it exists only via the working of the other body parts. The brain imagines and mythologizes it, the eye sees what is not there, and the mouth confirms the tail's presence for others. The finger points to it, the butt carries it, the heart fears it and the digestive system spews the bile of logic into the culture, giving folks the gall to accept my tail as an unmitigated fact.

So it follows that the tail is considered a sexual organ. Thus, the phrase, "chasing some tail"—yes, you can look it up on the Web— is used to describe men's casual sex pursuits. For pets, tail-chasing is described as behavior that happens when the animal does not recognize its own tail as part of its body. An understandable dilemma.

But not the dilemma of Black folks. Like chitterlings, the lindy-hop and the English language, we have taken this appendage and imbued it with magic, mystery, and humor.

And that is the tale of my tail.

FEELING TOSHA JONES

by Kenji Jasper

This moment stems from a series of movements more than sixteen years ago, during my eighth grade year, when I occupied the last desk in the row of seats closest to the door in Mrs. Sprenke's physical science class. I loved science back then. I hungered to master all knowledge of the way things worked. A few years later complex mathematics came into play. After that anything that wasn't lit or history-related became a white-hot pain in the ass to the tenth power. But I must stay focused. For this is not about math or science. This is about Tosha Jones.

Though the story to come may seem to contradict this paragraph, I always remember her face better than anything else: her flawless fudge complexion, her medium-length hair permed into a mushroom style with curls at the edges. She lived on Owen Street NE, just a few blocks from my mother's mother's house. And she had a man. They always had men.

The sky was a grayish white and our teacher's treble-laden voice was pontificating on the charges negative and positive of atomic particles. I was in "good student" mode, taking notes and thinking of questions to ask, when I looked down and saw it protruding from the seat in front of me. Two fudge colored cheeks with a sheet of khaki stretched across them, their mass squeezing through the chrome reverse "U" in her chair back. My thirteen year-old thought process went something like "Oh my God. That shit is huge."

What happened next was and continues to be uncharacteristic of the "me" I know best. I was a shy boy, a semi-brainiac wannabe writer with big lips, a peanut head and a propensity for being called "Robocop" by the boys in the lower-tracked sections of the student body, because I spoke perfect English. I had scored the extremely top-heavy Lateefah Hill's digits on the second day of the seventh grade only to find out that she'd sealed me in the "homie" box. I had lost in a love triangle between myself and one Julian Turner for the affections of Nikeva Lawrence, having been sabotaged by Julian's bald-faced but effective lie that I had called her mother a whore. Another strike and I was sure to be out of the game, though I had no clue of what "the game" nor being "out" of it might have meant.

Yet and still I found myself moving my knee toward the back of her desk until it kissed Tosha's soft and cushy prize. I felt the cap of the joint sinking into the warmth of the junk in her trunk. And then I pulled back, having held just long enough for it to be dismissed as a mistake, written off as the unintentional side-effect of me reaching down to retrieve a lost pen or pencil.

The back of her head remained static, her eyes glued to the teacher and what was being taught. I, however, had lost my appetite for learning as the still-maturing thing in my jeans doubled in size. Had it been as good for her? My anticipation took the form of a nervous scribbling on lined paper.

But Tosha hadn't noticed a thing. She was still taking notes, still getting her eighth grade education, the first in her final four school years before moving on to be a young, gifted and productive young woman in African-American society. She hadn't noticed a thing. So she wouldn't mind if I did it again.

I leaned into it this time, feeling the cleft between each cheek. It was warmer, more welcoming. I took my time, moving that knee from left to right to explore every inch, all caution dissolving in the bright red rush. I hadn't been this close since Kenisha Love had pecked me on the lips in the second grade. I hadn't been that hot since the 100-degree summer two seasons before.

Tosha still didn't move a muscle, though heads began to turn in other rows. It was pretty tough not to notice the bump and grind going down between the last two desks on the row nearest the door. But I paid them no mind, because Tosha was doing the same to me. I was "Ready for the World" and she was the digital display with which God had empowered me to tinker. So I did what most men do with wealth and privilege. I got greedy.

The next time I used my right hand. I splayed my fingers as wide as they'd stretch and took hold. Mrs. Sprenke's voice could have been a million miles away. I was no longer bothered by the stench of the wharf just outside of the third floor window. I didn't care that the V5 bus would be packed to capacity that afternoon, or that Robert Lampkin might want a Tae Kwon Do rematch in front of the HUD Building, where I'd be destined to lose, again.

I tried to squeeze all that ass into the palm of one hand. Play like I could carry it home and put it on the dresser. I felt like a man, or at least one of the older boys who got to tell their various booty tales on the sand and glass-covered playground back in the neighborhood. I held on because it was all that I'd ever had, and by the bleak story of my teens thus far, it was all I was going to get.

So I forgot that I was in a classroom. I forgot that Tosha had a man, and most of all, I forgot that I was not the kind of boy to whom these things happened. I forgot long enough to enjoy those three minutes of pleasure, moments in time ended by the folded note she slipped to me, a handwritten expression of two sentences that read: "You have to stop now. People are looking."

Tosha could've slapped me. She could've told the teacher or had her Man and Co. come up to the school to give me a quick stomp and shiner combo. Instead I'd only gotten a note to "Stop." I complied, and the two of us never spoke of what had happened again.

I was Sugar Ray Leonard scoring the decision against Marvin Hagler. I was Theismann throwing the pass that brought the Skins to the Superbowl. It would only be a matter of time before I could refute Darryl Gilliam's grade school dismissals that I didn't even know what a condom looked like. I, Kenji Jasper, defeated candidate in my recent campaign for student government vice president, had copped a feel, and gotten away with it.

The rest of my file on Tasha Jones is rather scanty: a fourteenth birthday party in the basement of her home I barely remember, a graduation pic with her name signed on the back long since lost. Word on the street was that she became a Jehovah's Witness. I, however, can only bear witness to the ass that was.

It's interesting that I've chosen to write on this topic, particularly since most of the world knows me as a breast man. Though when asked I will always list the eyes and lips as the features I observe first on a potential mate, the naked truth is that I normally drop my gaze a few inches to estimate hang and cup size. I long for the beautiful pause between the moment the bra is revealed and the moment I see the nipples harden in the flow of air. And though I am not alone in such a preference, the majority of brothers I know place their sights toward the rear, searching for the perfect parted curve between coccyx and quadricep.

Ass makes the world go 'round. Or at least that is what we're left to think after a healthy dose of all that is deemed black in this particular hemisphere. It is the focal point of every music video, even if most of the models in them are less than endowed in the afore-mentioned department. It has become slang for sex, even though traditional intercourse occurs through another orifice altogether. Ask the right man after too many drinks and he might be willing to argue that it's the black community's greatest asset altogether.

One of my old professors once lectured that the black woman's disproportionate behind was the product of water retention in the African body due to some reason or the other. This concept was somewhat supported by remarks from a relative friend of mine who, after living on the continent for a year or two, informed a group of men that all the women "grow that way" over there. The worst kind of bullshit from the worst kind of ignorance.

It is beyond my extremely limited scientific knowledge to even attempt to formulate a more suitable explanation. And even if I could, I don't think it matters. What matters is that the African female posterior has become a symbol of something, and that something is supposedly our greatest strength. If you're worried that this is about to turn into another Love Jones bullshit poem about the beauty of the black woman, you can slow your roll. My love for the African female form can be read within and beyond the lines. But this is about analysis and observation, through both of which I have arrived at the theory that follows:

Women are the givers of life and keepers of spirit, the sacred box from which second sight and intuition are born, and the engine behind each and every throne. Apply these facts to the history of African people, to enslavement and imperialism, to famines and floods, Queens Amina, Nzingha, and the sistas on the under-ground railroad. One foot scaling the proverbial mountain followed by the other. Feet guided by calf and thigh. Muscle tearing and healing to grow thick and wider, calisthenic development in bodies lower and upper building toward the waistline and that which sup-ports it. A perfect semi-circle ruining the Eurocentric ideal of a straight line.

This thing has whet the appetite of both overseers and fetish-driven opportunists alike. Its movement and vibrations are more seductive than the flowered face of sex itself. It is more engaging than the scowl of the thugged out MC or the perfect smile of the well-groomed and paid spokesperson. It subconsciously reminds all who view it of the greatest struggle, of the most captivating beauty there is, of all that is hated and loved, objectified and cap-tured, wiggling to the given score at whichever set of beats per minute.

Legs can go to frail or to flab. Breasts drop and flatten, to be replaced by synthetic circles that look far worse than what the Cre-ator had originally given. But the behind is forever. Even it if begins to jiggle beyond the realm of the enticing, or sag with the passage of time, it will always be there. Tosha let me hold a piece of forever for three whole minutes. God truly did smile upon me.

This is the power of the black woman's backside. This is what we men (and women) crave at the sight of a passing booty, a touch and taste of the forever between switching hips, the curve to caress at the tipping point of sensual overload. We want to have and hold this forever that extends from within her, this piece of space and time below the waistline.

In writing this I think about Tosha Jones, so much so that I've changed her name to protect her right to privacy. I think of the men who have known her better than I, and the kids who know nothing of her at all. She is far more than just that thing in the rear, more than a shard of my sexual awakening. She is a soul I barely knew at a time when she was changing a million times over. Wherever she is I hope she's alive and well, loved and loving.

STONES AND STICKS

by Carolyn L. Holbrook

. . . If we can shift the paradigm then we can
change the culture and the inheritance that the
coming generation gets.
—Luisah Teish

There are turning points in everyone's life, though we may not immediately recognize them as such. I experienced one of those moments in the spring of 1983 during a poetry workshop. Each student was required to write a poem, which the instructor would then videotape while the student read or performed it in a relevant setting. On this day, the class met in a cemetery to record a poem one of the students had written about rollerskating through a grave- yard. Little did I know it would be a life-changing event.

I have wanted to be a writer for as long as I can remember but it wasn't until I was in my mid-thirties—divorced, broke, and depressed with a teenager, three middle school kids, and a preschooler to raise on my own—that I was able to begin pursuing my dream.

I grew up in Minneapolis, MN. Like so many young people, I thought my city was the most boring place on earth and couldn't wait to move to a more exciting place. My opportunity came in a most unexpected way, after I gave birth to my eldest son at the age of sixteen. Because my mother and stepfather disapproved, I had no choice but to place my baby in foster care. Shortly after I was awarded custody, I packed my little son up and took off eastward, to try to start anew in my father's home.

After about a year, I gave in to the feeling that I was an outsider in both my mother's and my father's homes. I left Dad's New England town and moved to Boston in search of art and community. There I became involved in the Black Power movement and married a man I met while involved in a fashion show that featured afrocentric fashions and hair styles. He played trumpet with the jazz group that provided musical accompaniment and I coordinated the models and the fashions.

With him, I endured a level of violence that I did not know was possible. People who have not had to deal with physical or emotional battering often question why a woman stays with a man who abuses her. I can only speak for myself. I was trained to believe that, because I was different from most of the people in my family—darker skin and penetrating eyes which may or may not have been the result of having been born with a veil—I did not deserve to be treated well. Add to that, my father married a white woman after he and my mother divorced. It took me a lot of years to even begin to overcome the belief that I was not good enough for my mother or my first love, my daddy, and therefore could not expect to attract a good man.

Ten years and four kids later, I finally discovered that my kids and I deserved better. The journey, which was subtle but very healing, included writing poems and journaling. The result was that, once again, I packed up my kids and came back home to Minneapolis, which I discovered had become a mecca of art and culture in the midwest while I was away. The Guthrie Theater and the all-black Penumbra Theater had emerged, the phenomena of the *Mary Tyler Moore Show* and The Artist Known as Prince had occurred, and a number of organizations had sprung up to serve artists of all disciplines.

I was proud of myself for having found the courage to strike out on my own, not knowing how the kids and I would survive. But the initial euphoria soon wore off, replaced by the realization that I was in a severe funk, completely traumatized from those ten years of

CAROLYN L. HOLBROOK

insanity. Many mornings I struggled to pull myself out of bed to get my children ready for school. As soon as their school buses rolled away from the corner, I would lie on the floor, curled up in the fetal position, where I would stay all day until an inner sensor let me know it was time for them to come home. Then I would get up and plaster a smile on my face, genuinely happy that each of them had made it home safely.

Eventually I started to come out of the depression and decided to take some writing courses. To my dismay, I found out that artistic opportunities for a low-income single black mother were scarce back then. I decided to find a part-time job to help pay for classes, but quickly learned that I was not mentally healthy enough yet to join the workforce or to participate in college courses, even though I was fully eligible for financial aid. I started taking long walks while the kids were at school and slowly, between journaling and visits to a therapist, I began to heal.

One day, during a rare burst of energy, I decided to make use of the excellent secretarial skills I had acquired in high school. I rented a typewriter and put an ad in the University of Minnesota's newspaper that I was available to type papers, theses and dissertations. I then taught my kids how to type, proofread, and answer the phone properly, and we were in business. I also asked Lawrence Hutera, the director of the community center where my kids played every day, if he would be willing to add creative writing classes to the activities he offered there. He responded by putting the onus on me to create my own opportunity. "If you can find someone to teach a class," he said, "I will support you."

One day my son Julian came home from school and told me that a writer was visiting his fifth grade class that week. He had overheard her telling his teacher that she needed someone to type her poetry manuscript, and my sweet son referred her to me. A week later, when the poet brought her manuscript over, I asked if she would be willing to teach a class in our neighborhood community center. She agreed, and true to his promise, Lawrence allowed me to offer the class. He taught me how to write a press release advertising the six-week session, then sent it out to his extensive media list. He and I were both surprised that people from all over the Twin Cities showed up on the first night.

The success of the first six-week class inspired the poet to introduce me to more writers experienced in teaching poetry, fiction, creative nonfiction, journaling and playwriting. Before I knew it, and with no formal training in arts administration, I had created a first-rate writing program. The best part was that I was able to take all of the classes I offered to the public at low cost to participants, and no cost to me.

During the first year of the program, one of the classes that interested me focused on creating video poems. Students would spend the first few weeks writing and revising a poem and the second half of the class would be spent in various locations around the city creating videos of those poems. A young white woman whom I will call Gretel wrote a poem about rollerskating through a graveyard. Everyone in the seven-member class, including the instructor, was intrigued by the idea, and there was plenty of nervous laughter as class members threw words like "spooky," "macabre" and "eerie" around the room the night we discussed shots that might work well for Gretel's poem. At the end of the evening, we agreed to meet Sunday morning at the entrance of Lakewood Cemetery, where prominent Minnesotans such as members of the Pillsbury, Gold Medal and General Mills families, Vice President Hubert H. Humphrey, and now, Senator Paul Wellstone, are buried.

From the moment the decision was made, I felt disturbed, unable to come to grips with the thought that I might be complicit in the group's violation of the spirits of the deceased who lay peacefully in their graves. What right did we have to disturb them just because a callow young woman wanted to see herself on videotape skating through their resting place? And what about the mourners scattered throughout the cemetery? How would they feel when Gretel skated by with the rest of us walking closely behind her, gawking while they prayed for their lost loved ones or placed flowers on their graves? Would the instructor and I, the only blacks in the group, stick out like two flies in a glass of milk?

By the time I arrived on Sunday morning, Gretel had finished lacing up her skates and was about to lead the group into the enormous cemetery. I lagged slightly behind the class members, who strolled along as Gretel skated past curved, tree-lined paths and rows of granite plaques and headstones, large statues and imposing crypts as big as houses. The tall woman with shaggy white hair and a slight limp halted every few steps, appearing to be taken with the scenery and the powerful energy the place seemed to exude. And it was fascinating the see how the sun illuminated the golden highlights in the thirty-something man in tight leather pants' black and blonde striped mohawk. I was moved when I observed the young married couple who were taking the class together touch each other's hands affectionately when they slowed down to read the names of the dead and their dates of birth and death. No doubt they were contemplating a time when death might separate the two of them.

Gretel mugged for the camera, impressing us with her knowledge as she named birds that flew by and trees that were as twisted and bent as the people who lay in the graves they protected. The class members, usually quite vocal, were somber as they examined the elaborate monuments and pondered the messages written on both elegant tombstones and simple markers. Even without reading the dates, it was clear which graves had been there the longest. The older markers bore streaks of dark green, brown or black from having been exposed to the weather for many years.

Soon, Gretel took us down a narrow pathway that led to a thick cluster of trees bordered with pink, yellow and white azaleas. She stopped and turned to face the group, and said something was in there that was really interesting. She spun around and began skating slowly down the path, glancing back to make sure we were following.

I was the first to see the lovely, though weather-beaten, statue of a woman who looked like she had been carved by a sculptor in the Greco-Roman era. Her figure was draped in a gown, belted at the waist, allowing her skirt to fall gently over the pedestal on which she stood. Her right hand rested serenely over her heart, her left arm reached out in a gesture of peace. Her chiseled face was framed by long hair that was pulled back in a bun, and she gazed down at me with a soft smile. Her eyes, though devoid of color, appeared kind. She looked so real that it would have been hard to believe she was made of stone if not for the black streaks on her body that characterized the statues that had been there for a long time.

The class stood in a semi-circle and watched Gretel's eyes take on a ghoulish sparkle, which let us know that we were in for a joke. As the instructor's camera held her in focus, an impish grin spread slowly over her face. The group stood waiting, until finally the man with wavy blonde hair and goldrimmed glasses became impatient. "Well?" he asked. At that moment, Gretel's eyes grew wide. She turned and skated close to the statue. She lifted her arm and stuck out her finger in a gesture that reminded me of Michelangelo's *Creation* painting, God's finger almost touching the finger of man. Then, as suddenly as she lifted her arm, she snatched it back and said: "It's a statue of a black woman. If you touch her you'll die." Then, as though propelled by a tornadic wind, she skated away, leaving petals of laughter ringing in the air along with echoes of her words.

I was paralyzed, unable to respond. My breath halted as though a knife had been jabbed into my chest and slowly twisted into my heart.

I took another look at the woman locked in that dark body made of granite and, in my mind's eye, her shoulders began to slump from

CAROLYN L. HOLBROOK

carrying the weight of all that stone, to crumble from the burdens of overwork and underappreciation, from cooking and cleaning for the families of Gretel's ancestors while desperately trying to care for her family, the families of my ancestors. At that moment, I remembered every negative image I had ever heard of black women; *oversexed, breeder, wet nurse, mammy, hostile, nappy-headed ho.* Gretel's words named something I had felt vaguely all my life but could not describe with words of my own. Gretel's words made it clear that, in the eyes of the world, the black woman is poison: *"If you touch her you'll die."*

I have never been able to handle surprises very well. I couldn't gather my thoughts so I bore my shame, my anger and my humiliation in silence. I looked at each of my classmates and at the instructor, to try and gauge whether Gretel's words had affected them the way they had impacted me. No one else showed a reaction, not even the instructor, a black man. His silence was disappointing.

I can't blame Gretel. No doubt she was repeating what she'd heard all of her life. Truth is that throughout history, the black woman has had to fight the perception that her blackness makes her as venomous as a sting from the tongue of a poisonous asp— even as far back as Biblical times. In the *Song of Solomon,* one of the most beautiful love poems ever written, King Solomon's Shulamite bride has the misfortune of having to implore the daughters of Jerusalem not to look down on her. She says in defense of herself, "I am black, but comely." Unfortunately, we are still struggling with this perception.

I have three beautiful, intelligent daughters. I have had to help them maintain their self image over and over again, even as I attempt to heal my own self image. The day after my middle daughter, Tania, received her letter of acceptance to an Ivy League college, she left for school excited to show it to the African-American male counselor who had encouraged her to apply. To my dismay, when she came home, shoulders slumped, she tearfully related what happened. When the counselor proudly told his colleagues that she would be the first black girl from her high school to attend Vassar, none of the teachers or counselors showed any enthusiasm. One white female counselor started what turned into a chain reaction of discouragement, telling Tania that she was out of her league. When the news reached students, her black female peers, locked in their own minds and bodies, could not imagine that they, too, might be as capable as she. They insisted that Tania couldn't have gotten into a prestigious college because she deserved to be there. "They just let you in cuz you're black and they wanna look good," they asserted. Lord knows I understand the horror of what is happening to our young men, I have a son who is doing time in the federal penitentiary. But there seems to be a conspiracy of silence around our women. Could this be that, for the most part, our incarceration is invisible? That we are locked up in our bodies?

It took days and days of constant encouragement from me to help my daughter start to believe in herself again. Like countless black mothers, I have worked hard to train my daughters to be proud of who they are. The world would have them be ashamed of their darkness. For black women, loving ourselves and passing that self-love down to our daughters and our granddaughters is a difficult task. Centuries of negation often makes us feel like we need to adopt a hard, protective shell, which is either praised as strength or dismissed as hostility. In short, we turn ourselves into stone.

I left the cemetery that day wondering what it would take to liberate us. And today, as I see my four granddaughters move through a world where some are attempting to envelope America's first black First Lady in a tough cast, I have to ask again. What is it that will set us free?

CAROLYN L. HOLBROOK

MY DAUGHTER, MY SELF
by Anne Beatts

There is one black body in particular that I have come to know as
well or better than my own somewhat tarnished white one. As of
today it weighs fifty-two pounds and measures forty-five inches tall.
It belongs to my six-year-old daughter and I have it memorized. I
know every lump, bump and scraped elbow on it from toes to nose.
To me it is perfect in every way.

I never tire of looking at my daughter's body, naked or clothed,
and when, inevitably, she no longer chooses to share it with me
with such loving exuberance, I will feel the pain of separation. For
now, I greet her cries of "Mommy, wipe me," with merely feigned
reluctance, and her "power hugs" with heart-pounding joy. Ours is
a very physical relationship. We snuggle, we cuddle, we hold hands,
we squeeze hand signals for "I love you." I hold her when she cries,
I kiss her boo-boos to make it better, I rub her back so she can fall
asleep. We never part without a hug and kiss.

But sometimes she hits me. Hard. Meaning to hurt. She hits
and won't stop hitting unless she's physically restrained. These bat-
tles end badly, in tears, with her needing to be comforted by the
same person she's been lashing out against—her mom. The same
mom she makes handprint Valentines for and tells she loves
twenty times a day: me.

It's an ongoing struggle for both of us to get past her rage—and
the answering anger that being hit without being able to hit back
awakens in me—and return to our normal baseline of loving companionship. It takes all our emotional resources, plus therapy, plus
every trick I can think of or that anyone suggests to me. Distrac-
tion, mirroring, reward charts, taking away privileges, hitting

175

pillows, drawing pictures of her feelings—all of these work some of the time. None of them work all of the time.

But slowly, as she grows older, the hitting is happening less frequently, and when it does happen, she is able to let go of her anger sooner. So I am cautiously optimistic that we will survive this and that she won't be hitting me on her wedding day, which I hope I live to see.

Why is she so angry? Because throughout her short life people, starting with her Latino birth mother and African-American father, have neglected and abandoned her. Because until she came to live with me, she was in three different foster homes before she was three. I can hardly imagine it, yet this compact little package of fierce emotions, sharp intelligence, and tender vulnerability that I find so precious was rejected over and over. So her sturdy little body fills with rage, and hitting is the only way she can get it out. And there I am, a white woman being hit by a strong black woman-child. What a reversal of stereotypes! Revenge for all those loving mammies abused by the little white missus.

But it's not so easy. For now, I am convinced that her anger is color-blind. When she hits me, I am a stand-in for everyone who ever left her, black, white, or brown. And in that moment she is sure that I will leave her too, eventually. But no way is she waiting around for that another time. So she tries to take control by making sure it happens. My job is to convince her it won't. That's not easy either.

And I wonder . . . will there be a moment when her rage coalesces with the rage of the black community? Will someday she look at me with hatred across a racial divide? Will I become not just a bitch, but the white bitch who deracinated her and separated her from her culture? Maybe. Every teenage girl needs a reason to hate her mother, and she has some ready-made ones near at hand. So I am bracing myself to get past those hits too.

Whether or not I am harboring a mini Angela Davis in training, there may be trouble ahead. Especially since her stated ambition at the age of three was to drink wine, have big boobies, and ride a motorcycle by the time she was fourteen, a number she luckily considers nearly unattainable. On the other hand, maybe I shouldn't take this too seriously, as she also wants to be a veterinarian, a crossing guard, and a rock star. Some kids have imaginary friends—she has an imaginary roadie. His name is Kevin. After all, we live in LA. To add weight to the side of veterinary medicine, I am getting her a turtle, and have promised a dog sometime in the vague, motorcycle-riding future. We already have three cats. Her ambition to be a crossing guard I have chosen to ignore.

Meanwhile, here in West Hollywood, we go around in a bubble, in one of the bluest parts of a deep blue state, where "diversity" is a stated goal, and her kindergarten couldn't hold its graduation in the park because it was reserved for gay weddings. Here we are, white single mom and her black daughter, and no eyebrows are raised, no prejudice, if it exists, overtly expressed. The only inadvertently racist remark I have encountered came from a close friend who said, amazed, "She's really . . . *smart*."

And then there are those times in a crowd when people look around, concerned, and say, "But who is she *with?*"

"With me," I say, bringing up the rear with my load of essential items that she has handed me—her water, her blankie, her Spongebob ring-pop. "She's with me." It seems to be my job to follow behind her with baggage as she travels away from me into her happily-anticipated future, looking round only occasionally to check that I'm still there. Another ironic role for Miss Anne.

When I originally told a friend, another adoptive mother, that statistics indicated I would probably end up adopting a black child if I went through foster care, my friend raised an immediate objection, "But then nobody will think she's your daughter."

"Sure they will," I said. "They'll just assume I fucked a black man." I didn't realize that by the time I got my daughter, they would think

I was her grandmother and assume that her absent mother was the one who fucked a black man. "Are you the grandmother?" people ask me. She reacts to this with an impatient "She's my *mom!*"

"Why do they keep asking if you're my grandmother?" she says.

"Well, sweetie, I am older than most of your friends' moms," I say. "Make that all of them," I add to myself under my breath. "And, honey, also I'm white and you're brown, so they think that I can't be your mom and I must be your grandmother."

Once, some Japanese tourists in the lift line in Big Bear asked me if she was my grandson, despite her leopard-skin parka, pink earmuffs and mitts, and coordinating leopard-and-pink boots. But maybe I can chalk that up to the language barrier, or differing fashion standards in Japan.

I didn't set out to acquire that modern fashion accessory, a child with contrasting skin color. I applied to be a foster parent as part of the "fost-adopt" program, in which foster children unlikely to be reunited with their birth parents can be adopted out of foster care. In order to qualify, I had to lay bare my life to the scrutiny of social workers, outfit my home with a variety of childproof locks which it took my daughter roughly two minutes to learn how to open, and take a staggering number of hours of parenting courses, none of which truly prepared me for the reality of parenthood. I didn't specify a racial preference, I just said human.

But I knew that the pool of available foster children in California was predominantly black and brown. Just to give a perspective on race in America, the whites, light-skinned Latinos, and Asians get chosen first. And in a reversal of the Chinese practice, girls are more in demand than boys. My daughter is both black and brown. Her skin is a caffe latte in winter, much darker in summer. She has what some black people I've known call "good" hair, curly but not kinky. But in back, she's black. Her little behind juts out just like a picture in "National Geographic." I call it her cutie booty.

Once, she said she wanted to be white, not brown. I said that

ANNE BEATTS

was funny because I wished I was brown like her, that's why I got tan in the summer. I always tell her I love her beautiful brown skin. I took her to *Dreamgirls*. I never sing the praises of blond hair and blue eyes. Nonetheless, her favorite pop star is the very white, very blonde Gwen Stefani, of whom she once said, "Sometimes she sings like a black girl, but I know that she's not." I hope it's just the flip side of my once intense desire to be Joan Baez.

When she was placed with me, until she was adopted, I had an out. If the placement didn't work out, I had the option of having it "disrupted." In other words, she came with her own return policy, one the prospective adoptive parents before me had chosen to exercise when she hit and bit and didn't fit in with the picture of what they wanted, a matched set of fake girl and boy twins. The boy, whom they had since infancy, got to stay. She got to leave with me, a near stranger, amidst a lot of bright enthusiasm from the social workers: "Here's your new mom!" How brave she was!

After she was with me for two days, I would have lit out for the territories of Canada or Mexico rather than give her back. Meanwhile she had nightmares where monsters came to take her away. When I asked her what the monsters looked like, she said "old ladies." Well, when you're two, social workers do look like old ladies. We put up signs that said "Monsters stay out!" The social workers who visited weekly never knew the signs were for them.

When she was smaller, people would ask me, "Where is she from?" "Riverside, California," I'd say. "But where is she *from*?" they'd insist, expecting to hear "Sri Lanka," or some other new exotic destination where infertile white women could go to buy babies. "Does she speak English?" was another way of asking the same thing. "Incessantly," I'd reply. "But is she *American*?" they'd ask, still unable to accept the concept that I had not gone baby-shopping overseas but instead had chosen to think globally, act locally. "All-American," I'd say. "Half African American, half Mexican American."

However, according to the Department of Children and Family Services, my daughter is classified as African American. Bi-racial isn't a category on their forms. I am not sure why—could it be the persistence of that "one drop of black blood" theory of miscegenation? Even the Los Angeles Unified School District compels us to choose, though I jump at "other" on forms wherever I see it. Because being mixed is her truth, and also her beauty—apparently when races mix, the strongest genes from each side join forces. It's the genetic opposite of inbreeding, downfall of the Hatfields, McCoys, and Hapsburgs. Another sock in the eye for the Fuhrer.

This could account for all the beautiful, powerful bi-racial people in America today, one of whom is now President. My daughter identifies with him. "I know you like Hillary, mom," she told me confidentially toward the end of the 2008 primaries. "But I'm for Obama." It was a bittersweet moment when I showed her his picture on the cover of "People." "Who's that?" I said. "My dad?" she asked.

She knows she had two parents, and she even knows their names, names I can't reveal here. Does she remember them? Perhaps only viscerally. I've told her the simplest version of her past I can muster, that her parents were young and unable to care for her, that she needed a mom and that I needed a little girl of my own. When she asks where her birth parents are now, I tell her the truth, which is that we don't know. Will she ever see them again? she asks. "Maybe when you're older," is my all-purpose answer.

Recently she asked if we could visit the place where she was born. I know she hopes to find her mom there. Sometimes she says, "I bet my real mom would let me do that"—get a dog now, go swimming by herself, eat all the candy before dinner. I say, "I am your real mom. Your real mom is the one who loves you and takes care of you forever, and that's me." But I'd be lying if I said it doesn't hurt.

"But why are you white and I'm brown?" was one of the first questions she asked, while lying on my tummy in the bathtub, a tummy she now knows she did not come out of. There's no really good answer, other than the existential one—that's just the way we are. We are different from each other, as all children are different from their parents. Our difference is just more visible. She will never be the little me that I once thought I wanted, and maybe we are both lucky to have such obvious evidence of it.

That's something else people say to me, "She is *so* lucky." They mean lucky to be lifted out of poverty and neglect, lucky to be given an immediate pass to a mainly white world of comparative privilege and affluence. And of course, they're right, she is lucky. Nothing in the limited information I have about her birth parents suggests that she would be the brilliant, funny, musically and mathematically talented, highly verbal, artistic, imaginative, physically well-coordinated, healthy, strong, gorgeous individual that she is today.

Given love and attention, and security, she has flourished and bloomed, like a Japanese paper flower in a glass of water. It makes me wonder how many children like her are out there, never reaching their full potential, never getting their lucky chance to bloom. Maybe her parents were children like that. I don't know. I do know that at any given time there are over 60,000 foster children available for adoption in the state of California alone. There's a saying among adoptive parents: "You may not get the child of your body, but you get the child of your heart." Somehow my daughter and I found each other. "We are both *so* lucky," I say.

THE NEW MATH
by Werner Disse

I moved with my family from Northern California to South Africa in October, 1972. I had just turned thirteen. My father, an anesthesiologist, had accepted a teaching position at the University of Cape Town's medical school. There he would be working with Christian Barnard, the first surgeon to perform a heart transplant. My parents, my older sister and I were going to Africa!

Africa promised adventure. The first humans lived in Africa; Charles Darwin wrote that all of us have African ancestors. The nature shows on TV were full of lions and rhinoceroses and giraffes and elephants roaming majestically. There were also jungles and rivers and people in loincloths. Africa was ancient and exotic. Mystery would be my new home.

I remember looking at a globe and realizing South Africa was about as far as I could get from California. While that added to the allure, it also meant twenty-four hours in an airplane. By the time I was walking through Cape Town's airport, my ears were ringing. Everybody seemed to be wearing brown or white. People spoke English with either a British or Dutch accent. But the air smelled the same. I was scared as hell when we began driving on the left side of the street. I quickly noticed the cars on the right side were traveling in the opposite direction. I finally relaxed when I saw, shimmering in intensely bright light, an imposing mountain shaped like a table and, next to it, a mountain shaped like a lion lying down. It was magic: when I began the trip it was fall, and a day later it was spring.

We lived in an apartment complex that had guards. They wore khaki uniforms. Though they never initiated a conversation, they enjoyed having one. They always seemed easygoing. They weren't armed, but they kept watch. I thought they were black. In California I had learned that if anybody in your family tree was black, you were black. So it was possible to be mainly white, yet black. Whenever somebody had explained that to me I would feel puzzled, like when I watched a magician pull a rabbit out of an empty hat. I had the uneasy sensation that somebody was putting one over on me.

The guards were actually nonwhite. That was the essential distinction in South Africa: you were white or you were not. Actually, it was no different than what I had learned growing up, only the words were different. "Black" in California meant the same as "nonwhite" in South Africa. Maybe this was some universal truth that could cross continents.

It didn't make any sense to me. If I reduced it to an equation and showed it to my math teacher, he would flunk me. Imagine the following math test: X is white people and Y is black people; what does X times Y equal? In South Africa the answer would be nonX. In California the answer would be Y. It must be "the new math."

The guards intrigued me because they all had very large, sometimes massive, wives and girlfriends. Where I grew up, a slender look was prized in women. Dessert was a source of calories, not pleasure. Love handles were hated. So I didn't understand the guards' taste in women. I asked my favorite guard about it. He smiled, he always smiled, and replied wistfully, *Large women are so cuddly.*

Outside the city I did not see black people, except a few maids, guards and gardeners. This did not strike me as a big deal because in California I also rarely saw black people. There had been none in my school, and we'd had no black neighbors. Ok, that was California, but I was in Africa. Where were they hiding all the black people?

They live separately from white people, my father explained. I asked why. *Blacks are lazy and dirty.* I didn't share that thought. We were no different. I hated to clean my room and mom had to clean up after all of us. A few days later we drove past a huge expanse of shacks made of corrugated iron. The place was filthy. Smoke from burned-out fires hung like pockets of unnatural fog. I asked if that was the dump. My father smiled triumphantly. *That's a shanty-town—where black people live. See, I told you.*

He continued: *There's another reason we want blacks to live separately. They're violent. They're the only people that kill themselves.* I told my father that in all the documentaries I'd seen with him, World War I was white people killing white people. They'd line up opposite each other and start shooting like target practice. And World War II was the same. Well, maybe not Japan. My father sighed so strongly his bangs fluttered. *You're too young to understand,* he said.

Before I could show up at school I had to buy school uniforms, which consisted of khaki knee socks, khaki shorts, a khaki shirt, a blue school tie and a blue blazer with the school's insignia on the front pocket. As if this weren't sartorially festive enough, there was also a straw boater hat I was told I would have to wear outside of school grounds and tip towards any adult I recognized. I thought my parents were joking, but then I realized even they couldn't make this up.

On the drive to my first day of school I kept fretting about how uncool I looked in shorts. I mean, nobody in my previous school would have been caught dead in shorts. And the knee socks didn't help. As I got out of the car, I saw masses of boys wearing shorts. I spotted a teacher wearing khaki shorts, knee socks and a matching khaki blazer. I asked a boy if the teachers also had a dress code. *No, that's a safari suit. A lot of businessmen wear them to work.* I laughed until I realized he was serious, and then I laughed some more. At least there were no girls to see me. The schools in South Africa were single gender.

At lunchtime I went to the dining room, which looked like the dining room at Hogwarts, except it was smaller and there were only twelve to a table. The teachers ate at the far end of the room. They looked down on us from a table on an elevated platform. A nonwhite man handed a huge bowl of food to the guy next to me, who helped himself and then passed the bowl in the other direction. When the bowl finally reached me it was empty. I spotted an abundance of food at the teacher's buffet so I walked up to the head teacher, the housemaster, explained my predicament and asked him if I could have some of their food. He winced as if I was asking permission to sleep with his wife and said simply: *No*. Then he turned away and went back to filling his mouth.

I walked sheepishly back to my table. The boys screeched with laughter. They thought I had gone up there as a joke "to take the micky" out of the teachers. *No, this is serious*, I assured them. *I'm starving and they have tons of food.* That really cracked them up; I was a prankster. They proceeded to imitate my accent. More hilarity.

Except for the occasional accent mocking, school was pretty good. My classmates were friendly and fun. One had even used his body to shield me when an older boy had become incensed because I had called him by his nickname. What a difference from the sometimes relentless taunting of my previous classmates. They would yell or hiss that I was a Nazi because my parents are German. I remember asking a kid why he called me a Nazi when I was born in America ages, a whole fifteen years, after World War II had ended. He was entirely unfazed by my question: *Ya fuckin' Nazi.*

Once when I was eight I was waiting to be picked up from school. While sitting on the curb, I looked up and saw three teenage boys approach. They seemed to be in a hurry, probably late for baseball. I was stunned when they came within a few feet, but did not stop. I felt their rage before they even touched me. Two of them pinned my shoulders to the ground. Then all three began spitting in my face. *Nazi scumbag. Nazi piece of shit.* I was so befuddled that my whole world crumbled. I started to cry as their saliva, invective and loathing, kept slamming into me. I had no idea how long it lasted. I was such a sobbing mess I didn't even notice when they went away. I couldn't understand why they hated me. I couldn't understand why they hated me so much.

Before first period, my classroom in Cape Town was fertile ground for practical jokes. One day when I walked in I saw my classmates huddled around the window. On closer inspection, they were looking out the window and hiding at the same time. For the life of me, I couldn't understand the joke. I followed their line of vision, which was directed at the housemaster's office window on the other side of the courtyard. One of our friends was in the office. He bent over in front of the housemaster, who raised the cane in his hand and whipped my friend's ass. Four times in ferocious succession. *He's lucky*, a boy remarked. *Huh?* I asked. *He could've gotten six,* another boy responded. Like beauty, I thought, luck is in the eye of the beholder. I asked what our friend had done. *He talked back to a teacher.*

It was beginning to dawn on me that many things were not as I was told. "The Star Spangled Banner" sang of the land of the free; but wasn't that also where I was assaulted for being something I wasn't? My teachers in Cape Town were supposedly caretakers of my welfare; but didn't they let me go hungry rather than share food they would never miss? The school discipline was touted as tough love; but wasn't caning my friend for speaking what he believed really about fear?

I was only thirteen, so what did I know? I needed truth; in fact, I depended on it. As I was confused, I leaned on old reliable: obey authorities because they know best. Didn't they?

My father was driving me back from school when we stopped at a light. A nonwhite man in his fifties with hair more salt than pepper was selling newspapers at an intersection. He approached my window and asked me if I wanted to buy one. I shook my head. To my discomfort, the man wouldn't go away. *Please,* he said. I froze. He bent over so that his head was at my level. *Please buy a newspaper,* he said, his voice now even more desperate. The light changed and my father drove off. *You ok?* my father asked. *That's why we keep our windows up.* My father thought my shock was about safety. Actually, I was blown away that a mature man, older than my father, was begging me—me, a kid, the prankster—for a few cents.

I turned and observed the newspaper salesman through the rear window. He had retreated dejectedly to the sidewalk. A bull terrier was barking at him with the fierceness of a Rottweiler, yet he didn't react. He just stood there. His slumped chest made him seem frail.

I'd always sensed deep down that the status quo was wrong, but at that moment it became clear. The man's tormented eyes haunted me. Dread and despair resonated in my bones. I knew nobody deserved that. Nobody.

One day in math class we were studying Venn diagrams, which illustrate logical relationships between groups. The teacher drew two overlapping circles on the chalkboard. I yawned. The overlapping portion was called the "intersection." I'd never dealt with circles in my life. Suddenly, something clicked. This was my opportunity to find relevance. My teacher's favorite saying was that mathematics was the "paragon of truth." This was my opportunity to explore truth. I raised my hand.

I said, *If you look at the intersection, sir, it belongs to both circles, right?* The teacher nodded. *If you take any point in the intersection, then you could never say that point belonged to only one circle.* The teacher grunted. I pressed on: *Let's say the circle on the left is white people, and the circle on the right is black people. Then how can we say the people in the intersection are nonwhite?*

The teacher said kindly, *That's about the sophistry of politics, not the truth of mathematics.*

I asked, *But why isn't it? We get caned when we don't tell the truth.* The teacher smiled with compassionate pity.

I left South Africa after high school, but that smile remains in my vision. I see it everywhere in America: so what if it doesn't add up, grow up. Well, I'm almost three times older now and it still matters to me. How can we have meaningful discussions about race when our descriptions of race defy common sense?

I'm perplexed that my country continues to have the same racial definitions as those of apartheid-South Africa and slavery-America. Their original intent was to bolster racism, not reflect truth. Besides, how can anybody pretend African Americans are outside the white circle? Today, for many reasons, most American "blacks" are part white.

Of course, though nobody talks about it, the situation is much simpler than we realize. We don't need to concern ourselves with the "intersection" because it doesn't exist. As the first humans were African, there is only one circle: the black circle. We're all part of the same circle. Now *that's* "the new math."

WHAT YOU SEE IS WHAT YOU GET

by Hill Harper

Is it?

When it comes to the black body, especially the black male body, more often than not the images we've been force-fed have no bearing at all on reality. The danger in this is the high level of influence these images have on our perceptions, our expectations, and our prejudices. Simply put: people are inclined to believe that what they see is what exists.

Take a moment to think about it—the black male body, that is. What's the first thing that comes to mind? Probably not the most flattering or politically correct image, huh? You're not alone. A lot of us stumble over stereotypes before our mind's eye finally settles on an image that's more wholesome, more human. That's the damage that decades, if not centuries, of very specific and very destructive images—pimps, murderers, rapists, thieves, thugs, hustlers, junkies, drunks—will do. No matter how much you deny or dismiss it all, eventually it does seep in.

Thankfully, times are changing. This year may very well represent the emergence of multiple alternative images of the black male body. The election of the forty-fourth president, Barack Obama, and the formation of his new administration, has everything to do with it. It completely flips the script. Quiet as it's been kept, black men who are intelligent and hardworking and family-oriented and educated and successful have always existed; they just weren't visible. Mainstream media kept them skillfully hidden in the shadows of their more menacing counterparts.

So, what is the real significance of being able to see them now?

What impact will that have on our day-to-day lives, on the way we think about and treat each other, or on the way we think about and treat ourselves?

I'm not sure there are any quick and proven answers to those questions; at least, not yet. Even so, it's fascinating to discuss and take note of the many ways in which the black male image is currently being redefined not only in this society, but all over the world. This, for me and for most black men, I'm sure, is good news.

The onslaught of negative images of the black male form has always been troubling to me. The fact that I'm an actor and I work in an industry that manufactures—and, often enough, manipulates—images probably makes me a bit more observant, more sensitive about it. But the truth is that long before I decided to become an actor, while I was still in my youth, I became acutely aware of the black male body, of the images around me and the messages they were sending to me about my supposed possibilities—and limitations.

My older brother and I were raised by my divorced father, so there were three males in our home. My father, a psychiatrist and an entrepreneur, was a hard worker, a driven man who wanted nothing but the best for his family. He took a lot of risks with different careers and different projects in an effort to be what he considered successful. A number of those ventures worked, but a fair number also turned out to be complete disasters, economic failures. My father's was the first and most powerful image of the black male body that I had in my life.

Success was important to my father; it was something he desperately wanted. Everything about him and his actions was geared toward attaining and announcing his definition of success—even his wardrobe. Or maybe I should say *especially* his wardrobe. He was somewhat of a flashy guy. He wore a good amount of jewelry and drove flashy cars. He wore a tie everyday but he had jewelry underneath, and when he had his shirt open you could see lots of chains. My father was always impeccably dressed in the finest Italian suits; the finest everything, actually. He wanted the best of the best. To him, there was no such thing as flying under the radar. He wanted people to know he was there; he was present; he was successful.

Whether you want to say that it was a point of pride, of not being afraid to let people know you've got it, or that it was borne out of insecurity, of needing people to think you've got it, the image of the black male body that was introduced to me by my father is one that I've encountered often in my life. In fact, it's the entire focal point of the bling culture. And yes, part of it does have to do with our own insecurities, with our need to let people know that we have money, that we are successful.

With women it's all about big Gucci and Louis Vuitton purses, Jimmy Choo shoes and other things that are outward symbols of privilege, wealth and success. That's what the big chains are all about, getting it—something to announce our presence, our success. We created big chains that we laced with diamonds as a way of basically saying, "I've got money." And we all know the importance of money in this society.

If you're a brother with jeans and a tee-shirt, that doesn't say anything; if you're a brother with jeans and a tee-shirt and a $500,000 diamond necklace, now that says something. Especially if the person it's speaking to is a member of the opposite sex. So it's not just about insecurity; it's also about attraction, being a peacock and fanning your feathers, something that's customarily done by the male members of various species in the animal kingdom.

I was blessed to learn very early in my development that there are many different definitions of success and many different ways to negotiate the outward expression of one's success. That's because I had various images of the black manhood available to me. In addition to my father, I had my two grandfathers. My paternal grandfather was a physician; my maternal grandfather was a pharmacist. They were committed, educated, thoughtful, giving and hardworking. They were nothing at all like the black men I saw on television and at the movies.

I used to wonder who those men I saw on the television and at the movies were. They were so beyond anything I'd ever encountered. And I used to also wonder why people like my father and my grandfathers were so rarely portrayed. What was it about them that made them unworthy of being shown on television or plastered across a cinema screen? Because my family was steeped in the concept of community, my world was populated by more than just my brother and those three men, so it wasn't all that hard for me to figure out that they were not anomalies. What I didn't understand was why the public was being made to believe they were.

When I embarked on a career as an actor, I decided to make a clear distinction about what types of projects I would and would not participate in. Because I had been studying and attempting to dissect media images of black men my whole life, I had come to the realization that it was less about the individual role than it was about the entire project. Not every role can be that of a good guy; that's just not how the world is. Actors should be able to play a whole host of characters.

The important consideration for me has always been the message of the overall project. Is it celebrating a degenerative image of the black male? Or of black folks in general? If so, I don't want to play a part in it. And I fully understand that I might be much wealthier and much more famous than I am now if I had accepted a number of the roles that have been offered to me over my career. I don't blame the people who ultimately took those roles because everybody makes decision about what they do for a number of personal reasons—which they don't need to justify or defend to me. I only know that it's not for me.

Let me give you an example of what I mean about the role

versus the overall project. I chose to do *In Too Deep*, a Miramax film with LL Cool J, Omar Epps and Nia Long. The role I was offered was that of a drug dealer; I think everyone would agree that it's not an especially positive portrayal of a black man. But it's a character, and I enjoy playing characters, which is why I became an actor.

But before I say yes to any role, I look past the character and ask, what is this *film* saying to its viewers? Is it applauding a negative act? Is it promoting the disrespect and abuse of women? Is it implying that there is no down side, no price to pay wrongdoing? Is it broadcasting that: it's fine to deal drugs and cripple your entire community; call the women in your life Bs and Hs; father children you have no intention of supporting, emotionally or financially? I can tell you right now that if *In Too Deep* had ended with me and LL Cool J in a hot tub with a bunch of beautiful girls, our glasses filled with Cristal, toasting and drinking to the pleasures and benefits of dealing drugs, I would not have said yes to the role.

It ends with the investigative officer (Omar Epps) catching us and putting us in prison. After that he rides off into the sunset with the girl (Nia Long). It's a very simplistic message. You'd be surprised how quickly and how deeply images and messages, no matter how complex or simplistic, sink in and stay in. That's why this emergence of alternative images in our community is so exciting.

Not long ago, but definitely before the pendulum started to swing the other way, a friend of mine pitched a story to a major production company. It was a story with a central character whom he'd fashioned after his mother—a strong, beautiful black woman, a lawyer and activist. The executive told my friend that he thought the character was unrealistic, that there was no way she could be a great woman, and strong and smart and professional—and a mother. Since there had been many such white women portrayed on television, it was clear that race was also a factor. It was, in the executive's mind, unrealistic for a black woman!

With Michelle Obama's image and accomplishments being

displayed and spoken about nearly every day, the entire world—including that executive—is now aware that black women can be dynamic, educated, professional, maternal and beautiful all at the same time. This seems like such matter-of-fact knowledge, like something that should never have been an issue of concern or question in the first place. But positive and realistic representations of black people are so rare that when Barack Obama was elected as president there were articles written in major newspapers about how cartoonists did not know how to draw our new president in a way that was non-offensive. From the looks of the cartoons that I've read, they're still trying to figure it out; but thankfully, they'll have plenty of time to do that.

America will also have the time and opportunity to become accustomed to a wide array of true-to-life images of black women and men, images that will hopefully undo some of the damage that past negative images of the black body have done. Whereas once upon a time black men were constantly being depicted as criminals, now the prevailing image of a black man interacting with the justice system will be that of US Attorney General Eric Holder, an African American man whose duty it is to enforce the laws of the land.

If the images around us are reflections of what we can be and are expected to be, then this era of change can't happen fast enough. Young African American men are suffering. The graduation rate of African American males in the public school system is well below 50 percent. Too often the public faces of black male success have been relegated to the entertainment and sports industries.

It's amazing that African American boys now know that they can actually grow up to become president. But that's a pretty lofty goal for most people, black or white, so it's important that the images our society consumes show the black body in all its forms of success and health and productivity. It's important that they provide young black men with something to which they can aspire—and achieve.

I'd love to see more images of people like James Stewart, who is the top Supercross rider; and Lewis Hamilton, the first black person to win the Formula One Racecar Driving Championship; and Richard D. Parsons, former CEO and former Chairman of the Board of AOL Time Warner; and Kenneth Chenault, the CEO of American Express; and Marcus Samuelson, one of the best and most renowned chefs in the country. The list could go on and on and on. And it should. Maybe if more of these images of excellence were available to us, then we could say to young black children, to white Americans, to the rest of the world that when it comes to African Americans, what you see on the screen, on the television, in magazines, and in newspapers really is what you get. Now wouldn't that be something?

THE RIGHT SIDE OF THE DIAL

by Kenny White

I wouldn't be so presumptuous as to call it a spiritual awakening, first off, because white, middle-class families from Jersey just didn't have those sorts of things. Miniature golf outings, yes, coffee and cake, sure, but spirituality was something for the Sunday set and there was no alarm clock loud enough to rouse it there in Fort Lee. Consequently, it wasn't long before I came to see that church-going and an actual connection to the incorporeal had very little to do with each other. My friend Pam once told me that as a child she found it confusing to have observed her father being devout and all-loving during the hour of mass, yet nearly blowing a gasket minutes later while noting the lack of driving skills in "these god damned morons" who were exiting the church parking lot.

It was more of a nuts and bolts approach in my house. Not much talk of heaven, hell, or retribution of any type. Our understanding of right and wrong would come in a different form. In the nursery, when I was being outfitted with all the dealer options, guilt must have come standard. And say what you will, the specter of eternal flames and pitchforks doesn't hold a candle to the idea that you may have been the cause of someone's disappointment. Despite, or due to, this emotional fail-safe, my parents had a very close relationship for a near sixty-year run, during which I'd only seen them fight for a total of ten minutes. At the '64 World's Fair. Some might call that feat nothing short of a miracle, but again, that would be treading in those "other" waters. So I chalked it up to good management.

The World's Fair was out in Queens, right next to the new Shea

Stadium. The fourth and latest team of NY baseball legend, when the Mets began they were as hapless a franchise to ever play the sport. It would be another five years before they'd so dramatically bust out of mediocrity, but for now, the focus was on the fairgrounds next door, where pavilions sponsored by companies like General Electric, Bell Telephone, and General Motors were giving us exclusive glimpses into the future. These were glimpses that would not, as it turned out, become our future. The most glaring example, of course, being the "picture phone" . . .

Yes folks, within the next three to five years, every family in America will be seeing each and every person that calls them with glorious detail and clarity . . .

I suppose our obsession with vanity and privacy put the kibosh on that one. Imagine having to dress and comb your hair each time you wanted to make a *phone call!* And never mind that, how was I ever going to pull off the "is your refrigerator running" routine again? I knew this was a bad idea. The other erroneous assumption these companies were making (and this one was avoidable, as they had only to look at the clumps of tourists waiting in hour-long lines to get into these very exhibits) was that it was not now, nor would it ever become, a small world, after all.

It was decided during our parents' short, and ultimately benign skirmish, that my brother and I would have to choose Dad, if it came to that, since he did have the Bonneville and we'd still need to get around. Fortunately, the volume of kids' whispering is often louder than they intend it to be, so our pragmatism helped throw some cold water onto the argument and, just like that, it was over. Like they'd only been test driving those little-used vocal chords. You buy the extra horsepower but rarely can you find the road to open it up. You just like to know it's there if you need it. We sure knew that our neighbors had it. To many of them, it was the quiet moments that needed to be test ridden: *"Whatsa matter, you're not yellin'... somethin' wrong???"* So, argument over, it was time for another trip to the Belgian Waffle stand. We were all quite taken with this brand new slant on the old breakfast staple.

Since the word *divorce* was an unknown one in our family, it caught my ear when I one day heard my mother mention that the only person she'd ever leave my dad for was Harry Belafonte. I'm not sure to whom the comment was directed—it may have been the wall, for all I know. I knew that both my grandfathers' names had been Harry, like his, but besides that, I knew nothing else about the guy. So I checked out the album that had lately been in heavy rotation on our turntable. Big, bright red cover with a big, sculpted, pretty face on it. Harry Belafonte, "Calypso." Hmm, he didn't look one bit like the pictures of either grandfather Harry. Not only was he smiling . . . this guy was *black*. "Well, this is interesting . . ." As it was, being the only Jewish family in a square mile of Sicilians was enough spotlight for my low-profile lifestyle; having Harry Belafonte move in was just *not* going to be cool.

My parents' love survived Day-O. My musical foundation, however, did not. That these songs had such depth, such an immediate appeal, was clear. But the simplicity with which they were delivered was startling. I could see right into this Caribbean culture, with its syncopated beats as much implied as played. Yet oozing with movement. Suddenly the Pat Boone church of rhythm that I'd been attending would have to be brought up on charges: misleading the flock.

A very large door was cracking open for me. In my neighborhood, Vicky Carr's "It Must Be Him" came out windows of rooms with plastic-covered sofas, and Engelbert Humperdinck's "Lonely is a Man Without Love" filled kitchens where hot-off-the-boat nanas kept watch over pots of gravy on the day-long boil. But in my apartment, we were now discovering Miriam Makeba, in all her Zulu splendor.

The ornate outfits, lyrics formed by clicking the tongue, seductive poly-rhythms. I couldn't get enough. Figuring we'd soon be hearing our father plan his escape and eventual elopement to South Africa, we braced for the storm. *Pata Pata*, baby. Here we go again.

It was sex appeal. Defiant and irresistible . . . only I didn't yet recognize it, what with being just ten and all.

I'd been playing the piano for a few years already and was taken with guys like Peter Nero, Roger Williams, even Liberace. I didn't want to be them, I knew that. But I wouldn't have minded playing as confidently as they did. They'd play songs I knew, but would reshape them to fit their style. Fine, then. Just would have to keep practicing. Maybe a little less stickball, but do-able. The hair was another issue that I would have to someday address. Because if one of the requirements for success was to have all hairs neatly in place, as it seemed to be, I might as well have given up right then and there. Not with all the Dippity-do in the world.

Liberace also brought to the table some idiosyncrasies besides good hair that hadn't been included in my trainee handbook. My father, after watching Ray Charles on the Dinah Shore show one afternoon remarked, "Y'know, you're gonna need a gimmick in this business!"

"What, you don't think Ray Charles is blind?" I asked somewhat incredulously.

"Doesn't matter, it works. So does the name Garfunkel." I didn't like where this was going, but from then on I did come to notice just how many performers had already gotten this information. From Liberace's candelabra to Louis Armstrong's hankie, the world noticed and remembered. (To this day, I have to give Nelly props for having the most economically ingenious hook. I mean, really, a year's supply of band-aids would cost, what . . . 20 bucks?) Despite Dad's sagacious advice, I still seemed to be focused solely on the music. If I turned out to be a chump for that, well so be it.

One afternoon, I'm messing around in the living room, as I normally did after school. Listening to albums, practicing my rug-putting, whatever, as long as I didn't have to spend one extra second at school. That day *was* a little different, though, because of a new discovery. I had gotten an incubator and two fertilized eggs for Christmas that year from my Aunt Wilma. (Yeah, yeah I know . . . *Jews? Christmas?* Long story.) But the upshot is that the only chicken that did ultimately hatch in "30 days or your money back" survived long enough to have wriggled into one of our detachable stereo speakers and get stuck there for three days. Now what you should know is that from the moment my brother or I got home from school, until well into the evening, those speakers were *pumpin'*!

Anyway, the poor chick emerged days later looking like he'd been ridden hard and put away wet. Wobbly, disoriented, pissed off, but with the music in him . . . literally. I think he may have shown us some forgiveness in those few days before he succumbed to an acute case of chicken diarrhea. (I hope scientists are not finding any direct music/digestive tract links. Although, come to think of it, last week I heard a Barry Manilow song on the radio and felt a wave of nausea sweep over me.)

So I'm in the living room one day, still a little shaken by the whole chick episode, when I come across this new album I've never seen. Must be something my brother bought. He is older by four-plus years and becoming more sophisticated in his tastes. Jimmy Smith "Walk on the Wild Side." Let's just see about this. Whoa . . . what the hell . . . ? Songs I don't know at all, but man, this guy can . . . (I wouldn't know the word for a few years still) SWING. This was a whole different approach. Much more free. I felt something different when I heard this, and I did not recognize the feeling. But it made me do more than just listen and think of practicing scales. It made me run around the room.

Things were taking shape. There was a whole other world where, unlike my grandmother's favorite, Lawrence Welk, the musicians didn't have to smile when they played. They could grunt, groan and with foreheads knit, exorcise whatever they happened to be feeling. Well soon after, with the help of WABC, and more so, WWRL, up on the right side of the dial, came the flood. Otis Redding, Joe Tex, Jackson 5, Ivory Joe Hunter, Aretha, Stevie, Jackie Wilson, Al Green . . . the mother lode, a seemingly inexhaustible well. This was the 3rd dimension (as opposed to the 5th dimension who were closer to the 2nd dimension, if you ask me) that I was discovering. Some element added to a track or a vocal that could connect the ear to not only the brain, but to the arms, legs, and most importantly, to the heart.

If we'd been allowed to hear Little Richard's version of "Tutti Frutti" on the radio instead of Pat's, we'd have surely known something was up. But the country was having enough difficulty absorbing the shock of rock and roll as it came out of the mouths of white singers in Oxford shirts and saddle shoes. Albeit, white singers who seemed to borrow freely from the encyclopedia of Rhythm & Blues. It must have seemed out of the realm of possibility to expect pop radio and mainstream media to embrace this music in its unfiltered state. Louis Jordan? *No!* Louis Prima? *Hmm, possibly* . . . Louis Armstrong? *Can he be more fun?* Pat Boone? *Theeeere ya go! Now yer talkin'.* This was *still*, after all, picket fence, postwar time. The nation's rest period. And there was just no sane mogul who was about to do anything other than lease this musical madness from its rightful, yet racially unpopular deed holders (and that, at a *very* suspect price).

To think that we had been fed shells all this time. Well, the peanuts were here now, and I was savoring the flavor in a big way.

Let's fast forward a decade. The move back to my native New York, by way of Jersey and then later, the more provincial Boston, was more of a last ditch effort to overcome my intimidation of the place. I was writing music that I felt was sifting through all of my influences and this would be the place that could understand it.

Trouble was, the record biz was most practiced in the art of the pigeonhole, and if you couldn't fit into a particular marketing strategy, you were declared eclectic and of little use to most labels (some sour grapes inserted here). I thought this was short-sighted and short-changing the public by not respecting their broad range of tastes. That whole "we give 'em what they ask for" argument was so transparent and self-serving. Little did I know that this trend would worsen considerably over the next three decades.

I don't like to think of myself as a not-like-the-old-days kind of guy, because I know there are hugely talented people among us, but a glance at any top ten hit list from thirty or forty years ago would likely show you ten very different styles of music. Motown, rock, cabaret, instrumentals, C&W, novelty, spoken word (Lorne Greene's *Ringo* wouldn't stand a chance today), a variety not known to the modern listener. Not to say that it was all good, it wasn't, but you were given the full banquet. A chance to decide for yourself. Urban radio gave us a huge assortment of black music: the Detroit sound, the Philly sound, James Brown, Ruth Brown, Little Richard, LaVerne Baker, my two nearly family members, Harry and Miriam, Brother Ray, Marvin Gaye . . . you know how long it goes on. How have we learned to be satisfied with such a small palate? This low-carb, fat-free, Clear Channel (clear of any vision, that's for sure) staple that we have now. Every now and then someone will emerge with something to say, and a fresh way to say it. But it sure seems like the moment that occurs, the music industry, instead of encouraging and making room for other voices of distinction (more sour grapes inserted here) will instead try to find a slew of clones that can look and sound like that one maverick who somehow managed to slip through. And like shoes and tattoos, nonconformity again morphs into trends that reveal exactly the opposite intent.

As an "eclectic" and, therefore, "artist of little use," I found my way into the business of music in advertising. The *jingle* business.

Where I proudly hung my hat for more than twelve years. Aside from working with the simply stunning array of musicians, many of whom I'd listened to and idolized for many years (including Grady Tate, drummer on the aforementioned, "Walk on the Wild Side"), there was an equally stunning array of vocalists. And it was here that I got my first up-close gaze into the mechanics, or rather lack, of the black singing voice. An effortless act, like nothing I'd ever experienced. A vessel for both the deepest joy and anguish. It did not matter if we were singing the praises of the cleansing power of *Tidy Bowl*, or of the nutritional advantages of *Fruity Marshmallow Krispies*; this was a sublime force of nature, as pure as the rain, and I was struck dumb. Some of this group, the "NY Jingle Singers," had had some success in the record business. Guys like D-Train, Johnny Kemp, Frank and Babi Floyd, Curtis King, Fonzie Thornton, even Luther Vandross. Women like Ada Dyer, Vaneese Thomas (daughter of the funkiest chicken to ever walk the dog) Diva Gray, Jocelyn Brown, Valerie Simpson, Patti Austin, Lani Groves, Martha Wash, Catherine Russell, Lillias White . . . I could fill the page (and when I next see the one whom I've omitted, I'll wish I had!).

It was an indulgence for me. A kid in the greatest candy store. A parallel universe of voice, because nothing could sound like this. My thirty-second songs were given a life of their own. A phrasing turn, a slight pulling back of tempo could jack a song about fertilizer into the stratosphere. Damn, it would make you go out and buy a bag even if you lived in a sixteenth floor apartment! An emotional break in the voice, this creamy texture could suddenly stir some long dormant memory and you'd find yourself weeping during a paint thinner ad. If this energy could be harnessed we'd be long since free of our foreign oil jones. This was a precious resource of a whole different stripe.

Martha would barely disturb a facial muscle and solid brass would come out. Vaneese could simultaneously slack your jaw *and* jam radar with her gravity-defying high notes. D-Train's charm would be absorbed and transmitted by whatever he happened to be shilling. Ada could allow you a moment's peace from the most troubling day. Patti could stop a strobe tuner on any note while melting your heart. An ad-libbed "Yeah" would bust out of Johnny's mouth like a locomotive, stopping briefly at every station along the way. Every buoyant note from Lillias would immediately, like cream, rise to the top. Jocelyn could throw the spirit into the most cynical of bones. Curtis and Fonzie; the lacquer that gave the songs their finish. And Diva . . . Diva could fill even George W. Bush with the deepest . . . well, ok, there *are* limits.

But this was an involuntary act, like breathing. A sixth sense, an extra limb. Nothing manufactured or contrived. This voice had no choice and in the words of my personal ambassador to R&B, Peter Wolf, if it was in there, it had to come out. I was a beneficiary and I was proud and humbled to be part of their world. When they looked at me for direction, I may have felt like I could have been showing Monet how to work with oil, but I was happy to oblige and unabashed in my reverence. Sure, we were all paid well for our efforts, but for me, like them, it was never about anything but the music. Whether it was a Bach chorale or a jaunty little number for I Can't Believe it's not Butter, each note was shown nothing but respect. There was one goal; could we make it feel good? And the feeling that came across didn't always have to do with notes.

At a particularly tense recording session one afternoon, the "suits" were breathing down our necks to get it done, as usual. We used to tell them they could have the music cheap, fast, or good, but that they could only choose two of those three options. And trying to get to the bottom of what they'd find musically problematic was not always the easiest task, mainly due to their vagueness. Anyway, the late and great Frank Floyd was singled out and asked what note he'd been singing in the background harmony. "Well . . ." Frank began in is his inimitable not-at-all-but-completely serious style, "I wouldn't really call it a *note* . . . it's more like a *feel*." As much as the comment had furrowed the brows of the ad agency folks, the singers all found it riotously funny, both in its timing and its truth. Tension and productivity are not the best of friends, and a comment like this was invaluable in easing the strain and allowing the moment to proceed in a more creative setting. These were intangibles that people like Frank could bring to the table. And it was all part of what ended up on the tape. Though it may have seemed in the control room to be a momentary waste of studio minutes, it likely ended up saving lots of time and stress.

And so they listened when they needed to, they humored, they sang, they gave, and time after time, I'd come out smelling like a rose. And as I'm sure a phrase like that could straighten the hairs on the backs of a few historical necks by its implication, here it meant that we'd all get to keep our day jobs . . . in product sales.

Inspiration is revealed through many disguises. Some more recognizable than others. And when it's best worn, inspiration will propel and not intimidate. Greats like Prince or Michael Jackson have created styles all their own, yet styles that would have a very different look if James Brown or Sly Stone had not gone before them. Dee Clark's raindrops might never have fallen if Jackie Wilson's teardrops hadn't paved their way. I am a singer/songwriter. And how the gifts of these singers have affected me might not be starkly evident in my own craft. If those voices were Rolls Royces, mine would be a Yugo. Yet I don't think I could have witnessed the abandon, the ease, and the joy of these artists without digesting at least *some* of their spirit. I watched them raise the bar each and every time. And this bar is not set by technique or by note frenzies that would startle a hummingbird, a fact that is sadly lost on countless of today's hit-makers and wannabes. When grace is there to spot for the acrobats, it becomes quite a different event. And a multidimensional one at that. The black voice that I was privy to was not manipulated, devised, or embellished. It was merely let loose.

KENNY WHITE

And so I carry with me, even more than the sound of that instrument, the manner in which it was shared.

I've often wished that I hadn't drawn one of the shorter straws when it comes to singing. I have fantasized about how cool it would be if, along with property, talent and artistry could be willed upon our deaths. I would see myself someday bringing soup and muffins to Uncle Stevie or Aunt Aretha in the nursing home ("Yes sir, it *has* been a while," or "Yes ma'am, you're so right . . . *very* light skinned, I surely am!") in hopes of securing a portion of one of those creative inheritances.

But I also know that there is much more at play here. To be endowed with a great set of pipes is in no way a guarantee that you will be a great singer. That would require the necessary travel over life's hard bumps. And even then, if you're not capable of translating those road conditions into feelings, or you begin to over-think or adulterate them, you risk losing the immediacy. And that immediacy is what I think is soul.

Some singers with limited technical ability have gone on to define entire cultures (i.e. Frank Sinatra, Bob Dylan), yet some with enormous prowess, born with a true gift, seem destined to obfuscate any real sense of their own hearts (insert personal, jaundiced opinion here . . . i.e. Celine Dion, Michael Bolton). Of course this is music and music has always been and will always remain subjective. And that's what is so eternal about it. One man's ceiling . . . what makes one of us absolutely ache with longing, will hardly register with another. But having said this, I still cannot fathom how anyone could listen to Sam Cooke sing "A Change is Gonna Come" and not be driven to his knees.

P.S. During one of my mother's visits from Florida (when I couldn't sleep as a child—most likely due to her impending marriage to Harry—she'd tell me to think of *nice* things . . . like

Florida), I was scheduled to do a commercial for Jamaica Tourism. And although I didn't mention it, the singer that afternoon was to have been none other than Harry Belefonte. Unfortunately, a last second contract or scheduling dispute kept that session from happening. I wonder how she would've played it.

SOUL POWER

By Yolanda Young

I walk through the churchyard
To lay this body down;
I know moon-rise, I know star-rise;
I walk in the moonlight, I walk in the starlight;
I'll lie in the grave and stretch out my arms,
I'll go to judgment in the evening of the day,
And my soul and they soul shall meet that day,
When I lay this body down.
—Negro Song

When I was a child a deacon dropped dead at my church. Frankly, with all the time we spent in those pews (Monday was the only day the church was unoccupied, and filled even then during revivals and Vacation Bible School), I'm surprised it didn't happen more often.

As I recall, it was a routine Sunday with no programs or special celebrations to cause service to extend into the late afternoon. Sucking a peppermint, I had settled into a pew next to my slightly older aunt, Ruby. I was hoping for a bit of excitement in the form of a choir member catching the "holy spirit." (Ruby and I found shouting the most entertaining aspect of Baptist worship and mimicked these women often.)

I was quite young and had not yet experienced a close family member dying—I would understand the pain of grief soon thereafter, but on this particular Sunday, innocence made the event a spectacle.

Services were just beginning with the devotion. A tall, stout man in a dark suit and shiny shoes was winding down an Old One Hundred. These a cappella hymns have long gone out of style, replaced by rhythm sections and hip hop preachers, but before the black southern churches could afford fancy organs, fulltime ministers and tailor-made choir robes, they had to make do with paper fans, fish plate dinners and those slow drop cadences.

These hymns were the descendents of slave songs and the early 1700s melodies published by the English minister, Dr. Isaac Watts. The slaves, proving smarter than their owners could have imagined, turned traditional songs of salvation into freedom roadmaps. Songs took on double meanings. For example, "Swing low, sweet chariot coming forth to carry me home," sounded to the master like a wistful day coming when God's chariot would take one up to heaven, but to those toiling under a hot son and red moon, the chariot waiting was messenger of the underground railroad. So for utilitarian reasons, black folks' religion, rather than being contained in a building, went with them into the fields and slave cabins.

The end of slavery didn't mean the end of those songs. The black church repertoire did, however, expand to include *homiletic spiritual* arrangements. For a long time churches did without hymnbooks. Instead, the song's pitch and lyrics would be delivered one stanza at a time by a call leader in a sing-chant tone. So it was on "Death Sunday," as we came to refer to it.

One of the call leaders had begun in a slow, moderate tone with the line, *I know I am a child of God* . . . his voice grew stentorian as he reached the next line, *I'll wait until the spirit comes.* This verse was repeated again and again. Each time, the sound softening until it was a whisper, then a moan.

When the words were no longer discernable and the sounds merely a vibration in the air, Deacon Parker knelt to pray. He began by saying, "I come to you now, Lord," then in an instant, gave up the ghost.

After some attempts at makeshift resuscitation, a suit jacket was laid over his face. "His soul don' left him," I heard someone say.

A few churchmen rushed over to stretch him out in the pulpit below the choir. This movement was made a bit awkward on account of Deacon Parker's size. He was low and heavy with the vast majority of his weight being distributed in the area between his chest and hips, so several men were needed to lift him at the waist. A child could've managed the weight of his feet.

The funeral was held the following weekend. He was laid out real nice with a steel casket, several bouquets of rainbow carnations and a forest of plants. This kind of display garnered the admiration of black parishioners in much the same way driving a Cadillac or maintaining one's own teeth did.

Reverend Green presided over the burial and recited a scripture from Genesis as the metal box was slowly lowered into the ground: *And the LORD God formed man of the dust of the ground, and breathed into his nostrils the breath of life; and man became a living soul . . . For dust you are, and to dust shall you return.*

When I was very young, I thought a soul was something only a black person possessed. That was why, I reasoned, we referred to Big Momma's smothered pork chops and collard greens as soul food. But it was the music that persuaded me entirely. To understand the soul one must understand the feel of our music. Whether it's the organ notes on Sunday morning, or Don Cornelious's deep baritone signing off at midnight, "Peace. Love. And *SOOUUUL-LLLL.*" It was in the truth of the King of Soul's lyrics:

> *Know we need it, soul power*
> *We got to have it, soul power*
> *Know we want it, soul power*
> *Got to have it, soul power*
> *Give it to me, soul power*
> *We need it, soul power, we need it, soul power*
> *We got to have it, soul power*
> —James Brown

Later, when I learned to read and intuit, my feeling that white people did not have a soul was reinforced by the mean way they treated black characters in shows like Alex Haley's *Roots*, as well as, my older relatives' recollections of real experience. They had kept Big Momma away from her family on holidays, even Christmas, because the mistress of the house where Big Momma worked didn't want her children eating food cooked the day prior. My black schoolteachers supplemented my Louisiana Textbooks with stories of how white people kept Dr. Charles Drew out of the hospital and opera singer Marian Anderson from Constitution Hall. These folks were something else.

It also seemed to me that long after slavery had ended white people still maintained a preoccupation with owning us, even our souls. It was a great insult of the time to be called a sellout. In the seventies and eighties there was a code. A black person should never compromise their relationship with "the race" for success in the mainstream white world. The entertainer Sammy Davis Jr. was a member of Frank Sinatra's Rat Pack and a supporter of Richard Nixon, architect of modern day political race baiting. His talent was greatly admired, but among blacks, he was viewed as a sellout of historic proportions. Where was his integrity? Did he have any principles at all? During his quest for fame and fortune he lost an eye, his family's religion, and the respect of his people.

Today, nearly all black performers sell out, only now they call it "getting paid." Many of them make more money hawking products than they do performing. They market perfumes, liquor and fashion even to international markets where people are more likely to have roots in Seoul than soul. Worse still, hardcore rap artists glorify their vices—liquor, drugs, promiscuity, and violence—so our children grow up believing this is a part of our culture. Lucifer would be proud of such a change.

Over the last decade something has shifted within me and my

people. We're not soulful anymore. Cool? Yes. We put the "hip" in hip hop? Sho-nuff. But soulful? No.

The "haunting echo" that begins this essay was first used as such in "The Sorrow Songs," the last chapter in William E. Burghardt Du Bois' *The Souls of Black Folk*. Throughout the book, Du Bois wrestles with "the problem of the color line" or the brutal injustices that Negroes of his era had to continuously endure. At the same time he credits this cruelty with giving to us, and in turn to this country, the rhythmic cry unique to our music. "They are the music of an unhappy people, of the children of disappointment; they tell of death and suffering and unvoiced longing . . ." said Du Bois before going on. "There breathes hope—a faith in the ultimate justice of things. The minor cadences of despair change often to triumph and calm confidence. Sometimes it is faith in life, sometimes a faith in death, sometimes assurance of boundless justice in some fair world beyond. But whichever it is, the meaning is always clear: that sometime, somewhere, men will judge men by their souls and not by their skins."

I believe that time has come. Not for everyone, not in every situation and certainly not all the time. For generations we passed down such suffering just as we passed down those old songs, but what to do now that, as a group, we are no longer troubled or exiled, no longer in strife or hiding?

As I matured spiritually I came to understand that everyone has a soul, an inner awareness, a consciousness. Still, something was different about the soul of those said to be Ham's cursed descendents. Until now.

Today, there is no sorrow in our songs. We haven't suffered. I've been sad, but not sorrowful. I've known disappointment, but my soul has not ached. I have grieved, but only for a little while.

The way we worship today is entirely different from the way that was familiar to me as a child. We don't moan or sing hymns. When we shout out, it's more likely to be in praise than pain. We love

Jesus. Our parents *knew* Jesus, knew his suffering. They knew what it was to carry a cross, not only individual struggles, but a shared burden.

As the color line fades, so too does the suffering . . . and our soulfulness.

When his disciples were struggling to understand this type of sacrifice, Jesus asked them, "What will it profit a man if he gains the whole world and forfeits his soul?"

We just might find out.

THE SOUL SECTION
by Susan Hayden

*You can't sing about love unless you
know about it.*
—Billy Eckstine

It was easy to believe that everyone in the world was Jewish.

That's how I felt growing up in Encino, and my parents planned for it that way. We had Hebrew School, Sunday brunch at the Deli, shuls with pools and high school girls sporting the exact same nose job.

There was a clear code to follow that I couldn't interpret in a way that served me. I wanted more of something but I wasn't sure what. So even in the requisite designer clothes, I stood out, grasping for the intangible.

My family was considered to be upper middle class and on the fringe of Encino society. Dad was an entertainment attorney with his own sense of style, a hipster Rabbi in cowboy boots. He was strict and opinionated, yet generous to a fault. He made enough money to drive the newest model Mercedes and wear a signature Rolex. He'd take us to Hawaii every Summer and let me charge on his Neiman Marcus card.

He was also the proud owner of a weekend toupee.

I couldn't bring boys home because they'd always fall for Mom.

She was graceful and vivacious, an epic beauty. She never taught me how to cook or to sew, but she was a teacher of "Poise" at the Dorothy Shreve School of Modeling and Charm in Sherman Oaks.

She moved through her days with an effortlessness that was not passed on to me. I was a boy-crazy girl with a series of crushes on unavailable older men, like waiters, hairdressers and soap opera stars. There was simply no one at Birmingham High, and the selection in greater Encino was minimal. Love wasn't to be found anywhere West of Sepulveda.

It was waiting for me in Westwood Village, or so I'd heard.

I wasn't a fox, but I wasn't a dog.

In the Looks Department, I was what guys called "halfway decent," and, personality-wise, I was offbeat with an edge. When I finally got the courage to make the big trek into The City, it was 1979 and I'd just turned sixteen. I was sure that free expression lived "over the hill," where diverse communities converged and couldn't contain only one kind of culture.

I looked forward to getting to be myself, and if that didn't work, to reinvention.

For most girls I knew, the upgrade from a West Valley love-life was landing a boy from Beverly Hills, a doctor's son, with a Fiat convertible and Jack Purcell sneakers, whose parents were members of Hillcrest Country Club and came from a long line of Jewish royalty.

For me, love's blueprint came from records I played on a Technics turntable. Acoustic music of the Seventies revealed the existence of a newfound, sensitive male. Cat Stevens, James Taylor and Jackson Browne reinforced this idea by being unafraid to expose their feelings in song.

I was in search of someone who knew nothing about the unwanted geek I was in Encino. I'd never admit I lived North of Sunset, North of Mulholland, North of Valley Vista. I'd lie, pretend I was from Malibu.

But the guy I'd meet wouldn't care. He'd be able to see through to my soul.

Kim Pauli had been my willing accomplice since Second Grade. If I made a move, she'd follow. She was only one-quarter Jewish but held it like a talisman. It worked for and against her. She grew into a post-adolescent Playboy bunny with a quick wit, and all the Dads in the Valley had a thing for her, because she had Raquel Welch's tits and the innocence of *Gidget*.

A Star of David and a cross hung together on a chain around her neck.

No one offered to drive us to Westwood so we had to take the R.T.D. This turned a fifteen-minute car ride into an hour-long bus ride. Heading south on the 405, I couldn't escape Mom's voice in my head, like the soundtrack of *A Chorus Line*, instructing me on how to attract the opposite sex. I knew I should heed her advice because she got everything she wanted (even when she didn't want it) and seemed content the majority of the time.

She was a romantic of the highest order, with rules to live by; rules culled from her teachings at the Modeling School, Yiddish humor, and her own bare-bones experience as a Cosmo-lovin' woman:

1. "Upon entering a room, never look from side to side. Don't make eye contact with those around you. Walk with your head held high."
2. "Look for boys of your same race and religion. Love is complicated enough. Begin with a common denominator.
3. "If you want your dreams to come true, don't sleep.

The lowdown on The Village was widely known. Losers loitered inside the Arcade, "Vals" at Stan's Donuts, and City kids at Postermat.

If you were a druggie, Postermat was where you'd buy your bong.

There was a huge display case housing drug-paraphernalia-galore. The store was also known for selling vintage posters of rock stars.

They had movie memorabilia, concert T-shirts, and buttons with catch phrases. And they had the best-looking guys I'd ever seen.

They'd lean against walls, hanging out, stoned and flirting.

It was packed like a concert at the Fabulous Forum. The song "Baby, Hold On To Me," by Peter Frampton, was playing full-blast. I walked in, my head high, looking straight ahead, but got distracted and broke Mom's Number One rule by having extended eye contact with an employee.

I could almost taste his skin: darker than a caramel apple, lighter than Hershey's with Almonds. He was energetic and at least twenty, with perfectly faded Levi's and lean muscles showing through a UCLA jersey.

And he was noticing *me*, not Kim.

"I know I can't turn you on to a hand-blown glass hash pipe or a roach clip? Not your style. That's a good thing. So what *are* you here for?"

"I have no idea."

"Me neither, and this is my job."

"I do love music. Music . . . is my boyfriend."

"You'd like my dad. He's a famous jazz singer known as Mr. B. I play drums, classical percussion, keyboards, bass guitar . . . and I sing."

"Wow. My brother bangs on a practice pad."

"My mom, she's an actress . . ."

"Mine's a modeling teacher."

"She was in a movie with Clark Gable once."

"I love Clark Gable. *The Misfits* is the story of my life."

"Welcome to the club . . . Hey, who do you listen to? I like Joni Mitchell, Neil Young and Steely Dan."

"You would've fit in well at Woodstock."

"Truth is, my heart belongs to Roberta Flack and Donny Hathaway."

"Me too. 'Where Is The Love' is my all-time favorite song."

In 1973, Mom played their album of duets around a thousand times. It was the background music to every mother-daughter pow-wow we'd have. She was enamored of the Flack/Hathaway alliance, revealed in emotional songs, sung together and apart; Billboard hits, every one.

I'd taken ownership of the record, having memorized its hidden meanings.

"Sad about Donny, huh? Jumped from a window of the Essex Hotel last month. You'd have to be at the end of the line to do something like that," he said. "You'd have to feel so alone."

"When my Mom found out, she cried the whole night."

"I've got a great poster of the two of them. Wanna see it?"

"I'd love to."

"Meet me in the *Soul Section*," he said, then winked and walked away. I turned to Kim, who'd been rolling her eyes and glaring.

"Who do you think you are? Andrea Silver?" she sniped, before moving on to the gag-gift area.

Andrea Silver was this chubby, freckle-faced dork from Taft High School in Woodland Hills who supposedly had a one-nighter with Jermaine Jackson at the Heritage House motel. She told everyone about him, in graphic, unwarranted detail. Who cared what kind of boxers he wore?

The Jackson Five lived two blocks from me, on Hayvenhurst Avenue. Fans would park outside their house and wait for them to pull in or pull out.

Don't think I wasn't aware that I'd already broken Mom's Number Two rule. I'd fallen fast for the polar opposite of my race and religion; I'd found a City Guy who didn't treat me like a Val; who was drawn to some part of me, or the real me.

He just happened to be a different color.

"This is where I want to live. Right here," he told me, referring to the specific aisle where Marvin Gaye and Aretha Franklin shared a shelf with Bessie Smith and Billie Holiday.

I'd heard of these singers from my dad, who had a collection of 78s he used to play at night when he'd get home from work. It was a way for him to relax, until he found Transcendental Meditation. That's when he started listening to eight track tapes of gongs and rhythms of the rainforest.

In the Soul Section we sat on the floor, huddled close, his arm half around me as he spoke. "My father, he played with Dizzy Gillespie and Dexter Gordon, Miles Davis and Charlie Parker. We're talking bop big-band. He'd lived many lives before moving to the Valley."

"Wait. I live there! I thought you were a City Guy."

"I live in Brentwood now but I grew up in Encino. We were the first black family there, before the Jacksons moved in. I'm what's known as a 'J.B.A.'—Jew By Association."

I couldn't believe I'd never seen him in the produce department at Gelson's or browsing at Sunshine Records. I would have noticed. He stood out, and not because he was black, though in Encino, that alone must have made him feel otherworldly. His presence held an open-air kindness that was fresh and new to me. And his gaping spirit was as fragrant as the *Dreams* oil they sold in small bottles right around the corner.

"I've dated a lot of Jewish girls. You sure are a pretty one," he said, taking my hand. "There's just something about you. Well, back to work." And then he disappeared.

Maybe I wasn't as fat and ugly as my brother kept saying.

Kim was waiting for me outside. I was walking toward her when an arm reached out and handed me the Flack/Hathaway poster and a piece of paper with a name and number on it.

"Call me tomorrow when you wake up, before going out for *brunch*."

"How'd you know?"

"That's what you do in Encino on Sunday, even when you're not Jewish."

My curfew was Midnight and I made sure to be prompt. Mom and Dad were waiting to size me up, searching for signs of City trouble.

"It's true, I'm in love. He's from Encino, of all places. He works at Postermat and goes to UCLA."

"What's his name?" Mom asked.

"Guy Eckstine. His dad is a famous jazz singer."

"Billy Eckstine? Mr. B.? Oh . . . was he ever handsome."

"So is his son . . ."

"He's a *schvartza!*" Dad proclaimed.

It was like a force thrust me into our TV and I'd become Gloria on *All In The Family*, faced with Archie Bunker's ignorance. Or Joey in *Guess Who's Coming To Dinner*. Unlike those characters, I was too stunned to raise my voice, and besides, I wasn't allowed to talk back or I'd get grounded, indefinitely.

My parents had brought me up with integrity, a certain respect and without prejudice. Or so I'd thought. I'd learned about slavery in elementary school, persecution in Hebrew School.

Now, everything had become skewed and confused and Dad was acting like the anti-Semites he most despised. Is this how he felt in his heart of hearts about the non-Jews of the world? Is this why he chose for our family to live in a hermetically-sealed community of sameness?

I ran to my bedroom, slamming the door. Dad burst in behind me.

"You're *forbidden* to go out with him."

"You're a racist," I said calmly.

"It's *non-negotiable.*"

I taped my new poster to the wall and put on the Flack/Hathaway album. And I climbed into bed and cried, about otherness and two tribes, about racial divide. I cried about railcars and cattle-cars, about being chained and being branded.

We weren't so different, were we?

I wanted to call Guy, whisper into the phone, "Be Real Black For Me."

It was the name of the song currently playing and it seemed to apply. I wanted to tell him that I'd be at Postermat next Saturday night.

I'd meet him in the Soul Section, where we both wanted to live. But I didn't.

I went to sleep, breaking Mom's third and final rule, the one about having to stay awake to dream.

"DON'T SNEAK" were two words written in bold Sharpie and rubber-stamped on my conscience. I loved sneaking, especially pastries from the Continental Market, around the corner. I was overweight and sweets were off-limits. But rulebreaking was becoming a way of life and Guy Eckstine, a rare delicacy, worthy of stealing off a shiny platter.

I wanted to see what he tasted like, knowing the taste would linger.

His loose curls, sinewy arms, the warmth of his gaze; how he was able to take me in, without veering. This is what I thought of that following week, when I'd stare at my Trimline phone, pick it up, dial his number, then hang up before he'd answer. I wondered what I'd say to him the next time I was able to get out of the Valley and into the Village:

"*My dad's prejudiced against black people so I can't go out with you . . .*"

I'd secretly secured a car ride to Postermat for Saturday night.

Dad knew instinctively where my heart, mind and body were headed and he said this: "Before you breach someone's trust, play the scenario out in your head. Go through all of the motions, mentally, to see if it's worth it. Nine out of ten times, you'll find it's not."

He had a power over me I wasn't able to reconcile.

He had an ability to get his point across without ever raising his voice.

Perhaps it was his upbringing that limited his infinity.

SUSAN HAYDEN

He grew up in the Westside of Chicago at the tail-end of the Jazz Age. The sounds that streamed through his neighborhood reflected the Great Migration and the emergence of gospel and urban blues. Louis Armstrong, Tommy Dorsey and Mahalia Jackson were locals. They created the music of his youth, songs he was passionate about; songs on records he collected for years and then, one day, just stopped playing.

Papa Usher, Dad's Romanian father, ran a bathhouse on the Southside of town that was frequented by Al Capone and friends. I think Papa studied and stole the mean expressions off the gangsters that congregated to steam, and passed them on to his son.

Which is to say, you didn't want to make my dad angry. Monotone speech would be reinforced by a death stare. Mom called it "The Look."

My Austrian Grandma, Gertie, escaped the Holocaust, losing two brothers to Hitler. This subject wasn't discussed in Dad's house but it was blatant in her mood swings. When she'd get upset, she'd give her husband the silent treatment for two years at a stretch.

She and Papa Usher raised their children with an ardent pride for Judaism, yet in their old-country culture, there existed a territorial attitude about the so-called "chosen people" and it judged and excluded "outsiders." Dad was holding onto—and not thinking through—such beliefs.

These beliefs were being passed on to a new generation, unconsciously.

I'd never recognized this before wanting to date Guy Eckstine.

Soon I was playing the scenario out in my head, as Dad had suggested I do before sneaking. It was like a home movie that I could star in, produce, and direct:

In the beginning, I'm meeting Guy in Westside cafes, drinking coffee and reading lyrics, back and forth, from our favorite songs.

Music is our bond and it will no doubt lead to greater depths of closeness.

In the middle, we're meeting in Ventura Boulevard motel rooms, and Guy is showing me his boxers, same as Jermaine had supposedly shown Andrea Silver. Only this isn't a hit-n-run: He's looking into my eyes with intention; saying lines I'd only heard characters use on *General Hospital*.

Near the end, we're at Postermat, making plans for me to move out of my parents' house and into Guy's apartment, when Dad shows up in his 450 SL and drags me to the hidden chambers of Valley Beth Shalom Temple.

It is there that I receive The Talk from our Rabbi, about not going outside of one's race to look for love. It's the final scene, where the audience realizes these two "outsiders" from separate ethnic groups have taken a chance on each other only to find themselves once again persecuted.

In no uncertain terms, Dad's mind game worked on me. I knew it was a battle I couldn't win. So I chose to let it go.

And in the letting go, something shifted. I felt compelled to make Dad understand how wrong he was. I had to show him a new way of looking at something old. But how? He was, after all, fully formed.

Then I remembered: It was music that held the healing power.

In fact, the few flashes of true connection I'd ever had with my father were invoked by the shared love of a song.

It was in Dad's stack of old 78s, under Elvis and the Mills Brothers, that I uncovered none other than Billy Eckstine! On the record's sleeve, there was a picture of him, handsome as ever, and a quote underneath it that read, "The First Romantic Black Male Sings His Heart Out."

The night I was supposed to go to Postermat, I stayed home instead, and at some point, invited Dad into my room. I placed Mr.

B. on my Technics turntable and we both sat listening as a haunting voice, low and velvety smooth, sang to us about being a *"Prisoner of Love."*

And I watched as the tension left Dad's face, as his cheeks flushed with interest, as a closed mind opened, ever so slightly.

"Eckstine was the real thing. When he was living in Chicago and I was a kid, I got to see him perform with Earl Hines at The Grand Terrace Café. The place was run by Capone. It was called a black and tan club. It wasn't segregated. You could co-mingle there."

"What a concept."

"I love this song. And how you make me think . . ." Dad said.

Then the record ended.

I never heard my father use the word "schvartza" again; at least, not in my presence. I want to say that whatever took place between us over that brief span of time made him pause before rushing to judgment. And that he wasn't a racist, but a man who hadn't thought things through completely, until challenged.

And that perhaps it was a song, or a really great singer, that helped to shift his viewpoint.

BREAK SKIN, BREAK SPIRIT
by Meri Nana-Ama Danquah

I used to think that if you wanted to succeed in this country, be you black or be you white, all you needed was desire, and opportunity.

I used to think that a fair number of the black people who failed did so because of their own lack of desire and discipline—and it's true, there are those. But there are also those who have everything in place except a chance. They lack the opportunities that would open doors.

It wasn't until I became a mother that I realized that what binds these two groups of people—besides their race or, better said, as a result of their race—is the fact that at one time or another, most likely very early in their lives, somebody broke their spirit, shattered their sense of themselves as full-fledged human beings with the capacity to love, to learn, to achieve.

This breaking is an initiation into life inside your skin, life as a black person in America.

o o o

Here's a joke a former neighbor told Korama, my then-five year old daughter: What do you call white babies who go to heaven? Angels. What do you call black babies who go to heaven? Bats.

I'm not the sort who is easily shocked into silence, but . . . well . . . that shocked me into silence. Korama giggled politely, nervously, then turned and looked at me. I'm sure she wanted answers. I only had questions: what the f—? Why on earth would somebody tell a little black girl, my daughter, a joke as tasteless as that? Political incorrectness and racial hatred aside, the "joke" wasn't even funny.

To be sure, I never spoke to my neighbor again. But that wasn't the end. It was, in fact, just the beginning. Children aren't dumb. Far from it; they absorb everything, and they're quick with their associations.

Korama's favorite book at the time was *Stellaluna*, a sweet story by Janell Cannon about a baby bat who is separated from her mother. Until the bat and her mother are reunited, she finds herself living amongst birds, and it gives her the chance to notice that the two species actually share a lot of similar characteristics, that they're not so different after all.

That night when I tucked her in, Korama said she didn't want me to read *Stellaluna* to her. When I asked her why, she pointed to the small chestnut-colored bat on the cover of the book. "Is that what I'm going to look like when I go to heaven," she asked.

"No," I assured her, trying to find a way to change the subject.

"Then what will I look like when I go to heaven?" My first thought was to show Korama a picture of a black angel, but I didn't know where I could find one or if such a thing even existed. Had I even seen one before? I couldn't remember. A friend had recently given Korama a book of verse by Walter Dean Meyers titled *Brown Angels*. Included with the poems were various photographs of black children. I figured it would do. I pulled the book off the shelf and began reading the first poem. Korama propped herself up on the bed. "These are angels?" she asked. "Hey, this one kinda looks like me."

Until she grew tired of it and asked for another book, *Brown Angels* took the place of *Stellaluna* as Korama's regular bedtime reading. Weeks went by without another mention of bats or angels. I interpreted my daughter's silence as something of a victory. She had gone through the experience unscathed. Then we decided to eat cake.

It was a weekly ritual, our mother-daughter date. Every Sunday, she and I would bake a cake together. We went to the corner store where we usually shopped to pick up some cake mix. They were all out, so we went to a grocery store that, unlike the scantily stocked mom-and-pop shop, had an entire aisle devoted to baking.

Korama was beside herself as she stood there in an aisle, wider than her outstretched arms, full of cake-mix boxes, each displaying a single scrumptious slice of cake. It was a step up. She pointed to each box and asked me to tell her what the flavor was. One by one, I read the labels.

When I finished, I turned to ask Korama which one she wanted to buy. There were tears welled up in her eyes. "Mommy," she said. "Why is the angel's food cake white and the devil's food cake black? Are devils like bats? Does that mean I won't go to heaven?"

Again, I didn't have any answers. So I did what I do best. I wrote and asked for them. The article, which was published in the *Los Angeles Times*, presented the whole situation blow-by-blow from the joke to the book to the cake; then it ended with the question, *why is angel's food cake white and devil's food cake black? You tell me. And I, in turn, will tell my daughter.*

Reader response to the article was unbelievable. We got a ton of mail, letters from people sharing similar experiences, offering comfort and encouragement or attempting to explain why angel's food cake is white (*the cake is so light, like clouds; it tastes like a slice of heaven*) and devil's food cake is black (*so rich it has to be sinful; only the devil can make something that hard to resist*). We got packages and packages of carvings, drawings and other representations of black angels.

Korama was incredibly moved by all the kindness. She found it hard to believe that people who didn't know her, perfect strangers, could care so much, would take the time to reach out to her. It was a salve, that outpouring of love, a saving grace for my daughter's spirit which I'd noticed had been breaking a little bit more every time she stood in front of the mirror and stared at her black body, wondering if she'd make it to heaven or if her skin would relegate her to an altogether different fate. But that love, that love, corny as this may sound, it made her whole again.

o o o

When I was nine and a half years old, a friend's father used the word *nigger* in my presence. He wasn't calling me a *nigger*, not directly anyway. He was recounting a story about how he'd almost gotten into a car accident earlier in the day. The *nigger* to whom my friend's father referred was the individual driving the vehicle with which he almost collided.

I wasn't at all offended; of course, I had absolutely no idea what that word meant. It'd only been three years since my family had emigrated from Ghana, so I was still relatively new to the country. Also, ours was a household with little tolerance for assimilation. We didn't even speak English in our home, so *nigger* had not yet become a part of my new American lexicon.

My friend was embarrassed. "Dad," she whined, rolling her eyes and tilting her head in my direction to remind her father that I, a black person, was present.

"You said she's African, right?"

"Well, yeah," his daughter confirmed.

"Then she's got nothing to worry about." He sounded so certain. It made me curious. "You see," he continued, "it's true that all *niggers* are black, but what a lot of people forget is that not all blacks are *niggers*. Africans are Africans, plain and simple. A completely different breed, straight outta the jungle. You guys aren't like the common black folks we got here. And I'm sorry to say, a lot of them are *niggers*, just no good. Nah, if you hear us talking about *niggers*, don't think twice because we're not talking about you."

What could I say?

"Oh, okay. Thank you." That is what I said, even though what he said made no sense to me. How could he have possibly known where that black person in the car was from? He could very well have been African. Even so, what was it about being African that supposedly shielded him—and me, for that matter—from being a *nigger?* I really didn't understand. I wanted answers but I didn't know where to get them. My parents were far too literal, too logical. They didn't understand the nuances of racism in America.

A couple of months later I watched *Roots*, the miniseries that was based on Alex Haley's novel with the same title, and made some disturbing associations. In the first part of the miniseries, Kunta Kinte, a Mandinka from the Gambia, was captured into slavery. After he and the other captives were loaded onto a ship as human cargo, they sailed the middle passage to America, where they were then sold at auction to the highest bidder. In Kunta Kinte's case, that was John Reynolds, a plantation owner who immediately decided to change his new slave's name to Toby.

Of course, Kunta Kinte refused to answer to, or even acknowledge, his new name; he refused to relinquish his identity, his sense of self. So they beat him. They cracked a whip, again and again, over his bare back until the flesh was bruised and swollen. Then they beat him some more, hoping that when the skin broke, so too would the spirit. Time and time again, after having beaten the new slave within an inch of his life, they asked him his name. He used what little breath there was left in him to answer, "Kunta. Kunta Kinte."

Not long after one of these beatings, Fiddler, an older slave whom John Reynolds had chosen to oversee and train Kunta Kinte, told his young charge, "Things start looking better once you stop being African and start being a nigger like the rest of us." Suddenly I remembered my friend's father and what he'd said. I wondered what it all meant to me and to my future in America.

The next time they beat Kunta Kinte and then asked him his name, he told them it was Toby.

o o o

Granted, there's nobody standing over us with a freshly oiled whip waiting for us to say the new name that we have been given—but we still don't have total freedom. Freedom to name who we are. Freedom to name what it is we want to be. Being black in America can still so easily be about the surrender of identity, the relinquishment of your sense of self. It can still so easily be about using whiteness, definitions of the dominant culture, as your Rosetta Stone, as a way to translate yourself to others and, sometimes, even to yourself.

o o o

When my daughter was twelve years old, she decided that she wanted to attend a junior boarding school. I know it's not a common practice among most Americans, especially African Americans, but in my family sending one's kids to boarding school is commonplace. My parents, my aunts and uncles, their parents—all of them attended boarding school. Blame it on the colonial upbringing.

When she was in first grade, Korama went with me to visit Foxcroft, the Virginia secondary school I'd attended my freshman and sophomore years. The school, which is all-girls, boasts a beautiful and serene 500-acre campus, complete with a breathtaking English-style garden named after the founder, Miss Charlotte. When Korama laid eyes on that garden, she fell hard and fast, vowing that she would one day attend Foxcroft. She made it her goal. Every grade, every year brought her one step closer; and each summer, she'd announce her progress. "Only seven more years until Foxcroft." "Only five more years until Foxcroft."

This whole idea of a *junior* boarding school, though, was something new. It had not been a part of our plan. I worried that maybe she was too young, but she insisted that she'd be fine. She begged and pleaded, sobbed and whined. Korama is a strong-willed girl, has been from the day she was born, the sort of kid who knows exactly what she wants and makes it known. Even when she was nonverbal, Korama never left any room for doubt. She'd slap the bottle of soy milk out of my hand whenever I tried to feed it to her; bob and duck her head and flail her arms about as I, always a tad chilly, attempted to slide a sweater or turtleneck on her before going for a stroll in our favorite Los Angeles park in the heat of August.

In fact, with the exception of the brief period of doubt and uncertainty that followed the bat joke, my daughter had always been fearless. She was also extremely personable and extraordinarily bright. And she yearned for more companionship than the life I'd built for her offered. She was the only child of a single parent. To make matters worse I was hermitic, a full-time writer, a borderline misanthrope who preferred books to people. No wonder she wanted to rush things along and leave home three years ahead of schedule.

Like Foxcroft, this school was also all-girls, except it was located in a small Pennsylvania town. We discovered rather quickly that it wasn't as academically challenging as its catalog and its administration would have had us believe. Korama, who was the youngest student in her seventh grade class (which also made her the youngest student in the entire school), was far too advanced for the courses in her grade level. The school was ill-equipped to handle high-achieving students, so they simply placed her in courses that could accommodate her aptitude—one course at her grade level, two at the ninth grade, and a few more courses at tenth, eleventh and twelfth grade levels. It was socially disastrous. No sane educator would allow a seventh grade child, no matter how smart she is, to be skipped into the twelfth grade. But in essence, that's what this school did; they had my twelve-year-old daughter taking classes with seventeen and eighteen year olds—and still getting A pluses at that. Ah, to be young, gifted and black.

I'm not sure which of these three things—young, gifted, or black—pissed her classmates off the most, but it didn't take long for the bullying to start. Korama was the lone black student in pretty much all of her classes, so race was the easiest and most obvious difference to hold against her. The other students called her names—*nigger*, rabid rainforest monkey—when school officials were not around. When

Korama left the schoolhouse to walk to her dorm, books clutched to her chest, they walked closely behind her and whispered those names. When Korama returned to her dorm room after school she was greeted by the same racial slurs, this time scrawled onto the dry-erase board on her door. It was 24/7 harassment.

The instant I found out, I told her she had to come home—but she wanted to tough it out. "I can do this," Korama assured me. "If I leave, it's like giving up. I'm not gonna let them win." I backed off, took my concerns and complaints to the school's administration, which was as inept on that issue as they had been on the issue of proper academic placement. "Teenage girls can often be mean," the headmistress told me. "There's not much we can really do."

One evening Korama called to tell me that the girls had not only been calling her those hateful names, they'd also started kicking her. When I told my sister, Paula, who was based in Maryland at the time, she jumped in her car immediately and made the six-hour drive to central Pennsylvania to get Korama. It was a straight-up rescue mission. They left behind Korama's microwave, her mini-fridge, her toiletries, and a fair amount of her clothing. Paula knew, just like anybody who knows anything about real racism (as opposed to armchair racism) would and should know, that if Korama hadn't gotten out then, with little more than the clothes on her back, she would not have gotten out with her life.

o o o

It is next to impossible to get a child accepted into a magnet or charter program in the Los Angeles Unified School District in the middle of the academic year, but somehow—with tears, shrewd maneuvering, and an obscenely short skirt—I managed to pull it off. It also didn't hurt that Korama had taken the requisite tests in elementary school and been officially identified as a "gifted" student. So upon her return to Los Angeles, Korama was enrolled into a magnet program for "highly gifted" students.

This program, as it turned out, was one of three programs housed under the roof of one school building. One of those others was the regular neighborhood school program, into which anyone who lived within a certain zip code range could enroll. The students in the regular neighborhood school program were predominantly black and Hispanic. In addition to the regular neighborhood school program and the highly gifted magnet program, there was also a charter program for gifted students. That's right, students who had been tested and identified as *merely* "gifted," not "highly gifted." And it's worth noting that the students in both the gifted and the highly gifted programs, with the exception of no more than a handful of blacks and Hispanics, were either white or Asian.

These three programs that operated under the same roof were run separately, each following their own designated curriculum. The students were essentially segregated except during non-academic elective classes, PE, and lunch—the perfect times for teasing, bullying, and other such potentially life-threatening childhood activities. And how it all worked, the social pecking order, at this particular school was fascinating; predictable, yes, but fascinating nonetheless. The regular neighborhood school program kids teased and bullied the "gifted" program kids. The "gifted" program kids then joined forces with the regular neighborhood program kids to tease and bully the "highly gifted" program kids.

I'm not sure why there were so few blacks and Hispanics in the "gifted" and "highly gifted" programs, but if Korama's experience was any indication, then it was because they were made to feel like traitorous freaks. There were only two students of color in Korama's seventh grade class—her and a bi-racial (black and white) boy who successfully passed for white until Back-to-School Night, when his tar-skinned daddy, of whom he was a spitting, albeit lighter, image, showed up and left no room for doubt.

Not that I could blame the poor boy for trying to slip through the cracks. There's something completely deflating about being the only one. No matter how nice and welcoming everyone is, you're still the "other." You're still the one on the outside looking in, the one who probably won't have a date to the dance, the one who will probably never go out with the most popular guy or girl in your class or get voted homecoming king or queen.

"You tryin' to act white," the black girls in the regular school program accused Korama. "You not really black."

When I was in school, I'd also been accused of acting white, of not "keeping it real." When I'd told my father, he just sneered, acted like it was the most ridiculous thing he'd ever heard. "If you're not really black, then what are you?" he wanted to know. "Tell them you're an African, born and bred. You can't get any blacker than that." He further explained to me that if "keeping it real" meant failing or not otherwise rising up to my full potential, then it was high time we found another reality. And I believed him, that tall African man standing before me; I believed him.

But Korama wasn't a recent immigrant from Africa. She was born at Cedars-Sinai hospital, bred in Los Angeles. Nothing I said seemed to console her, or managed to convince her that she had every right to be talented, to be bright, to simply be. She'd been all alone at that boarding school, shuttling from class to class in different grade levels, not being able to truly bond with any of the other girls. And now, she was alone again. There were no other black girls her age, in her grade, in that "highly gifted" program, to whom she could look for friendship or even affirmation.

o o o

Korama's downward spiral was swift. There were nightmares. There was screaming. And a whole lot of crying. Tears in the morning as she was getting ready for school; tears in the car as we were driving to school and I was listing all the reasons why she couldn't stay home with me instead. She cried every day, throughout most of the day, and she was sad all the time.

It amazes me now that I didn't figure out Korama was cutting, using sharp instruments to bruise herself, to break skin. The signs were right in front of me. I'd seen the random drops of blood on her sheets and just assumed, no matter where they were located on the bed, they were from menstruation. It would never, not in a million years, have occurred to me that they were from self-inflicted wounds, that my daughter was even capable of hurting herself in such a way. But she was, and she did.

Thankfully, there has never been much room in our relationship for secrets, so Korama told me about the cutting—right about the same time that I found out she was flunking out of the "highly gifted" program. Since she kept up with the assignments and I checked her homework every night, I found it rather surprising; then it was explained to me that Korama hadn't handed in any of the assignments. We eventually found them all, stuffed in her locker. I lobbied to have the assignments accepted and her grades recalculated; Korama, on the other hand, wanted to keep the failing grades. "I thought that if I did really poorly they'd kick me out and then I could be normal and go to the regular school with all of the black kids. I want to be normal, Mom."

And the cutting? "It hurts so much inside," she told me. "When I cut myself, the physical pain makes it more real."

The school administrator, a middle-aged white man who seemed genuinely kind-hearted, suggested therapy. I balked at the idea. Ordinarily a huge proponent of therapy, I didn't see how it would help in this situation. "It would give her the opportunity to discuss her problems," he offered. I explained to him that I didn't think the problems were hers, and I didn't want Korama sitting around for an hour week after week claiming ownership of them.

"The fact of her blackness," I said, "is not a problem. The fact of her brilliance is not a problem." But the fact that society did not know how to deal with people like Korama *was* a problem. And unfortunately, it was our problem.

My downward spiral was swift as well. Instead of writing, I spent what little free time I had reading books like Mary Pipher's classic *Reviving Ophelia: Saving the Selves of Our Adolescent Girls*—books that, in their efforts to detail all the ways we need to protect young girls, ultimately left me feeling overwhelmed by all the ways the lives of young girls could fall prey. Korama had promised me that she'd stop cutting and I believed that she would try, but could it be as easy as that? I feared that if something else happened before the end of the school year it would push her over the edge. I worried that she might try to kill herself. I worried that she would never recover, she would never regain her self-esteem. I couldn't sleep at night; I couldn't eat during the day. All I could do was worry. My hair started falling out; alopecia, the doctor informed me, the result of stress.

One morning in the midst of what had become our usual teary, drama-filled school drop-off, I screamed, "Let's just go home." Korama thought I meant home to our apartment, which is where I drove that morning, and where she spent the day playing hooky. But I meant home to Ghana. I'd had an epiphany. Ghana was our Gilead. We were both coming undone; we were both hurting in such un-nameable ways. I wanted whatever protection, whatever balm, whatever healing it had to offer.

o   o   o

Accra, the capital of Ghana, is a modern, cosmopolitan city with a huge expatriate community. Korama attended the Ghana International School, a truly multicultural institution with black, white, Hispanic and Asian students from all over the globe. Even though the majority of the students were black, you'd be hard-pressed to categorize them. Their backgrounds, experiences, and interests were so diverse. There wasn't the illusion of one black reality to sustain or betray.

The protection, the balm, the healing that Ghana offered Korama was, ironically, the very thing that in America she'd been made to believe was her downfall, her burden, the cross she'd been cursed to bear—her black body. We stayed in Ghana for two years—two very pivotal years in an adolescent girl's life. During that time, Korama's self-esteem soared, her confidence returned; she was able to engage her intellect; she was expected to succeed, not because she was black, but because she was smart and capable. Perhaps more important than any of that was her new and improved social life. She had girlfriends with whom she shared novels, lip gloss, and secrets. She had crushes on boys who might possibly return her affections; she attended dances, organized sleepovers. She started to feel normal.

You'd think with everything that had happened, Korama would have gladly forgotten about America, gladly forgotten about her goal of attending Foxcroft—but she didn't. She was actually more determined than ever to realize those dreams she'd almost allowed herself to believe were impossible, out of her reach. She applied and was accepted as a sophomore.

Three years later, as I watched Korama walking in her tea-length white dress through Miss Charlotte's garden to receive her high school diploma, I couldn't help but exhale a sigh of relief. She was graduating cum laude, as the vice head of the school, had been lauded with various awards and honors, and she was on her way to an Ivy League college; despite all the obstacles, Korama had made it. My daughter had made it. But how many other black children, I wondered, had not?

Korama had, in fact, stopped cutting. But I remembered the days when I thought she might kill herself. It made me wonder if other black children had used sharp instruments to do more than break skin? How often can your spirit be broken until it's beyond repair?

The month before Korama's graduation, an eleven-year-old boy from Georgia committed suicide because he couldn't deal with the bullying anymore. A couple of weeks before that, an eleven-year-old boy in Massachusetts committed suicide, also as the result of bullying from his classmates. We don't need any more black angels, little African American children dying for no reason other than our society's inability to see beyond confining stereotypes of the black body. But the list of suicides and attempted suicides goes on. And on.

We've all heard of the proverbial straw, the one that breaks the camel's back. When I tell white people about Korama's experiences with racism and with bullying, I like to start from the very beginning, from the first word that was spoken by that ignorant neighbor. I like to explain it all step by step, because I don't think a lot of white people are aware of the hurtful and compromising positions into which black people in America are placed every single day. I don't think a lot of white people understand how truly remarkable and oftentimes miraculous, black survival is, black success is. Usually I find that I am right; they're not aware. They don't know.

When I tell black people about Korama's experiences, they nod knowingly. They finish my sentences. It's a story they've heard before, a story they've lived themselves. They have their version of a similar narrative—a different town; a different decade; a different destructive habit to deal with the intense emotional pain; always going back home, whether it's moving up North or down South, with grandparents or to another school district in order to make it stop, to start fresh someplace else.

"There's not one person I know," a friend of mine said, "who hasn't been through that. I think every one of us, from Ruby Bridges on, has had to deal with it in some way. Maybe that's the price of the ticket."

MERI NANA-AMA DANQUAH

∘ ∘ ∘

After Korama's graduation ceremony my father placed his arm around her and said, "I'm so proud of you, sweetheart. The sky's the limit now." Korama looked up, as though she was already planning, accepting the invitation to soar. She turned toward her grandfather, smiled; and I could tell she believed him, that tall African man standing beside her. Korama believed that the sky was her limit, that her future was, indeed, hers to name.

THE BLACK BRAIN
by Greg Tate

The question of where to begin discussing The Black Brain (upper cased because It, like, Came From Outer Space—more on this later) actually turns out to be a no brainer since, as we all well know, the first brains on the planet showed up in the Kalahari desert region of southwest Africa about 20,000 years ago. Those brains specifically belonged to the Bantu-speaking black brains of the Kalahari's Khoi San people—folk who modern genetics and genealogy tell us possess the oldest "Y" chromosome markers on earth. That being the case, we've all got bits of black brain floating around inside of us no matter our more recent ancestry on other continents. The old saying 'It ain't the meat, its the motion,' may explain why we all can't dance like our more coordinated and rhythmic brothers and sisters of the human tribe—myself surely included.

From what we know of early Khoi San culture they seemed to have put those brains to good use in pursuit of many things we still chase after today—sex, drugs, rock and roll, cave painting, a hot meal and the holy ghost. The language of dreams also seems to have been as epiphenal to them as it was to Freud. From what we can tell from our vantage point two hundred centuries removed, they put great stock in what their shamans and priests were dreaming about while under the influence of some variation of wacky weed and that laffy taffy.

Thinking and drawing in metaphor also seems to have been a major pastime on evidence of the many highly stylized and highly evocative (and anything but simply mimetic) cave paintings they left on walls throughout the region. They also created an extraordinary music tradition—which, on evidence of the CD *Bushmen of the Kalahari* that I recently downloaded from Itunes, seems to these somewhat knowledgeable ears to have anticipated every subsequent significant body of music from Mozart to Motown, Mambo to Coltrane, Krunk to Kwaito.

Mathematician Ron Eglash has elaborately traced the origins of fractal geometry and the binary code, the algorithmic number system behind all of today's computing devices, to ancient African architecture and divination systems—the formulas for which were imported to Spain by a Moorish scholar and used by the Spanish philosopher Liebniz, whose work in turn inspired the work of Alan Turing, inventor of the first binary computing machine. Meanwhile, back in the jungle, indeed.

Since slavery days in America, however, the Black Brain has been on the defensive. The first great Black Essentialist Thomas Jefferson noted the same in his "1791 Notes On Virginia." Therein Ol Massa Thom assessed the New World Afrikan's reasoning capacities as inferior to whites based on his observations as a patriarchal slaveholding believer in the rights of men:

> *Comparing them by their faculties of memory, reason, and imagination, it appears to me that in memory they are equal to the whites; in reason much inferior, as I think one could scarcely be found capable of tracing and comprehending the investigations of Euclid; and that in imagination they are dull, tasteless, and anomalous.*

In reply to this drivel, African American math wizard Benjamin Banneker—clock builder, solar-eclipse-predictor, architect—had already, by the time Jefferson spewed those words, utilized Euclidean geometry to design the city of Washington DC, all well within spitting distance of Jefferson's beloved Monticello. When

Banneker wrote as much in a letter, Jefferson gave Banneker a polite reply, agreeing with all that brainy and black Banneker implored Massa Thom to ponder (like the need for Jefferson to renounce slavery in deed and not just self-abnegating words), but in private, Jeff let on that he basically considered Banneker to be some sort of freakish nigger-anomaly. (So fear not, The Black Brain, because like The Mythical Highlander, There Can Only Be One.)

There is some evidence that Black Brains did continue to proliferate in the New World after Bannker's time (1731–1801). One of the strangest of these was possessed by a man named Nat Turner who led the bloodiest slave revolt in US history in 1831. What's often recounted when Turner's name comes up is that his revolt led to the merciless slaughter of fifty-seven white men, women, and children. Less scrutiny actually attends the lucid but phantasmagorical words of his confession, which may constitute the first great American surrealist poem:

> . . . while laboring in the field, I discovered drops of blood on the corn as though it were dew from heaven—and I communicated it to many, both white and black, in the neighborhood—and I then found on the leaves in the woods hieroglyphic characters, and numbers, with the forms of men in different attitudes, portrayed in blood, and representing the figures I had seen before in the heavens. And now the Holy Ghost had revealed itself to me, and made plain the miracles it had shown me—For as the blood of Christ had been shed on this earth, and had ascended to heaven for the salvation of sinners, and was now returning to earth again in the form of dew—and as the leaves on the trees bore impression of the figures I had seen in the heavens, it was plain to me that the Savior was about to lay down the yoke he had borne for the sins of

men, and the great day of judgment was at hand. About this time I told these things to a white man, [Etheldred T. Brantley] on whom it had a wonderful effect—and he ceased from his wickedness, and was attacked immediately with an acutaneous eruption, and blood oozed from the pores of his skin.

Turner was also, his confessions point out, a prodigy as a child:

The manner in which I learned to read and write, not only had great influence on my own mind, as I acquired it with the most perfect ease, so much so, that I have no recollection whatever of learning the alphabet—but to the astonishment of the family, one day when a book was shewn to me to keep me from crying, I began spelling the names of different objects—this was a source of wonder to all in the neighborhood, particularly the blacks—and this learning was constantly improved at all opportunities—when I got large enough to go to work, while employed, I was reflecting on many things that would present themselves to my imagination, and whenever an opportunity occurred of looking at a book, when the school children were getting their lessons, I would find many things that the fertility of my own imagination had depicted to me before; all my time, not devoted to my master's service, was spent either in prayer, or in making experiments in casting different things in molds make of earth, in attempting to make paper, gun-powder and many other experiments, that although I could not perfect, yet convinced me of its practicability if I had the means.

Turner's confessor and his lawyer, Thomas Gray, notes that when he asked Turner for more details about his knowledge of casting, paper-making and dynamite, he had little doubt Turner could indeed have manufactured such items if he had the means.

Other formidable nineteenth-century Black Brains deserving of recognition and respect here would certainly be those of the well known Henry "Box" Brown, Frederick Douglass, Scott Joplin, Harriett Tubman, and Paul Laurence Dunbar. Less well known would be those of the men who made up The 'Glory' regiment as depicted in the film for which Denzel Washington won his first Oscar. Though the brothers as depicted in the film give little evidence of being above average intelligence, if even, the men of the actual unit left behind letters whose witty and direct use of language will likely embarrass many who call themselves professional writers today. One of them, known only as the private soldier GES, wrote the following letter from Jacksonville, Florida to a Philadelphia newspaper to protest the inequality shown to Union soldiers versus Rebel prisoners during the war:

There are a great many men, who were rebel soldiers, employed in the various departments here, and our Commissary furnishes hundreds of rations to the poor. They pretend to be in the most destitute condition, and there are some drawing rations from the Government who are well to do and fully able to provide for themselves. I cannot fail to contrast this treatment which rebels receive at the hands of our authorities, with that meted out to the negro soldiers by the rebel authorities. A flag of truce was sent out to the rebels the other day, and when asked about the negro prisoners and officers, the reply was: 'We will hand [hang?] every d—d negro officer we catch.' We can learn nothing of the colored prisoners. It is reported that they were killed on the field. When shall this weakness and folly on the part of our authorities cease? And when shall these atrocities be met with that vengeance and retaliation they so justly merit? Where are the colored prisoners captured on James Island, July 16th, 1863, and those captured at Fort Wagner, July 18th? And, lastly, where are those captured at the Battle of Olustee, February 20th, 1864? Can any escaped prisoner answer? Can any Federal spy answer? Can any one in authority answer? Can any man answer this question? If, while we are pampering and petting rebel prisoners, Federal prisoners are hung and enslaved, we are exchanging smiles for kicks—paying gold and honor for dross and dishonor. . . .

There are comparatively few contrabands coming into our lines. The rebels had been expecting our force here in Jacksonville a fortnight before its arrival, and ran all their negroes off into Georgia. As soon as the male contrabands reach here, they are put into the army, and the females are sent to Hilton Head, or permitted to go to Fernandina. Poor creatures! They are the most wo-be-gone set—no shoes, hats or clothing, and, what the most impoverished slave-woman seldom fails to possess, turbans. I have noticed a strange peculiarity among the people here. They are all the most outrageous stutterers. If you meet one and say, "How are you?" as you pass, you could walk a whole block before he could sputter out the Southern, "Right smart, I thank ee."

There have been four inflictions of the death penalty on colored soldiers since the landing of the expedition, February 7th, 1864. Is this not strange?

I might write at greater length, but long letters are tedious. Trusting that the cause of justice, for which we all struggle, may meet no detriment by the hands of our wicked enemies,

I remain yours, very truly,
G.E.S.

Another of them, Corporal James Henry Gooding, wrote letters of such powerful reasoning that some Civil War scholars, we're told, remain "baffled" as to where Gooding—who records show to have been merely a "common seaman" before the war—might have received his 'classical' education. This excerpt from a rather droll and cheeky complaint he wrote to President Lincoln about the unequal pay doled to all black soldiers, whether they were Freeman or Ex-Slave (or Contraband in the parlance of the times) may help explain why Gooding's way with the pen still has those scholars babbling in shock and awe:

> Now if the United States exacts uniformity of treatment of her Soldiers, from the Insurgents, would it not be well, and consistent, to set the example herself, by paying all her Soldiers alike? We of this Regt. were not enlisted under any "contraband" act. But we do not wish to be understood, as rating our Service, of more Value to the Government, than the service of the ex-slave. Their Service is undoubtedly worth much to the Nation, but Congress made express, provision touching their case, as slaves freed by military necessity, and assuming the Government, to be their temporary Guardian—Not so with us—Freemen by birth, and consequently, having the advantage of thinking, and acting for ourselves, so far as the Laws would allow us. We do not consider ourselves fit subjects for the Contraband act. We appeal to You, Sir: as the Executive of the Nation, to have us Justly Dealt with. The Regt, do pray, that they be assured their service will be fairly appreciated, by paying them as American SOLDIERS, not as menial hierlings.

One can only chuckle imagining how different a film experience *Glory* would have been if the African American soldiers' language skills had been as accurately represented as their battlefield mien. (Likely, they would had to have come out with subtitles and then a translation of those subtitles, as in the Jamaican patois film, *Rockers*.)

What may be most ironic about the recurring drubbing, doubting, and outright dissing The Black Brain continues to be confronted with is the fact that the human brain actually contains a very key component known by the medically Latinate assignation Le Substabtia Nigra, or roughly translated, That Black Stuff. Now the Nigra is located in the brainstem, the part of the brain that controls a person's reflexes, autonomic breathing, body temperature, sleep, wakefulness, and blood circulation. It is so called because its neurons contain a high amount of melanin—which give it "a particular dark color"— and of what's known as black substance dopamine. The Nigra is one of three primary producers of the neurotransmitter dopamine, which turns to be rather crucial when it comes to such critical activities as behavior and cognition, motor activity, motivation and reward, inhibition of prolactin production (involved in lactation), sleep, mood, attention, and learning. Deterioration of The Nigra is thought to be instrumental in the onset of Parkinson's disease, and in fact most of the research you will find on the Internet about The Nigra is mostly concerned, surprise, surprise, with what happens when The Nigra goes bad. Once again, no love for the common Nigra.

Dig deeper than the dopamine and Parkinson's researchers, however, and you'll find the writings of one Italian scientist who believes that all life on earth originated in star-hopping superblack carbon-based aminos that generously traversed mad galaxies enveloped in cosmic dust solely intent on producing The Nigra, the rest of the buckwild human family that followed, and all other organic life as we know it.

More Afrocentric researchers of The Nigra also feel that its presence in folk with more melanin content than the waisaichu may account for why children of phenotypically African descent develop coordination and motor skills at a faster rate than children of phenotypically European descent, and may also be the source of the mythical and mystical powers of the pineal gland, also known as 'the third eye.'

HUNGRY
by Kenneth Carroll

*I would hurl words into this darkness and wait
for an echo, and if an echo sounded, no matter
how faintly, I would send other words to tell, to
march, to fight, to create a sense of hunger for life
that gnaws in us all.*
—Richard Wright

"This is my pillow," says my five-year-old son, laying his head on my stomach. He absent-mindedly pats the roundness of my gut as he heads off to sleep. The stomach my doctors vehemently advise me to lose is one of my son's favorite places. Whether watching cartoons, picture-book-reading his way to sleep, or just jabbering in five-year-old verbosity, this is his place. Sometimes he mocks me, stands shirtless in the mirror and mimics my exasperated examination of my paunch. My son knows nothing about the days when my stomach was flat and barely full. He knows nothing of the agitated conversations of parents who fret about job security, evictions and future clouded by the twin evils of racism and poverty. Back when my stomach was flat, like the world, when my seven siblings and I lived so close to the hungers that poor children are faced with that we could hear them whisper at night.

Growing up in the sixties and seventies in DC's rapidly disintegrating public housing, I never knew a really fat kid. They were the oddities, the kids to pick on. Fat kids either had a medical condition or their parents were able to secure extra food by hustling. In the seventies hustling meant the criss-crossing of legal and illegal jobs to make ends meet. Kids weren't beyond hustling also. Poverty rarely allowed us children the opportunity to be lazy. Between the three, but more often two, squares our parents squeezed from the dollars they had, we kids had to provide our own "in-between meal snacks." Sometimes this required procuring five-finger discounts from "mom and pop" stores owned by other black families. Most often, however, it required legal hustling, holding the two full-time and one part-time jobs that black folks had resigned themselves to doing since Reconstruction. But no matter how hard families hustled, legal or illegal, there was seldom excess. So we kids understood early, as all poor kids do, that we would have to find our nickels and dimes through our own devices.

I began working at about age eight, carrying grocery bags from the store for women. I also had a paper route and collected soda bottles. My friends and I spent ALL our hard-earned money on snacks. Sometimes the more conscientious among us actually bought food for their families, but the rest of us ran to the "mom and pop" stores to buy up every pastry and penny candy available. Those who had no money resorted to the "cuts" game. If one of your friends said "cuts" before you said "no cuts" you had to break them off a piece of your snack. But the game was just that. It was for play because we'd never let one of our friends go hungry, unless it was payback for some previous act of being stingy on their part. We kids knew the cyclical reality of hunger and family dysfunction. Eventually we'd all have to deal with one or both. So we shared, partly out of love, partly out of necessity.

But just like the carefree laughter of my friends, the candy only temporarily assuaged my real, unarticulated appetite. I craved for something all children need as much as well-balanced meals. I hungered for stability. I hungered for the security of knowing that running home straight from school and throwing open the refrigerator wouldn't result in disappointment. I hungered for the knowledge that my father, unlike the fathers of most of the kids in my neighborhood, would be there, in the home where we lived, in

KENNETH CARROLL

the stands or bleachers where we played. A full stomach, like a full refrigerator, had meaning beyond its contents. It connoted a normalcy we could only wish for. It said that everything was all right, at least temporarily. I knew, sure as the changing of the seasons, that I would come home and find an empty refrigerator or a home empty of a father. There were times,when my alcoholic father, on a shame-filled binge of drinking because he'd lost the rent money gambling, would be gone for days, and the refrigerator and cupboards echoed his absence.

Those salad-less days were the times when I fell in love with my mother, who turned batter, leftovers, sliced vegetables, and rotting fruit into salves for the chorus of bellies that demanded responsibility and miracles from her. Our eight mouths excused the deprivation a father who was out in the street feeding or succumbing to his own hunger. My mother turned day-old bread and hard crust into pudding, and rotting apples were sliced for the good portions and fried in cinnamon. Flour rose like Lazarus in my mother's kitchen to create hearty biscuits.

We never were malnourished and we never went without a dinner, but sometimes we only got one chicken back and a single serving of veggies and potatoes. Beans of all varieties were a staple in our home. This was not enough for eight rambunctious children who hurled themselves through the day in perpetual motion, as if eluding some unseen pursuer. Between paydays, my father's mounting debts and his descending ego, our stomachs, impatient and insolent, howled. This compelled us to relieve its temporary discomfort with remedies that often violated the tenets of my mother's morality.

My best friend Erroll and his brothers had sickle cell anemia, a condition that caused them to be hungry all the time. They were the only kids in the projects who regularly drank sugar water. Earl's belly jutted from his slender frame like one of those starving African or Chinese kids that our parents conjured when we turned up our noses at squash. Erroll was quick-witted, industrious, and perhaps egged-on by hunger, was fearless. He was certainly not going to wait for his meals, nor did he trouble himself with worries about familial stability. He answered every call of his distended belly with visits to the Safeway grocery store on the avenue. He taught me how to shoplift, admonishing me to, "Never to steal more than you can eat." This was his strategy should the indolent security guards awaken and actually care about their jobs. I learned to heist fruit and pastries, which would be flattened inside my underwear. I got pretty good at stealing, and by my seventh grade year, I stole nearly every day. I augmented my school lunch with snacks and fresh fruits. I don't know if it was the proximity of my church, St. Francis DeSales, to the grocery store I stole from daily, or just my mother's *Raisin In The Sun* teachings kicking in, but I felt bad about not feeling bad about stealing. Satisfied with the knowledge that I was now wise enough to make the pangs in my stomach cease even when I was broke, I decided to stop stealing everyday.

Located between St. Francis, where I went to seek answers and salvation on Sundays, and the Safeway grocery store, where I went to increase my daily caloric intake, was the Woodridge Branch Public Library. The building was a nondescript rectangle of 1950s functional design. It had one floor of books and a basement for meetings. On a day when there was nothing for lunch and my stomach expressed itself with a militant sound that rumbled through my classroom, I decided to go to the library after school to kill a few minutes while deciding whether to steal something to assuage the noisy tremors in my belly or simply hope for a filling meal at home. Normally I'd go to the library and grab the Sepia and Jet Magazines. I'd flip through them, looking for stories on athletes or entertainers, though more often I'd end up looking at the "Beauty of the Week" and trying to suppress an erection that seemed to arbitrarily find a reason to make its presence known. Thanks a lot God, I sarcastically thought, another hunger to feed.

KENNETH CARROLL

But this day in the library, I picked up a book called *Black Poets*, an anthology edited by Dudley Randall. I cracked its spine and there in front of me was a short poem. "Wild Negro Bill." The first line of the poem went, "I'se Wild Nigger Bill." I looked around the library, sure that somebody was going to tell me to put away the book with the word my mother forbade us to use. Wild Nigger Bill proclaimed his freedom from slavery, from white folks, from work, and, it seemed to me, from an unjust world. There was no other information on this anonymous poem about Bill, but I was sure that he did not let hunger lull-a-bye him to sleep. "I eats up raw goose widout apple sauce!" By the end of the poem he's no longer Wild Nigger Bill, but "Runaway Bill," an elevation in status due to his rebellion and initiative. In *Black Poets* I discovered Langston Hughes, Lucille Clifton, Amiri Baraka, and many more voices, angry or analytical, voices that screamed unabashedly about all that they lacked and were determined to have.

When I was nearly finished with the book, I went back to the literature section and grabbed the book that was next to it called *Negro Writers*, edited by Langston Hughes and Arna Bontemps. There I found more poets and new poems with different voices warming my chest. I mumbled the words of the poems beneath my breath, eager to hear them, to hear the music my eyes told me was there on the page. While I was reading Langston's "I am the darker brother," the librarian tapped me. I jumped, and she jumped at my jumping. "We're closing," she said. "If you want to continue reading those books, you'll have to check them out." I looked up, and blinked myself back into the world. The sun sunk into the hills of the playground behind the library and an eager moon sat in the April sky. I looked quickly at the grocery store. It was shuttered like a state secret. I knew that whatever meat my mother had cooked, my portion had probably been doled out to my siblings as a lesson to me about getting home on time. We were not the Cleavers, who would have had a stern warning and heated plate of food waiting for the

Beaver had he tarried from school. Of course missing dinner would be the least of my troubles if my mother didn't buy the homework excuse I had prepared.

I decided to check out the books. I walked the quarter mile home, reading the poems from *Black Poets* again. The streetlights came on as I read, and this time I recited the words aloud, laughing or being empathetically angry with the authors. I loved these people who wrote these poems, I thought, and nearly cried at the idea that they had written these poems for me. These writers, who I could no longer consider strangers once I read their poems, articulated the distance between desire and acquisition. They spoke with such power of their own hungers. They said it was something in the world, not just in my home or in the projects, that was creating my appetite. My hunger, they asserted, was not a natural hunger. They said my poverty was not the sole responsibility of my father or the divine roles assigned to black folks. Their poems talked as frankly about racism as my mother's friends gossiping in our kitchen. Their poems were a stark contrast to my parents, who whispered truths they thought I couldn't handle, or teachers who repeated myths and dared me not to believe them. They told me the truth. Not like St. Francis church, where the truth was hidden in Latin and archaic ritual. These poets sounded like Friday night card games in my kitchen, or shit talking barbers on Saturday morning. Their rhythm belonged to Otis Redding and Aretha Franklin.

I entered the noisy village of our housing projects, and realized that my stomach had not grumbled once while I read the books. Not in the library. Not in the twenty-minute walk home. After that day, a day where I was sated by verse and stanza, the library became my sanctuary. I discovered more black poetry anthologies and added Larry Neal and Amiri Baraka's *Black Fire* to my "favorites" list. I checked these books out so often that the Librarian invoked some rare rule disallowing me the chance to have them out for more than thirty days at a time. Finally, I decided to make them

KENNETH CARROLL

mine. I did the same thing I did when I had no money for food. I stole the books.

South African writer Nadine Gordimer remarked, "Truth isn't always beauty, but the hunger for it is." What I hungered for and what the poets gave me was stability. Unlike my father, unlike my next meal, they would be there guaranteed with more words than I could consume in one sitting. Their words were a sympathetic echo to my pain. I also discovered my own voice—a way to articulate my own needs. I began writing poetry about the hunger associated with being poor and black, and how it leads many to sickness or death. But this glorious hunger, this desire for truth and beauty, had lead me to a library and to a skill, a strategy, that would keep me from ever worrying about my next meal or the expectant emptiness of home. I often missed meals with no regret while I sat in my room and wrote or read. I pasted my poems on my walls, using every available space in my bedroom.

Some days I would come home and find my father sitting on my bed, quietly reading the poems on my wall. When he noticed me he would wordlessly leave my room, never commenting, not even on the poems about him. My mother, however, found great joy in my poetry. She and her friends filled my face with home-cooked desserts as I read them in our kitchen.

While my father continued to use alcohol to fill the chasm that sent him away from his children's eyes and into the streets, I considered his reading my poems a kind of skewed dialog—the same way my poems became a skewed and one-way dialog with a country I loved, but a country I was sure despised my existence.

But my son, who is asleep now on my stomach, will never know the deprivations that sought to define and confine my life. I have taken the advice of the black poets, and I have not let my own hunger diminish my capacity to give what I was deprived of as a child. My son, who has my father's head, sleeps soundly. I place a kiss on his cheek and notice his stomach, quiet, flat, filled.

FEAR AND LOATHING
by Stephanie Covington Armstrong

I spent more than half my life despising the black female body, my black female body. I blamed it for attracting and allowing the most heinous crimes. These feelings of loathing began in childhood and continued on into my adulthood. I thought that by whittling down my black girl curves, shaping them into my own masterpiece, nothing bad would ever happen to me.

We lived in the Bedford-Stuyvesant neighborhood of Brooklyn. In the seventies, Bed-Stuy was an uneasy mix of the seedy and the sophisticated. It didn't have the safe homespun feel of a Spike Lee set. Vietnam vets returning from the war littered the corners with beer cans, Mad Dog, and Newport butts; they reeked of urine and danger. Like all little girls, I wanted the fairytale; I knew instinctively that it didn't exist in my neighborhood, so escape was always on my mind.

To the men in my neighborhood, women were merely objects that could be broken down into parts and then reassembled. At will, they could turn those Bed-Stuy streets that we called home into a war zone. I grew up watching my mother steel her body as we traveled through the minefield of catcalls and whistles. Back then she had the kind of traffic-stopping figure adults referred to as a "Brick-Shit-House." At five feet eight, one hundred and twenty pounds, stacked like a Vegas showgirl, my mother commanded male attention whether she wanted to or not. She rarely responded to that sort of attention, but whether she ignored it or spoke up, it seemed as though nothing could stop these men from loudly commenting on her body, from head to toe, part by part. As a child, witnessing this was frightening and traumatic, especially the vulgar hand motions,

261

and the way they reached out to touch her. It wasn't just as if they wanted to have her; it was as if they intended to have her.

I decided early on that I did not want my mother's body. I did not want to be rendered powerless, like my mother, like all the other black women in our neighborhood. I wanted to be able to walk down the street and not have men call out to me, reach out for me. I wanted to be untouchable.

By the time I came of age, my body took on a life of its own, bending toward womanhood at a much slower pace than the bodies of my two older sisters. They were both tall, slim—and stacked. They were buxom, with cinched waists and that classic black woman backside. I was shorter and a lot less busty. In fact, I was completely flat-chested, even past the age of fifteen. Nevertheless, that didn't discourage the unwanted advances of men. Particularly one man, our uncle, the man who had turned himself into my molester. I had already started identifying the female body with helplessness, and seeing it as an invitation to trouble. The more my figure developed, the tiniest hint of breasts budding and that tight bubble butt, the less comfortable I grew with myself.

I came to view each rite of passage into womanhood as a betrayal. It became harder and harder to pretend that I was somehow immune to my ancestry. I was growing into my future, stepping fully into myself, a black woman, which meant that I could no longer be flat and insignificant. I could no longer be invisible.

"Can I get some fries with that shake?" the men would sneer as I walked to the subway station.

"You must be a member of the itty bitty titty committee," they'd taunt as I walked home, "but don't worry 'cause a mouthful is all I need."

The inevitable had happened. I had become prey.

I developed an unhealthy scorn for my body. By my early twenties I had tried every quick-fix diet and miracle remedy. I was determined to fight my body's natural instincts, its God given assets. Despite all the negative attention it sometimes attracted from men, my mother and my sisters celebrated their womanliness. They seemed secure with themselves and with who they were. I envied them this freedom. I wanted my body to be off-limits to even the most discerning, prying eye. I wanted men to see me as too fragile to assault with crass words or insulting hand gestures.

The journey from diets and potions to laxative abuse happened quickly. Before I knew it I was popping handfuls of laxatives, swallowing them as though they were sweets. I was drinking gallons of dieter's tea, the kind that makes your stomach cramp and keeps you in the bathroom for hours. Slowly, I starved myself away. Weighted down by my past and by that familiar feeling of helplessness, my weight became the one thing I could control in my life. Or, at least, that's what I thought.

What I wanted was to be admired, to be adored and revered. Rarely had I seen that happen to anyone in real life, certainly not the women I knew and certainly not by anybody in my neighborhood. It happened to the waifish women on television and to the butt-less, stick-figured supermodels who graced the covers of fashion magazines. To me they appeared sacred, glamorous, absent of any flaws; it was as if nothing bad could ever happen to them. If I couldn't be like them then I wanted to be ignored, just left alone.

To me the black female body was identified with overt sexuality. Whether the blame rests squarely on the media, rap music, hip hop videos or our history—slavery, miscegenation, rape—I wanted to distance myself, my body, from those images. It seemed that no designer had yet created an outfit that could successfully downplay the curves of most black women. I began to stay away from colors that accentuated those curves, bold colors like reds, yellows and oranges. I started dressing in darker, more neutral colors. Blacks, whites, tans, browns and denims were the perfect camouflage. Some people might think it was my blackness that I resented. It wasn't. I love my dark skin and nappy hair, which I have usually opted to wear natural. What I resented was my state of poverty. Interestingly the two, poverty and blackness, often go hand in hand. But it was poverty, not blackness, which robbed me of the ability to trust that any of my needs would ever be met. It was poverty, not blackness, that imprisoned me in those circumstances, in that neighborhood, with those men.

It makes perfect sense to me now that I equated heaviness, and powerlessness, with poverty—just as it makes sense to me that people mistakenly equate blackness and black culture with things that are in reality synonymous with, and symbolic, of poverty. The fried rice and fried chicken, the meat patties and coco-bread, all that carbohydrate-rich, high-fat, high-sodium, MSG-laden food could easily be found in my neighborhood, or any other black neighborhood. It was a psychological trick on the poor. Soul food was the stuff of nostalgia; never mind that it came at a cost, that far from sustaining us, it was what killed us. It was what made us obese, made us sick. Overweight women bragged about being happy, comfortable with the extra padding. I just couldn't relate. At family gatherings, my female relatives would remind me that "men prefer a little something to hold onto." If I dared to defend the positive aspects of being slender, I was told, "the only thing that likes a stick is a dog."

Wallis Simpson, the American-born Duchess of York, once said, "You can never be too rich or too thin." I had never been either. But I felt that I had paid my dues; I had done more than my fair share of time in the poverty zone; I had survived on food stamps and government cheese. And now, I was done. Now, I wanted the opposite, and the way I would get there was by being thin. Thinness would be my ticket.

Nothing is more tiring than self-loathing. Every moment of every day is spent wanting to be something or someone other than who

STEPHANIE COVINGTON ARMSTRONG

or what you are. Hating the financial realities of my life was one thing; hating myself was another. It would take me years before I learned how and why I linked the two together in my mind, how and why I thought that I could change one by controlling the other.

Here's the truth: lots of women would have given anything for that body, that black female body that I tried to starve away. Lots of people told me that, but I never believed them. No amount of compliments could convince me that my body was bangin'. That's because all those years of playing games with my weight, of dieting, starvation, abuse of laxatives and diuretics, and compulsive exercising led to body dysmorphic disorder. I became unable to view my body as others saw it. In the mirror, a small tight butt appeared large and shapeless. It didn't matter if I was one hundred pounds or one hundred and forty pounds, I was always heavier than I wanted to be; bigger than I deserved to be.

Those rare times when the scale tipped in my favor, my imagined perfection left me elated. But it never lasted. The scale that had one day been a friend would quickly become an enemy, chastising me for a blatant lack of control. I hated the way my inner thighs seemed to meet no matter how much I exercised. I hated the way my stomach would sometimes become soft and mushy. I hated myself, my life. I fell into a deep and utter despair, pained at my inability to control anything in my life. I had failed miserably at the one thing that seemed easy, the one thing I should have been able to do, relieve myself of the body I so despised.

I wonder how many little black girls feel that way? How many look in the mirror and hate what they see? How many try to erase themselves from head to toe, part by part? I took it to the extreme; I know this. But there are so many levels of that type of suffering, of that type of feud between the self and the body. So many ways for a young black girl to remedy the powerlessness that is imposed on them. I realized this only after my whole life had fallen apart. Only after I had nowhere to turn, when I could barely stand tall anymore, and there was nothing left for me to do except surrender. I dropped down on my knees, clasped my hands together and cried "Oh God, please help me."

I learned to love my body, to accept it for all its flaws and to appreciate it for all its beauty, all the things that make it a classic black woman's body. These days I love my butt, the power of my thighs, and slight sway of my breasts. I love my body clothed and naked. But all of that took a while to happen, years of therapy, prayer, and self-discovery. Forgiveness became the key that set me loose, not only of my eating disorder but also of the guilt and shame I had been carrying for years. It also shifted how I viewed myself in relationship to men. I stopped expecting them to disappoint me, to judge me or to wound me. When a man noticed my body it stopped being a scary reminder of the rape. I stopped identifying every man who could present a threat with my uncle. I came to understand that being raped altered my sense of safety in the world. It made me paralyzed, afraid of losing control, afraid of being vulnerable.

When I became pregnant with my first child I developed an even greater love and acceptance for the black body. My black body, which was housing my baby's black body. I appreciated the strength my ancestors passed on to me. Being an expectant mother allowed me to connect to my own mother, to her body, which I had once considered powerless, an invitation to trouble. Her body had been strong enough to bear three daughters, strong enough to bear the sole financial responsibility of their household, the isolation that came with that responsibility, and the unwanted interest of strange men. It had sheltered her daughters from the pain of fatherlessness. My mother was a strong black woman who had always recognized the power she held in her body. I, on the other hand, was just learning.

Each day of my pregnancy I fell in love with the way my body swelled and conformed to support the needs of my growing child.

STEPHANIE COVINGTON ARMSTRONG

I fell in love with the idea of pushing forth yet another black female body into the world. As my thighs stretched toward each other I never, not once, worried that I was growing fat or obese. I was a healthy mother, something I never thought I would be, and that's what mattered most.

Recently I went for a run in my neighborhood. I was dressed in baggy sweats, a t-shirt and running shoes. A day laborer, with a stack of menus in his hand, flagged me down. "Excuse me." He spoke in the accent of the newly arrived. I removed my Ipod head-phones and answered him, "Yes?"

"I live on Venice," he said, pointing toward a neighborhood fur-ther south. Not quite understanding his question I leaned in closer. "Yes, are you lost?"

"How much?"

"Excuse me?" I still couldn't comprehend.

"How much for you to go to Venice Blvd?" He smiled up at me, his face full of hope.

"For what?" I couldn't seem to break through the communica-tion barrier.

"Twenty dollars?" He offered the price up as if he were sug-gesting an item off one those menus he was carrying. In that second I understood. It finally became clear. I hurried away, shocked by his ignorance. But I didn't turn it into *my* issue as I might have done once upon a time. I knew, all too well, that it was *his* issue, *his* problem. I was free to go about my day, my life and that's because I love myself. I know my worth.

IN SICKNESS
by Gail Wronsky

Sometimes you're lucky to have a job at all. My brother says in Cincinati these days you've got to have an MBA to work at the Wal-Mart. But most of the people I know have held minimum-wage jobs at some point—while they were students, or between other gigs, or sometime in their twenties before they figured out what else to do. Most of those jobs were in food service or offices or retail stores (all of which have their own bragging rights). Why I decided to work at a hospital in Virginia, schlepping bedpans instead of cocktails while going to school, I don't know. It had something to do with wanting to learn about the body—wanting to face the facts of our physical lives as human beings—wanting to touch skin and hair, take temperatures, feel pulses, tend wounds. It had something to do with being raised in a middle-class, white, suburban world in which the body was almost systematically denied and ignored.

In my house, we didn't smell bad (we wore deodorant!), we didn't menstruate (or at least we never mentioned that we did), we didn't fart (overtly), belch (never!), and nobody but nobody died (if they did, there wasn't an open casket, or a wake, and the dead person wasn't talked about after that unless in euphemism). Breasts were bound up tightly in cotton armor; hips and buttocks encased in girdles. Nothing on my body was ever supposed to shake or seem soft.

I applied for the job as a nurses' aide because I wanted to learn what I felt had been hidden from me during childhood. It happened, because of geographical location and population densities, that the people who would teach me about the body would, for the most part, be black people. The hospital where I worked was in Charlottesville. Many of the patients were black—some from the city and some from Blue Ridge Mountain mining towns or farm towns. The staff of the hospital was divided almost exclusively in terms of race: the doctors were white or Asian; the RNs were white; the nurses' aides, orderlies, food workers and janitorial staff were African American. And me. But I was used to being kind of a fish-out-of-water—it was 1977 and I was Charlottesville's only punk-rocker. My hair was blue; I wore so much eyeliner that I looked a little bit like Uncle Fester; I dressed in combat boots, thrift store men's clothes, and festooned myself with costume jewelry.

At the hospital they gave me a white scrub dress, told me to get white stockings and sneakers, and didn't say a thing about the hair or makeup—which was the first thing I loved about the place. The other nurses' aides wore wigs, or dyed their hair bright orange or red and lacquered it up to the heavens in fantastic loops and sweeps. The truth was, I fit in better there than in my classes at the university, where I was considered weird and/or crazy. The women I worked with at the hospital sometimes even asked me where I bought my jewelry, or how did I do that to my hair (not *why*).

I had as my teacher, my hospital guru, a black woman named Rema, who was (and I know the dangerous water I'm treading here in terms of racial/gender stereotyping) a genius and a saint. Rema had raised umpteen children and had worked at the hospital for decades. She was tall and thin with gray hair and thick eyeglasses. One of the luckiest things that has ever happened to me was her taking me on to be her protégé. Out of a training class of ten or twelve, she zeroed in on me, the only white girl, and made me her student. I always felt that she saw me as kind of pathetic. Which I was, truly, in terms of care-giving experience.

Rema's relationship with the bodies of her patients was absolutely matter-of-fact. There wasn't a physical condition anyone

GAIL WRONSKY

could have which surprised her, or grossed her out, or made her embarrassed. She taught me how to give shampoos to people who were paralyzed or comatose. ("Never say anything personal about the ones in comas," she said. "They're listening!") She taught me how to prep people for surgery, which mostly meant how to shave crotches and bellies. Showing me how to give my first bed-bath (to an enormously obese white woman), she lathered up a washcloth, pushed it between the woman's legs, and went to work. The woman hadn't had a bath in days. Rema handed me the washcloth after she was done—I was supposed to rinse it—and said, "Always soap up that perineal area good." I could see how uncomfortable the experience was for the woman getting the bath, how embarrassed she felt, and how the tone of Rema's voice, her professionalism and expertise, made the bath seem normal; it was just a matter of course, and thus somehow not a thing that called forth judgment or condemnation. Her nasty crotch was "a perineal area." Her obesity was something Rema never let on that she noticed.

Rema treated the black patients and white patients with absolute equanimity, and everyone preferred her care to the care of anyone else on staff. I was accepted, even later when I wasn't in training and was no longer working with her, because I'd *been* trained by her. The training consisted, for the most part, of my imitating her—I moved my hands and arms the way she moved hers, carried on conversations the way she did (friendly but not too friendly—not ever so personal as to be condescending. She'd enter a room saying something like, "Who ever heard of making lime juice out of real limes—the world's gone crazy, I swear!" to which everyone had some kind of reply). Watching her, I learned how to give CPR, wipe butts, rub backs, spoon-feed people who don't want food, tend bedsores, and change colostomy bags.

But it was what accompanied my aping of her behavior that was the real miracle of getting to work with Rema: a profound internal change. I soon found that working with hospital patients I was calmer than I'd ever been doing anything. I felt like a Zen monk, in fact—just doing what I was doing. Nothing frightened me or disgusted me. I didn't get embarrassed by nakedness or sexual organs. I still found some smells hard to stomach, but I didn't make it a big deal, even in my own mind. They were simply smells the body produced and they had to be endured. When I got home after my shift I always stood in a hot shower for ten minutes. But I didn't experience any of it as awful. I didn't resent having to scrub myself down, and I think I would have if I hadn't been transformed by watching what I came to think of as Rema's holy dance of healing.

Unlike Rema, who didn't seem to care who her patients were, I preferred taking care of black patients. I know it's not cool to make generalizations like that, but the truth is, I always felt a little more upbeat walking into the room of a black patient. To put it simply, black people seemed to be more at ease in their bodies than white people did. They seemed less embarrassed by their illnesses, their body odors, their excrement. They laughed more easily.

The difference between walking into the room of a black man and a white man with a straight razor in my hand, having to shave their pubic hair before surgery—well, it was beyond huge. The white men, as a rule, were horrified, even when they pretended not to be. The black men were both resigned and ironic, sharing, mostly wordlessly, or with a comment like, "If you don't hurt me, I won't hurt you, baby," an awareness of both the delicacy and the humor of the situation. They'd give me a grin and a shrug, and I'd get to work, shielding the penis with my left hand while I cleaned the hair off expertly with the razor in my right. It was what had to be done. Black men accepted the unpleasantness with grace. On a couple occasions white men even refused to let me do it, demanding a male, or an older woman. "Get this castrating freak out of my fucking room!" one of them yelled out once. I heard that the person they sent in to replace me gave him a heck of a shave.

After a year in the regular hospital I was transferred to the psych ward and put on night shift (11 p.m. to 7 a.m.). I no longer had to wear the scrub dress; I no longer had to empty bedpans or give baths or shave crotches. Mostly what I did, in fact, was play cards with the patients who couldn't sleep. Again, as in the regular hospital, many of the patients were black. All of those were women. It occurred to me, after working there for a while, that black men were probably put in prison for doing the things that landed white men in a psychiatric hospital. But that's another essay.

As a young feminist I was appalled by the treatment of the women on the ward. Most of them were depressed, had attempted suicide, and most were treated with a combination of electroshock therapy and mind-killing drugs. I worked on that ward for about six months and never once saw a man treated with electroshock. Yet another essay.

Within the hierarchy of the place, black women were clearly at the bottom. They were ogled, and probably fondled, if not worse, by orderlies (black and white) routinely. They were subjected to sexually explicit comments and crude insinuations by hospital staff and other patients much more consistently than white women were. When I brought this up at staff meetings I was ignored. The chief of staff was an Indian man from Bangalore; I used to picture him throwing widows on funeral pyres, which is bigoted of me, but he was the one prescribing all the ECT.

The patients I remember most from my time there were black women: Delores and Mary. I remember them because of the ways in which both of them were victims of the black, female body. I remember what I learned from them about what it means to inhabit that body.

Delores was a fierce woman in her twenties, claimed to be a hooker, who'd been brought in through emergency because she'd slashed her thighs with a steak knife. She was incredibly beautiful—dark skin, almond eyes, the voluptuous body of a goddess. The whites of her eyes were chrome yellow from hepatitis, which made her look like an exotic cat of some kind, or a creature from another planet. She was only on the ward for a week, on suicide watch, meaning she couldn't have anything sharp in her room—nothing glass that could be shattered, no razors, no nail scissors—and her visitors were frisked before being allowed to see her. (I only ever saw one visitor, a skinny, depressed-looking black man who was either her father or her pimp—she never said which—and he'd clearly spent more time than he'd have liked to visiting Delores in places he didn't want to be.)

What was stunning about her behavior to me was the way she seemed to call out all the sexual harassment that was constantly coming toward her. It was as if she felt, or knew, that her strength was all in that body. She pushed her breasts in people's faces; she swayed up and down the corridor shaking her ample ass. Clearly that was how she'd managed to get along in the world as far as she'd gotten. If everyone was going to see her as a sex object, hell, she'd out-sex-object herself. She'd be threateningly sexual. Brilliantly sexual. And she was.

Playing cards with me and a couple of the other aides at 3 a.m. was the only time I saw her relax a little. Not completely—she kept her eye on the men, if there were any in the room, and sexualized the conversation between herself and them if they hadn't sexualized it first. She was in control (cheated at cards like crazy, too; I always tried to be her partner). She made herself so outrageously an embodiment of female sexuality that most men backed down rather than go further with their banter. As if to offer proof of her prowess, she eventually broke out of the place by cozying up to one of the orderlies and getting him to help

GAIL WRONSKY

her—I don't know if there were any sexual favors involved, but I imagine there were.

The only thing that keeps her story from being a story of triumph is, of course, the self-destructive behavior with the steak knife. I've thought about her for years, thought about her trying to turn her body, probably her most available resource, into power. It could almost work, couldn't it? Like the black community taking racist language and making it a weapon used by them not against them? But Delores was not only female, she was black and female. The absolutely devalued nature of her status in the urban, Southern world was something she'd clearly internalized; slashing her own thighs, she hurt herself better than any man could hurt her. Or perhaps before someone specific could hurt her. I sometimes wonder whether she cut herself on purpose in order to spend some time in the hospital—the whole thing being a way of hiding out maybe. It would have been another way of turning her body, her one bit of collateral, of capital, into something useful to her. It would have been a smart move in that case, if a painful one, and not simply a demonstration of intense self-loathing. To this day it hurts me to think that there wasn't any other place for her incredible energy and audacious alacrity to go.

Mary was a thirteen-year-old girl who'd been brought to the ward because she'd stuck thumbtacks into the bottom of a baby's foot in her foster home. She refused to speak. I'd been assigned to conduct her admissions interview and write up a report, but she wouldn't say a word, so I had to just describe her physically and try to assess her demeanor. She was in some ways the opposite of Delores: she was not yet a woman. Her breasts were small, her feet and hands too big for her bony frame. She reminded me of a Dalmation puppy—the way she hadn't even grown into her limbs yet. Even though she wasn't beautiful, she was adorable. She looked at me sideways, without actually giving me any eye contact.

The report that came with her from the police said she'd spent her entire life moving around among various foster families, but had been at her most recent place for more than a year. The baby, a new foster, had just arrived. I can imagine the rage she felt—and the fear that her already so-tentative place in the world might be threatened by the newcomer. Tragically, the violent demonstration of her anger and fear guaranteed that she wouldn't be allowed back there. In fact, her foster parents never even visited. Her only visitor, and he came every day, was a shy young black man who was in love with her.

The doctor on staff—the Indian guy—gave her a physical exam and discovered she was sexually active, a fact he brought up at the first staff meeting after her admittance. Since she wouldn't speak to anyone, he insisted she be given birth control implants in her arm, without consent. To me that seemed an outrageous violation—putting chemicals in her body, controlling her fertility—it wasn't quite as bad as forced sterilization because it wasn't permanent, but that's what it evoked in my mind. I objected strenuously, and eventually a couple of the nurses supported my objections. Backing off somewhat, the doctor told me I had twenty-four hours to get her consent, but after that time, even if I hadn't gotten it, he'd put the rods in her arm.

No one had even bothered to ask Mary or her boyfriend whether or not they already used any form of birth control. Or talk to Mary about whether or not she wanted to be having sex at all. All that mattered was that she not be allowed to get pregnant. We were all supposed to be trying to break up the relationship as well because the guy was at least twenty (although he seemed much younger). This was also outrageous. The young man seemed to be the only person in the world who cared about her. They were in love. When he came to her room they sat in silence together holding hands. She seemed to be devoted to him, not afraid, not reluctant, not even submissive.

GAIL WRONSKY

At any rate, I spent my next shift sitting on her bed talking to her about love, and relationships, and sex, and birth control. She stayed silent. I explained what the doctors were planning to do, and told her she could prevent it if she wanted to. I told her I understood how the new baby at the home had made her feel, why she had done what she'd done. Why she shouldn't act out that way in the future. I talked about my life, my boyfriends, what I was reading. Why it wouldn't be a good thing for her to get pregnant at such a young age. How handsome I thought her boyfriend was. How nice he seemed. She just listened. But she managed to look me in the eye a couple of times, which felt like a reward, like permission to continue talking.

The next day they gave her the implants, without having gotten consent, and when I came to work two days later she was gone. I don't know where she was taken. I have no idea what ever became of her. Deeply upset about not being able to say goodbye, I sat in her room feeling that I'd failed her, worried about where she'd gone. One of the nurses from the day shift came in on her way out and handed me a paper lunch bag. *"Mary left this for you,"* she said. Inside the bag was a small, pink, ceramic horse Mary had made there during an occupational therapy session, and a note, written in a spidery, childish hand that said, *I want you to know that I am living.*

The nurse said, "I think she meant to say that she was leaving."

No, I thought. She's telling me she's alive.

What would a horse mean to a thirteen-year-old black girl from the slums of Charlottesville? Had she ever even seen one? What does a horse mean to any of us—freedom, power, beauty? Why paint it pink? Because she was just a girl and she must have thought it looked pretty. As I write this, her horse is on the windowsill behind my desk. I think it's the only artifact I've kept from those years. All the times I've moved, crossing the country in part to get away from some of those memories, the mindset I associate with the South, I've wrapped it carefully, and carried it with me, in my suitcase. It represents resilience and generosity to me. It reminds me that Mary was alive, and wanted to remain alive, that after all she'd been through, she was still capable of loving her boyfriend, of making a wordless but very human connection with me, *and* of making art, because the horse sculpture is an exquisitely beautiful and imaginatively rendered thing.

I want very badly for her to be alive somewhere being loved and making art. And for Delores to be alive and healthy. And for Rema to be enjoying a comfortable retirement, being taken care of as well as she herself took care of so many other people. As I say that, I know the chances are pretty slim that any of those things are happening.

GAIL WRONSKY

SACRED RHYTHM

by Tajamika Paxton

I grew up in a family that prizes the curves of shapely women. I looked at my mother's curves and those of my aunts with deep admiration. When my body began to develop in junior high, I felt like a golden child. On my maternal side I would hear the phrase, "Don't nobody want a bone but a dog. And even he don't want it if there ain't no meat on it." That phrase would give me validation for my naturally thick thighs. On the paternal side, as soon as I entered the door, the uncles and aunts wanted to "get a look at-cha" to see "had you gained any weight," advanced beyond your training bra, or grown a moustache (mostly for the young men but not always). My curves passed the tests. I was born with my mother's posterior and long waist, and ample breasts courtesy of my favorite aunt. My family was proud of me.

Each of my parents had six siblings and I have no less than sixty cousins within thirty miles of each other. There was always a struggle for attention, each child wanting to carve out visibility. Being prized for my shape was how I created value for my life. I understand it now as my currency, the way that I achieved a place of recognition within the family. But to think of my body as an object of value because of the responses it received meant that I was beholden to those responses. As I grew, I came to crave the positive responses, and in order to receive them, I acted out in ways both healthy and not. I do not think the currency gained me anything of true value except the fleeting satisfaction of admiration. And when I finally discovered a way to understand my body beyond its physical form, I was relieved to know it served a function that was more rewarding than any of the sounds of admiration I heard, first at home, then in my romantic relationships with both men and women.

As a child, I was also admired for my intelligence and curiosity. So in fairness, my currency was my brain and my body. One was cultivated, the other genetic. But in a working class African American family dynamic, being smart comes with the stigma of being uppity and unapproachable. Too afraid to threaten my sense of belonging, by age ten I was learning to sacrifice my nerdy urges for tight tank tops and Jordache jeans. And this served me well as I entered junior high and high school. Outside my nest was similar to inside the nest. Brain wasn't valued nearly as much as body and knowing how to work the booty for the latest dance or swing your hips in the direction of the cutest boy. In seventh grade having a 34C cup upped my stock far more than being able to list all the presidents and vice presidents in chronological order. I was a little girl longing for validation in this new world, and I craved a way to stand out. I found it in my physique.

Standing out this way seemed as though it could carry me throughout my entire life, as it does many women. But using this currency didn't buy anything lasting. There was always someone who wanted to wrestle or find a way to get you alone in a crowded school. A young girl's body certainly doesn't seem a fair item for trade. I see the same struggle for recognition in video girls, with their bodies glossed and shined and reveling in their brief moments on the world's stage, or in the high school girls who parade down the Los Angeles street where I live, skinny jeans, cleavage and piercings on fierce display. They are all trying to find value, struggling to answer the question, *Is what I have to offer important to someone? Anyone?* I see the hunger for validation in adult women who offer themselves in exchange for things that feel real and are socially sanctioned—financial security, marriage and social standing, and/or fame. The oldest profession, prostitution, set up the idea of a woman's body having a price; the Middle Passage and the ravages of slavery showed us that the Black body was a proven commodity. But there is another way to think of the Black body, besides as a tool for pleasure or profit.

I'm intrigued with the ways we can think of the body as a symbol of self-care, even a tool of self-actualization. I practice this self-care through studying and teaching yoga. When I began to practice yoga, my body was longing for an expression that was not about sex, another's response, or another's enjoyment, but about a form of movement that felt liberating, free, and full. I wasn't a trained dancer, was never an athlete; I much preferred books to balls and still do. When I was invited several times to a private home for yoga instruction, I suspected the beautiful teacher was hitting on me. My skeptical subconscious thought: "'Yeah right, yoga." She sounded just like the junior high boys who wanted to "study" with me. But when I took the class, I discovered my heaven. I had stepped through an unknown portal into an uncharted world, like that episode of *The Twilight Zone* where the little girl puts her hand through the wall in her bedroom. Unlike that little girl, however, I controlled when I entered and exited. And I delved into the practice without reservation. The standing poses emphasized strength, the energy metaphorically taking root through the lower parts of the body and ascending through the torso. I felt surges of power stronger than any previous sensations my body had known. As my hips stretched in poses like Pigeon and Happy Baby, I was flexible and invincible. And inverting my body with my feet in the air and my head on the ground, I was surprisingly at peace and confident. What were these strange poses and these breaths we were taking that felt like the call of the ocean? Our teacher asked me to breathe through my back, as if my skin was like gills on a fish. With these aids, I began to see my body through a much larger scope. I could practice yoga, and its related science, meditation, any time I needed to access a feeling of power, calm or feel an upsurge in energy. My body was becoming a tool for healing long seated emotional blocks through yoga's emphasis on exhalation and letting go. And I could keep my physical form in optimum shape as well. I studied diligently for years with a small group of dedicated yogis in a class that felt like a cocoon from the demands of life outside its hillside doors. We were lovingly encouraged to be curious about all the sensations that arose, and constantly urged to let go.

I became a teacher years after that first class. As a teacher, I transmit that same loving encouragement to the students who trust me to guide them as I see their bodies taut with the tension of urban landscapes, holding onto all the identities and spaces we think we must hold onto in life. It is through watching those bodies that I learn so much about the human condition and the undeniable link between the mind and the body.

In yogic teachings, the back of the body is the gentle yin side, that which receives from the Creator, the Source or one's own interpretation of higher power. The front of the body is more representative of the ego, the side we present to the world, as evidenced by the phrases *poking one's chest out* or *putting your best foot forward*. Yoga teachers commonly use forward bends to help students get length in their spine, stretch out the vertebrae and their connective tissues. In science, the spine is known to have the highest concentration of nerve endings and supports all the rest of the systems of the body. All of this informs yoga's concentration on keeping the spine supple. The idea of the spine as a receptor in yoga is not so different from feeling a chill in your spine in traditional Christian faiths when one is receiving the Holy Ghost.

In a weekend workshop for high school girls in the juvenile justice system, I asked the young women to fold forward from a standing position, to stretch the spine and invite a sense of calm. I demonstrated the pose, only to look up and discover many of the girls gawking, shocked that I was asking them to bend over in this way. I realized it was the vulnerability of the pose, the embarrassment of their behinds sticking straight up to the ceiling. They had not been shy at all about describing their sexual exploits just moments before. But this level of still quiet gentle movement was unavailable to them. It had no reward, no value. There wasn't a lover on the other end praising them, or feelings of sexual gratification and their flash moments of power and control. It was just each of the young women alone in her body, in a room with other women, and they were unable to relax.

When I saw these young women unable to perform the forward bends, even those from a seated position, I wondered about their ability to hear the sounds of their own instincts, their ability to trust themselves and to feel safe. And I wondered what or who had robbed them of this at such tender ages.

When I'm teaching, I'm trained to see beyond the physical poses, into the emotional body, psychological body and mental body. I see arms lifting above the head in Mountain pose to bring more air to the brain and open the heart and lungs. And when I take a closer look, I know these same arms reach out and hug children. They cook meals for children who don't belong to them biologically, but who they're raising anyway, because bloodlines have never been the way Black people determine who is or who is not family. I see hearts open up in the deep back bending poses like Camel or Bow. I know Black hearts usually only get talked about when one of them has been broken by somebody likely called "no good," but there's so much more to a Black heart than heartbreak. Sometimes it takes months and months of classes before someone can do a backbend without being supported, or exhaling "whew" when it's over. But I see those hearts.

I ponder frequently the condition of the Black body. I think of one stretched out like Miriam Makeba or Odetta or Isaac Hayes after a life well lived. Or I think of a body like Sean Bell's, riddled with bullets and cut down when there was so much more he had to give.

From what I can gather, the Black people in my classes can see what I see, too. That's why sometimes they resist yoga so intensely; yoga, with its emphasis on sensations and mindfulness, is going to put them in a position where all they can do is feel. When feeling is not about feeling good, that can be troubling for a people who, in the face of onslaught, have learned to take refuge in their pleasures and distractions. In these moments I'm grateful that yoga is a slow and methodical practice. It gives the patient practitioner time to release tensions. Tensions born from worrying when we'll ever be thought of as right before wrong, as correct before incorrect, as welcome before suspect. That sort of thinking can wear down your shoulders, neck and spine over time. It can make letting go a delicate process.

"Let go" was my teacher's constant refrain. I have come to understand some of what she meant. As my body matures and changes, which is the polite way of saying I'm getting older, I'm changing my relationship to it. I practice with more patience than strength, more surrender than push. There's still an egotistical pride in being able to rock a pair of jeans, but it's now coupled with a graceful acceptance of myself and of life as it is. Most times. I allow the practice of yoga to emerge from a place on the inside that is gentle and soft, instead of coming from the outside with a rigid focus on perfect alignment and competing with the person next to me to see who can hold the difficult poses the longest. Most times. My practice has become my devotion and my body has really become my temple, occasional Filet-O-Fish aside. With the openness and freedom the poses provide, I can embrace yoga's all-encompassing philosophy—its ethical precepts of contentment, non-violence, and truthfulness; of using only what one needs; of the cessation of endless desires; of self-restraint, management of the breath, deep concentration, sense withdrawal, and meditation. I measure my body's value and my overall value by a yardstick that has nothing to do with another's approval or desire, but everything to do with how I care for and treat myself. That's the currency now. I figure out how to keep this body healthy and alive and vital, because whether the backside is big or small, without health there's nothing at all.

My deepest desire is for all people to experience this freedom in their bodies. When I practice, I see my favorite aunt from my childhood, all the aunts, my mother, my sister, and sisters unknown—all living inside of me. I want them to feel as resplendent as I do. I want every little girl with a body that she thinks only has value when she gyrates it for her *boo,* to experience an intimacy with herself, all of her gorgeous self—hands, arms, neck, shoulders and feet. My hope for those girls is the same hope I hold for myself—that we will each unlock the innate wisdom and sacred rhythm of our beautiful bodies. And in understanding our unique sacred rhythms, we learn to be sourced by those rhythms; sourced by our divine instincts, not the base ones; sourced by the soul, and not hatred of person or groups, seething consumption, endless greed, or insatiability. I have hope that through this practice of stilling the chaos of the mind, we will experience ourselves as pure goodness, whole, complete. Our actions will stem from this place, creating a harmony with ourselves that has the possibility of extending to our families, communities, and to all those with whom we are inextricably connected. That harmony, that joining together, is the literal definition of yoga, a binding together. That harmony, that binding together, has immeasurable value.

THE JOY IN THE JOURNEY
by Tonita Austin-Hilley

My mother, Ethel, was a shoe addict. She owned every color, every height, every texture, and every style shoe imaginable. You see, as a young child living in the projects, there were many days when she walked barefoot to school because it was her older sister's turn to wear the one pair of shoes they shared. So when she was able, she made sure there would never be a reason for her to go barefoot again.

Her father, William Vaughn Jr., was well known for being remarkably stylish. He would wear a three-piece suit and dress shoes just to sit outside on the porch and smoke a cigar. He was as tall and smooth as a drink of iced coffee with a smile as bright as the early morning sun, and just as warm. Mom acquired her sense of style and fanatical passion for shoes from him. As teenagers, Mom and her older sister shared both shoes and clothes. My aunt entrusted her with selecting the shoes to match the outfits they purchased together, because she said Mom always picked the perfect pair. Mom believed that the shoe completed the outfit. You could not call yourself dressed if your shoes did not make a statement. She understood that shoes told a story about where you were on this life's journey.

Less than twenty-four hours after I watched the last breath escape my mother's diseased lungs, I was chosen—expected—as her only daughter, caretaker and, as she had always referred to me, her guardian angel, to select the shoes that she would wear and the garments that would drape her for eternity. I summoned her spirit to help me make the right choice. I, unfortunately, had been to several dozen funerals in my lifetime and knew what the church folk in Burlington, New Jersey expected to see: a nice pastel tailored suit and a pair of stunning high-heeled shoes to match. I have never been able to comprehend why our folks feel that we should be dressed in uncomfortable shoes and constricted clothing when we are laid to rest. At the end of my life's journey, if I have to wear anything forever, I want it to be a pair of pretty satin pajamas, preferably red!

I knew the choice I made for Mommy would turn heads and cause the church ladies to gasp, but then again, I also knew that it would make my momma smile. One of my aunts thought I should've dressed her in a suit.

"Do you see a suit in her closet?" I snapped. Anyone who really knew my mother was aware of her recent love affair with African-inspired prints and clothing. She had given away all of her unyielding business suits, most which were now in that aunt's closet.

I was drawn to one of her favorite traditional African dresses, full of life and saturated in the bright colors of grass and sunshine. The dress went from shoulders to ankles, with a head wrap to match. I knew Mommy was going to a better place, and Ethel was always well-dressed when she knew she was going someplace special.

"Which pair of shoes are you going to put on her?" was the next question I was confronted with.

Feet are synonymous with strength, movement, change and journey. They represent the base of our bodies, the foundation of each movement we make, and the support that allows us to hold fast and stand tall, like oak trees in the midst of a rainstorm. I think of how many callused feet there must have been during the bus boycotts when we chose to walk for freedom. How many corns and bunions ached through the shoes of those who walked from Selma to Alabama? I think of the strong feet supporting the flesh-torn

TONITA AUSTIN-HILLEY

backs of field hands pulling carts and moving quickly through the tobacco fields and cotton plantations. Stepping and humming, whistling and praying; feet blistered and bleeding from the jagged ground beneath them. Feet that were once used for dancing and praising their gods were forced to strain their arches and support the backs of the slaves pressed up against them in the diseased belly of slave ships. Feet once bronze and beautiful were now swollen and hardened from walking the stony walkways up to the auction blocks. Oh how they must have cried at night, wondering when the days of rest would come, wondering when this life's passage would end—even if it was through death.

Mom had the worst feet. They were long and narrow, size ten double A, though sometimes she wore an eleven. She had corns and calluses, thick toenails and extremely dry skin. I thought Mom's feet had become so tough from neglect, until I learned about her childhood.

Ethelyne Vaughn was the name my mother was given at birth—but oh, how Mommy hated to be called Ethelyne! She was born in the New Jersey projects on October 1, 1943, the same year that the National Congress of Racial Equality (CORE) was organized and five years before Martin Luther King was ordained as a Baptist minister. Mommy's skin was the color of milk chocolate. She had legs as skinny as a chicken's drumsticks and she never struggled with weight as I do; she was a perfect size six the years before she married. Those big eyes, brown as chocolate pudding, were one of the visible gifts she passed on to me. Her hair was black as burnt toast, thick and long, as silky as that of her namesake, her paternal grandmother. The elder Ethel Vaughn was half Blackfoot Indian with long black braids down to her waist. Ethel Vaughn always intrigued me. Even meeting her only a few times, I felt that I was in the presence of a quiet warrior. Her great-great-grandmother was pure Blackfoot, and was mistress to the great Chief Sitting Bull, or so that story goes. I remember sitting around the kitchen table at night with Mom, listening to her tell stories about her childhood and family.

She talked vividly about the projects, her home, and how she loved to linger around her own mother, my grandmother, while she played cards and drank with her husband and some of the other men in the family. Grandma Dean preferred whisky and pinochle to sewing and soap operas. My father was one of the many men in the family who admired her ability to feel at home with the guys, yet still be respected as the woman of the house. Mom was also a tomboy. She loved to play with cars and run around outside collecting insects and getting dirty with the best of the boys. I think that's why she was never completely comfortable in high heels.

She seldom spoke of her mother, Leathia Denaural Vaughn (also known as "Dean") who died shortly after Mom's fifteenth birthday. I think the memories were too painful. She had complications after childbirth, and although she was a nurse herself, the white hospital nearby would not admit her, so she didn't get the care she deserved. That killed her. I wished so much that I had been able to know my grandma Dean. My mother beamed when she spoke of her, and I knew I would have loved her too.

After her mother's death, Mom's father, Grandpa Vaughn, struggled to raise five children on his own, including the newborn. Mom, unlike her older sister, felt obligated to help her dad and dropped out of high school to help take care of her younger siblings. Her older sister had just recovered from a long spell of tuberculosis and did not want to assume the responsibility. It strained their relationship. Mom silently mourned the loss of her mother, yet at the young age of sixteen she was forced to walk in her shoes. So many of us Black women have a hard time allowing our nurturing nature to flow into our own lives. We are so good at taking care of other people, and when taken to the extreme, it transforms into unconstructive care-taking and self-neglect. She

TONITA AUSTIN-HILLEY

abandoned her emotional and social needs to take care of her family.

Yet Mom knew how far those mistreated feet had carried her, and she was proud of them. It could explain why even though Mom owned more shoes than Macy's, she felt most comfortable in her bare stocking feet. Every day when she walked into the house from work or school, or a PTA meeting, her shoes would be the first to come off. She would remain barefoot until she had to leave the house again. She wouldn't soak her feet or scrub her calluses, yet she polished her toenails, and felt no shame about wearing sling backs and open-toed shoes in the summer.

Not until her retirement, when she finally had the time to sit and soak her feet, did Mom ever bother to get pedicures. Whenever she'd put on a pair of sandals with newly polished feet, I would say, "Mo-om! Would you please soak those feet?" During my teenage years, I learned from my friends in my neighborhood and at boarding school that a lady was to always keep her toes well manicured and polished, especially when she showed them in public. My mother knew that I loathed her feet, and it tickled her to pieces! Just to irritate me, she would rub the bottoms of her dry, callused feet on the arches of my feet, or clip her thick, sand-colored toenails right in front of me, laughing uncontrollably as they flew across the room. Sometimes just to really drive me nuts, she would rub the rough heel of her foot against the side of my stocking foot just to see if she could make my hose run.

As a teenager, dressing for parties and wanting to look cute even while hanging out on the front steps, I became infatuated with clothes, and like my mother, had to hunt down perfectly coordinated shoes. But unlike Mom, I hated buying shoes. I have large feet that I inherited from both of my parents, but instead of my mother's narrow heel, I have a high instep. And, like my father, my feet are wide. It has always been frustrating to shop for a size ten and a half wide. Over and over again, shoe salesmen would tell me that they were all out of my size or didn't carry that width. Like Cinderella, I would try on pair after pair, hoping and praying that the gorgeous ones would miraculously fit. So many times I would force my wide, long foot into fabulous pumps, walking around the store convincing myself that they weren't really that tight and they would loosen up as I wore them. Sometimes I would take the shoes home in defiance, determined to finally have stylish shoes in my closet, regardless of the pain it would cause my poor toes when I walked in them. But most of the time I would walk away, exhausted from going store to store, trying on shoe after shoe.

I was a knockout in my teens. It was so important to me to dress so that I would turn a head, even when I walked to the corner store. I had every color and style of costume jewelry to accent my outfits, and I went to my summer jobs dressed better than my managers! Because of my love of fashion and my shapely figure that turned heads, I began to get signals from friends and family to not be so enamored of myself and my appearance. I began to look differently at the woman in the mirror, and I started to feel insecure about the physical gifts my parents gave to me. Most of my life I have loved everything about my body: my eyes are big and brown with thick, arched eyebrows, the envy of every woman who has had to take the torture of wax. My legs were so shapely that I was often asked if I ran track, and my breasts were a perfect C cup (at least until I had my first child!). But I was cursed with the feet for which no one stocked shoes! Why would God give me the feet of a sumo wrestler?

It has become clear to me that I needed such strong feet to carry me, to move me successfully and effortlessly through the ecstatic joys and the tremendous losses that I would encounter in my first few decades on earth.

My feet inspire me to move. They propel me to the next space. If I could think of one single thing that I could do to put me in tune with my inner voice and allow me the feeling of soaring over the clouds away from fear, stress and trivial life, it would be dancing. The movement frees my soul and spirit; I feel like I have been baptized again. My first love has always been dance.

I once had a teacher at Philadanco who said that every movement begins with the foot. In all modes of dance it is the placement of the feet that leads the movement. For the movement to be successful, the feet must be firmly planted, yet also light enough to unreservedly move the body through time and space; free to escape the confinement of what is expected of us, what is required of us, and move us towards our true destiny.

How it must have felt to be Gregory Hines with feet as quick as lightning! Watch his face, and the faces of Alvin Ailey or Judith Jamison as they move through time and space. I love to watch the late Gregory Hines dance. His feet are mesmerizing. They seem to move all by themselves, effortlessly, as though they are separated from his body. So quick—so smooth—then slow and melodic. I am torn. I watch his shiny shoes, wanting to figure out how he knew his feet could do that! Yet I am also captivated by his face. He is lost in the moment. The permanent smile tells me that he couldn't feel freer, yet he's also content to be planted in the moment, enjoying where he is right now on his journey. He knows the ability to express joy through movement is a blessing. His face echoes the faces of field hands on southern plantations who, in spite of their struggles in life, so appreciated the few opportunities they had to make music with their hands and feet. To grab a handmade instrument, brush off their finest clothing, and dance under the moonlight. You can almost imagine watching the stress and strain—the burdens of captivity—move from their weary eyes through to their toes, where they told the story of their journey.

Watching Alvin Ailey or Judith Jamison is a similar experience, though they expressed their release in a different way. Their freedom was in the physical journey they took across the stage. Up and down, around in whimsical spins and soaring leaps. So beautiful and heavenly. They used their bodies to express the anxiety, the sadness, the elation and the excitement in their movement. Their souls endowed them with the yearning to express themselves, and they trusted their feet to move them. They celebrated the joy that's in the journey.

There is this knowledge that we have, even within the womb. From the moment we realize there is the possibility of freedom, we kick our feet, eager to stretch our heels. It is in our nature.

My mother was laid to rest in October, five days after her fifty-eighth birthday. A few months later I felt the first kick. I knew if the baby had any of my genes, I'd be dealing with some big feet. In the last few months of my pregnancy, I had feet and limbs so far up my diaphragm that I had to learn to fall asleep while sitting propped up on pillows. If I laid down, I was suffocated by the toes and heels of this little person who was attempting to occupy my entire being. I learned to live with it like so many before me, and I slept.

When my mother saw the first sonogram, she laid her head in my lap and cried like a baby. I know that she had been praying to God for me, her one and only daughter, to have the incomparable experience of childbirth. Mom embraced life the first seven months of her illness; it was only the last two months, when the cancer spread to her brain, that she spent most of her time resting. I am sure she knew that she would have to guide and care for her grand-baby from above, just as my grandmother's spirit ushered me into this world. Mom kept thanking God and hoped she would be able to see this miracle happen. I would soon walk in my mother's shoes and give birth to a child who would never feel the loving arms of his grandmother.

My mother's best friend, Louella, sat with me among the dozens of shoeboxes, searching for the right shoe. Nothing we saw

TONITA AUSTIN-HILLEY

matched the comfort and peaceful nature of the garment that would drape my mother's body. I sat quietly, waiting for my mother's spirit to give me direction and guide me to the shoe that would be fitting for a woman who had moved through her entire life with grace and determination. This was a woman who had survived the loss of her own mother at an early age and had to take on the role of mother. A woman who grew up feeling lost and alone, without direction, yet raised four strong children and guided them toward success. My mother survived innumerable deaths and a difficult marriage. She triumphed over all adversity to claim her Master's degree at the age of fifty-two. Why would she need anything on her feet now?

I was ready to go home and lay down. The hormones were sending a wave of nausea through my gut. I pulled one more box out of her closet. It was a pair of beautiful satin slippers that she wore on her second wedding day. As her maid of honor, I bought them for her so that she could dance the night away. This is it, I thought. This is how you reward the feet that have carried you. After all, shoes help your feet carry you on your journey through life. My mother's journey had come to an end. What she deserved now was ease, rest, relaxation, all the things those slippers symbolized. So that's exactly what I chose for her.

NOTES ON CONTRIBUTORS

Elizabeth Alexander has published five books of poems, including *The Venus Hottentot* (1990), *Body of Life* (1996), *Antebellum Dream Book* (2001), and *American Sublime* (2005), which was one of three finalists for the Pulitzer Prize and was one of the American Library Association's "Notable Books of the Year." She also co-authored with Marilyn Nelson the young adult collection, *Miss Crandall's School for Young Ladies and Little Misses of Color*. Her two collections of essays are *The Black Interior* (2004) and *Power and Possibility* (2007). She was the inaugural poet for the presidential inauguration of Barack Obama. She is the first recipient of the Alphonse Fletcher, Sr. Fellowship for work that "contributes to improving race relations in American society and furthers the broad social goals of the US Supreme *Court's Brown v. Board of Education* decision of 1954." Her other awards include a National Endowment for the Arts Fellowship, two Pushcart Prizes, the Quantrell Award for Excellence in Undergraduate Teaching at the University of Chicago, the Jackson Prize for Poetry, the George Kent Award, given by Gwendolyn Brooks, and a Guggenheim fellowship. She is the chairperson of the African American Studies Department at Yale University.

Stephanie Covington Armstrong, a Brooklyn native, is an author, playwright and essayist who lives, mothers, and writes in Los Angeles. Her work has appeared in *Essence, Sassy, Mademoiselle*, and *Venice* magazines, among others. She has also written a commentary titled "Eating Disorders Affect Us All" about black women and eating disorders for NPR. Stephanie sold a TV treatment, *Kimchi and Cornbread*, which led to a talk-show deal with MTV. Her memoir, *Not All Black Girls Know How to Eat*, was published in the summer of 2009. Covington Armstrong has spoken about eating disorders at colleges and universities throughout southern California. She has been a fellow at both the Dorset Colony for Writers in Vermont and the Dorland Mountain Retreat Writers Colony in Temecula, California.

Tonita Austin-Hilley is a native of Philadelphia, PA and currently lives in Upper Providence, PA with her husband James and two children, James III and Janai. Tonita loves poetry, angels, children, dance and butterflies. She is an alumnus of the University of Pennsylvania and is currently self-employed. *Joy in the Journey* is her first published essay.

Anne Beatts is a TV writer-producer who won two Emmys as a writer for the original *Saturday Night Live*. She created and produced *Square Pegs* on CBS, and co-executive-produced NBC's *A Different World*. She and her producing partner, Eve Brandstein, recently executive-produced and co-directed *John Waters Presents: Movies That Will Corrupt You*, a premium cable film series. In 1999, she returned to *SNL* as a writer on NBC's Emmy-winning 25th anniversary special, for which she won her third WGA Award. In 1995–96 she was executive producer of *The Stephanie Miller Show*, a late-night talk show. She was the first woman contributing editor of the National Lampoon and both performed and wrote for the "National Lampoon Radio Hour." She has been published in *Esquire*, *Playboy*, *Los Angeles Magazine*, *Vogue*, *Elle*, and Salon.com. In 1997 and 1998, her humor column "Beatts Me!" appeared weekly in *the Los Angeles Times*. She co-edited the best-selling *Saturday Night Live* (Avon, 1977), *Titters: The First Collection of Humor by Women* (Macmillan, 1976), and *Titters 101* (Putnam, 1984), and co-authored *The Mom Book* (Dell, 1986). Her work has appeared on Broadway in *Gilda: Live* and the Tony-nominated rock 'n' roll musical *Leader of the Pack*. She is an adjunct professor in the Writing Division of USC's School of Cinematic Arts.

Annie Burrows was born in New Orleans, LA. She has lived in Los Angeles since 1987. She has been married to Jonathan Burrows since 1999. Ms. Burrows worked as a photographer and photographic researcher before the birth of her two children, Zane and Lili. She still misses Louisiana and visits her beautiful home state at least twice a year. The brick plant in Slidell still exists and many of the buildings in New Orleans were constructed from St. Joe bricks. Visit the website at http://www.stjoebrickworks.com for information about its history.

Kenneth Carroll is a native Washingtonian. His poetry and plays have appeared in numerous publications including, *Role Call, In Search Of Color Everywhere, Spirit & Flame, Bum Rush The Page, Potomac Review, and Beyond The Frontier*. His short stories have appeared in *Its All Love* (2009, Random House), *Stress City* (2008, Paycock Press), *Children of the Dream* (1999, Simon & Schuster), and *Gargoyle Magazine*. He is the 2009 DC Area Writing Project Honoree and was awarded a 2008 literature fellowship from the DC Commission on the Arts and Humanities. He is married and the proud father of a daughter and two sons.

Nzingha Clarke is a writer based in Los Angeles and Mexico. She is currently at work on a novel that may be called *The Family Business*.

Meri Nana-Ama Danquah, a native of Ghana, is the author of the ground-breaking memoir, *Willow Weep for Me: A Black Woman's Journey Through Depression*, which the *Washington Post* called "a vividly textured flower of a memoir that will surely stand as one of the finest to come along in years." She is the editor of two critically acclaimed anthologies: *Becoming American: Personal Essays by First Generation Immigrant Women* and *Shaking the Tree: A Collection of New Fiction and Memoir by Black Women*. Danquah is currently completing *All Anyone Wants*, a nonfiction book about her return to Ghana, and *The Nine Lives of Nina Brown*, a young adult novel. She divides her time between Los Angeles, California and Accra, Ghana.

Werner Disse was born in San Francisco and has lived in Switzerland, South Africa, France, Germany, and England. He received a BA and an MBA from Stanford University and is also a graduate of Oxford Law School, where he was a Rhodes Scholar. He is currently finishing his first novel, *The Oculist*, a fable about a girl who repairs the lens through which she sees herself. He is also co-writing, with Bonnie Serratore, an emotional intuitive, *The Way Back Home: How to Clear the Energy of Our Emotional Wounding*, which is devoted to the description and healing of what Eckhart Tolle calls the "pain-body." He currently lives in Santa Cruz, California.

Lynell George is a journalist and essayist based in Los Angeles. Her work has appeared in various magazines, newspapers, and essay collections. She is the author of *No Crystal Stair: African Americans in the City of Angels*, and is a former features writer for the *Los Angeles Times* and *L.A. Weekly*. Her work has also been featured in the *Washington Post* and the *Boston Globe*; *Vibe*, *Essence*, *Ms.*, and *Smithsonian* magazines; as well as the following essay collections: *Writing Los Angeles: a Literary Anthology*; *Sex, Death, and God In LA* and *Step Into a World: A Global Anthology of New Black Literature*.

David Goldsmith, proud father of daughter Maddy (Wheaton College 2012), is a graduate of Opera/Music Theatre from the College Conservatory of Music at University of Cincinnati. A music theatre lyricist and television producer/writer and screenwriter, David's musical *Having It Almost* was performed at the 2006 New York Musical Theatre Festival and was an official selection at the 2008 National Alliance for Musical Theatre showcase. He also wrote the lyrics for the American version of *Hot Shoe Shuffle* (North American tour); *Li'l Devil* (ASCAP/Disney Music Theatre Workshop); *Hats! The Musical for the Rest Of Your Life* (Denver Theatre Center); and many others. For television, David served as co-producer/writer of *Beautiful People* (ABC Family Television) and wrote for *The Fearing Mind* (Fox Family) and *The Dead Zone* (USA Network). His most recent musical, *Imagine This*, about a family of Jewish actors trapped in the Warsaw ghetto in 1942, enjoyed its World Premiere in 2007 at Theatre Royal Plymouth in the UK, and opened at the New London theatre in the West End in the fall of 2008, where it received four What's On Stage Theatregoer's Award nominations, including Best Musical, and was a finalist for the prestigious Fred Ebb Award.

Hill Harper is author of the *New York Times* bestseller *Letters to a Young Brother* (Gotham Books, 2006), which was named Best Book for Young Adults by the American Library Association in 2007, and *Letters to a Young Sister* (Gotham Books, 2008). Both books won two NAACP awards. Currently starring in *CSI: New York* as Dr. Hawkes, a role for which he won the 2008 and 2009 NAACP Image Award for Outstanding Actor in a Drama Series, Hill has appeared in numerous prime-time television shows and feature films, including *The Sopranos*, *ER*, *Lackawanna Blues*, *He Got Game*, *The Skulls*, *In Too Deep*, *The Nephew*, and *The Visit*. Hill graduated magna cum laude with a BA from Brown University (and was valedictorian of his department) and cum laude with a JD from Harvard Law School. He also holds a master's degree with honors from Harvard's Kennedy School of Government. He is a motivational speaker who tours around the country. He was named one of *People's* Sexiest Men Alive, and he currently lives in Los Angeles.

Peter J. Harris, founder and artistic director of Inspiration House, is an African American cultural worker who has since the 1970s published his poetry, essays, and fiction in a wide range of national publications; worked as a publisher, journalist, editor and broadcaster; and been an educator and workshop leader for adults and adolescents. Currently, he and his daughter Adenike are writing a memoir called *Ghost on the Door: A Father and Daughter's Healing Conversations After Sexual Abuse*, a candid, ethical, loving dialogue between a black father and a black daughter confronting, surviving, and transcending her rape by a black stepfather. Harris is author of *The Johnson Chronicles: Truth & Tall Tales about My Penis* and *Safe Arms: 20 Love/Erotic Poems (and One Ooh Baby Baby Moan)*. His work has often explored the lives of black men. His magazine, *Genetic Dancers: The Artistry Within African/American Fathers*, published during the 1980s, was the first of its kind. His book *Hand Me My Griot Clothes: The Autobiography of Junior Baby* featured a philosophical elder black man ruminating on life, love, and ethics, and won the PEN Oakland award for multicultural literature in 1993. His personal essays about manhood and masculinity have been published in several anthologies, including *Tenderheaded: A Comb-Bending Collection of Hair Stories*, *Black Men Speaking*, *Fathersongs*, *I Hear a Symphony: African Americans Celebrate Love*, and *What It Means to be a Man*.

Susan Hayden is a poet, playwright, fiction writer and montage artist. Her novel, *Cat Stevens Saved My Life*, made the Top 100 (out of 5000 entries worldwide) in the inaugural Amazon Breakthrough Novel Award. Most recently, her play *Gypsies, Tramps & Thieves* was recorded and aired on KPFK's Pacifica Performance Showcase. A book combining her poetry and art will be released later this year. She is currently at work on a play about the sudden loss of her husband, actor Christopher Allport, and her journey through grief toward healing. She lives in Santa Monica with her son, Mason Summit.

Carolyn L. Holbrook lives in Minneapolis, MN. She is a writer, educator, and long-time advocate for the healing power of the arts. Her passion for providing grassroots accessibility to the literary arts inspired her to create SASE: The Write Place, a community-based organization for writers. She served as Artistic/Executive Director from 1993–2005 and spearheaded the organization's merger with Intermedia Arts in 2006. Her personal essays have been published widely, most recently in *Black Renaissance/Renaissance Noire* (New York University April 2008), *White Teachers/Diverse Classrooms* (Landsman/Lewis, Stylus Press 2006), *Teachers as Collaborative Partners* (Tutwiler, Erlbaum Press 2005), and *Speakeasy* (Loft Literary Center 2005). A chapter of her memoir-in-progress inspired a choral piece composed and performed by the Twin Cities Women's Choir in 2004. She teaches English and creative writing at Hamline University in St. Paul, MN. She serves on the program committee of the Givens Foundation for African American Literature for which she established an artists-in-the-schools program in 2005. She was named one of "100 People to Watch" by *Mpls/St. Paul Magazine* in the year 2000.

Kenji Jasper is an author, journalist and screenwriter who has been writing since the age of nine. His is the author of four novels, including *Dark*, a *Washington Post* and *New York Times* bestseller, and *Snow*. He is also co-editor of *Beats, Rhymes and Life*, a collection of critical essays on hip hop culture published by Broadway Books. His writings have appeared in *Newsweek*, the *Village Voice*, *Essence*, and on National Public Radio. A native of Washington, DC, he currently lives in Los Angeles.

Brent Jennings is a writer, actor, director, and teacher. He is the author of the solo play, "The Resurrection of Jimmy Spills." He has appeared on television in several HBO projects such as the Emmy Award–winning *A Lesson Before Dying*, *The Soul of the Game, Don King: Only In America*, and the Peabody-Award winning civil rights drama *Boycott*. He co-starred in the classic film *Witness* and appeared in the movie *Life* and the horror classic *The Serpent and the Rainbow*, among others. He has held starring and recurring roles in various television dramas and movies of the week and has made over fifty guest appearances on network television shows such as *ER, The Practice, NYPD Blue, Brothers and Sisters, Gray's Anatomy, Bones*, and *Boston Legal*. Mr. Jennings is an adjunct professor at the American Academy of Dramatic Arts in Los Angeles, where he resides with his wife and two sons.

A. Van Jordan is the author of *Rise*, published by Tia Chucha Press, 2001, which won the PEN/Oakland Josephine Miles Award and selected for the Book of the Month Club from the Academy of American Poets. His second book, *M-A-C-N-O-L-I-A*, published by W. W. Norton & Co., 2004, was awarded an Anisfield-Wolf Award and listed as one the Best Books of 2005 by the [London] *Times Literary Supplement* (TLS). Jordan was also awarded a Whiting Writers Award in 2005 and a Pushcart Prize in 2006, 30th Edition. *Quantum Lyrics* was published July 2007 by W. W. Norton & Co. He is a recent recipient of a John Simon Guggenheim Fellowship, 2007. He is a Professor in the Department of English at the University of Michigan.

Steven Kotler is a New Mexico–based writer. His articles have appeared in places like the *New York Times Magazine*, the *Los Angeles Times, National Geographic, GQ, Wired, Discover, Popular Science, Details, Outside*, and *ESPN the Magazine*. He also writes The Playing Field, a blog about the science of sport for PsychologyToday.com and has authored two books, the (1999) novel *The Angle Quickest for Flight*, which was a *San Francisco Chronicle* bestseller and won the 2000 William L. Crawford IAFA Fantasy Award, and the (2006) non-fiction work *West of Jesus: Surfing, Science and the Origins of Belief*, which was a 2006 Pen West finalist. He has a BA from the University of Wisconsin, Madison in English and creative writing and an MA from The Johns Hopkins University in creative writing. He lives on a tiny farm with his wife and too many dogs.

Joel Lipman is a writer, producer, and director specializing in adventure, non-fiction reality series, and entertainment specials. Currently the president of Liberty Pictures, Joel is an Emmy-nominated producer who has produced over

200 hours of television. He was vice president of Development at Autonomy/A2TV from 2002 to 2007. He was also co-founder and vice president of Sachnoff-Lipman Entertainment from 1996 to 2006. Joel has written ten plays and directed more than twenty-five. In 1980 he was commissioned by the Kennedy Center to write a play for their traveling exhibit, "The Child In America." In 1981 he was given the exclusive rights to the story of Sgt. Jimmy Lopez, one of the original fifty-two Iranian hostages. The play he wrote about Lopez's experiences, *Made In America*, was optioned by PBS. Over the years, Joel's poetry has been published in various literary magazines.

Philip Littell grew up in New York and London, joined the army in 1969, went straight—I mean directly—into acting school, then found more great teachers, started teaching right away and then started working, moved to LA in 1976, shuttled between the classics and performance art, segued to clowning in clubs (the immortal Weba Show), started writing furious songs to easy listening tracks, then wrote with and fronted several bands, wrote and directed and performed in a series of contrarian music theater pieces, stumbled into opera as a performer and found himself writing texts for a host of modern American composers (Previn, Susa, Torke, and Larsen among many) until that stopped being interesting, still performs, acts, sings, directs, translates and adapts, and is currently writing a sequence of maddened plays. He is also an obsessed and obsessive photographer. None of this makes any sense, and yet it does.

Jason Luckett is an essayist, poet, and performing songwriter based in Los Angeles. His latest musical release is MMIX. In 2007 he founded TheObamanation.com, a blog dedicated to a discussion of "Mulatto Moments in Post-Racial America." His work has appeared in the poetry anthology, *Voices from Leimert Park*, and other publications. He also composes music for films, including the 2005 short *Primary Next of Kin*, with Danny Glover. In 2004 he established GroovysoulCreative.com as an umbrella for his creative ventures.

Susan E. Matus is from a mixed culture of Nicaraguan and Danish/Irish descent. She grew up in San Francisco in the seventies in a "singles complex" that didn't allow children. She somehow was the exception. She credits the isolation of her childhood as an only child for helping to develop a seemingly innate tenacity and grand imagination. A love for poetry at a young age inspired the creative writer in her. She has written numerous short stories, poems and a lifetime of journals. Currently she is working on a children's story called "Honu" about a female sea turtle that discovers her true creative purpose. She hopes that it will inspire young girls to realize that just being a woman is a great honor and a journey they should cherish. She lives in Southern California with her husband, son and two dogs. "Ace in the Hole" is her first published essay.

Tajamika Paxton's career has included positions in film, television, music and the healing arts. She is the former head of production for Forest Whitaker's Spirit Dance Entertainment; she produced for Star Jones's first television show, and was the Production Manager for MeShell Ndegeocello's critically acclaimed Peace Beyond Passion. Currently, she is making peace with being a television writer and a yoga teacher all at the same time.

S. Pearl Sharp "works words, conjures vision." Her commentaries and essays have been broadcast on National Public Radio. Published works include the nonfiction *Black Women For Beginners* (Writers and Readers), the poetry w/jazz CDs *Higher Ground* and *On the Sharp Side*, four volumes of poetry, including *Typing In The Dark* (Harlem River Press), plays and short stories. She adapted the essays of esteemed actress Beah Richards to stage in *There's a Brown Girl in the Ring*. An award-winning independent filmmaker, Sharp married poetry and history with film, creating *Back Inside Herself, Life Is A Saxophone* on poet Kamau Daa'ood, the semi-animated *Picking Tribes* and the documentary *The Healing Passage/Voices from the Water*, among others. She conducts workshops that blend the writing craft with holistic healing and the perpetual pursuit of wellness.

Kimball Stroud is a political strategist, fundraiser and writer in Washington, DC. She is co-founder of Impact Arts + Film Fund, a non-profit organization created as a platform for artists and filmmakers to engage with the political and policy arenas. IAFF hosts film screenings, panel discussions, and promotional events to educate and enlighten its audiences and create a climate for meaningful social impact. Stroud has raised funds for several films. She was most recently executive producer for the documentary film *Outrage*, a work by Academy Award–nominated filmmaker Kirby Dick that examines the hypocrisy of closeted politicians who actively campaign against the LGBT community to which they covertly belong. She has raised millions of dollars for progressive organizations, including The RFK Center for Human Rights, The Creative Coalition, and Rock the Vote. This is her first published essay.

Greg Tate is a writer and musician who lives, thrives, jukes, and jives in Harlem. He is currently working on a critical biography of James Brown, The Godfather of Soul.

After a long and successful career as a New York studio musician, record producer and composer/arranger for film and countless TV commercials, **Kenny White** found himself at the starting gate of a new vocation: that of a troubadour. A touring singer/songwriter. In the advertising world, he composed or arranged hundreds of national and international commercials and garnered many industry awards along the way, including the Clio, the Mobius, and the prestigious London International Award. His record productions resulted in a Best Vocal Performance Grammy nomination for Shawn Colvin. White's work on Peter Wolf's "Sleepless," contributed to its selection by *Rolling Stone* as one of the "greatest 500 albums of all time." As a songwriter and performer, he was quickly signed by folk icon Judy Collins to record for her Wildflower Records label, where he is currently working on his third record. This is Kenny's first published non-musical work.

Gail Wronsky worked as a nurses' aide at University of Virginia Hospital in the late seventies. She is the author, coauthor, or translator of nine books of poetry and prose, including *Dying for Beauty*, *Poems for Infidels*, *The Love-talkers*, *Volando Bajito* (a translation of poems by Alicia Partnoy), and *Blue Shadow Behind Everything Dazzling*. She lives in Topanga, California, and teaches creative writing at Loyola Marymount University.

Yolanda Young's essays have appeared in the *Washington Post*, *USA Today*, and *Essence Magazine*. A columnist, she's shared her radio essays with listeners of NPR's "This I Believe" and "News & Notes." In 2003, Random House published Yolanda's memoir, *On Our Way to Beautiful*. The Washington, DC Commission on the Arts and Humanities honored her with an Emerging Artist Award. Yolanda was born and raised in Shreveport, Louisiana. She is a graduate of Howard University and the Georgetown University Law Center.